Practical Teaching Skills for Driving Instructors

Eleventh edition

Practical Teaching Skills for Driving Instructors

Developing your
client-centred learning
and coaching skills

John Miller and Susan McCormack

KoganPage

Publisher's note

Every possible effort has been made to ensure that the information contained in this book is accurate at the time of going to press, and the publishers and authors cannot accept responsibility for any errors or omissions, however caused. No responsibility for loss or damage occasioned to any person acting, or refraining from action, as a result of the material in this publication can be accepted by the editor, the publisher or the author.

First published 1993
Second Edition 1995
Reprinted with revisions 1998
Third Edition 2000
Fourth Edition 2002
Fifth Edition 2006
Sixth Edition 2007
Seventh Edition 2009
Eighth Edition 2011
Ninth edition 2014
Tenth edition 2017
Eleventh edition 2019

2nd Floor, 45 Gee Street
London
EC1V 3RS
United Kingdom

122 W 27th St, 10th Floor
New York, NY 10001
USA

4737/23 Ansari Road
Daryaganj
New Delhi 110002
India

www.koganpage.com

ISBNs

Hardback   9781789660609
Paperback   9780749498580
Ebook   9780749498597

British Library Cataloguing-in-Publication Data

A CIP record for this book is available from the British Library.

Library of Congress Cataloging-in-Publication Data

A CIP record for this book is available from the Library of Congress.

Typeset by Integra Software Services, Pondicherry
Print production managed by Jellyfish
Printed and bound in Great Britain by CPI (UK) Ltd, Croydon CR0 4YY

CONTENTS

ABOUT THE AUTHORS

John Miller has been involved in the driver training industry for over 35 years and was an ADI for more than 30 years. For most of that time he ran his own driving school for both car and lorry drivers as well as an instructor training facility in Chichester. He is now a training consultant to the industry.

As well as *Practical Teaching Skills for Driving Instructors*, John is the author of *The Driving Instructor's Handbook* (also published by Kogan Page).

Both books are listed by the Driver and Vehicle Standards Agency as essential material for the ADI examinations.

John Miller can be contacted at johnmiller07@btinternet.com

Susan McCormack has been in the driver training industry for 30 years. During this time, she has taught learner drivers, trainee driving instructors, fleet drivers and other qualified drivers, and developed training materials and courses. Susan has completed an MSc in Driver Behaviour and Education at Cranfield University. She is Managing Director of Tri-Coaching Partnership Ltd, which delivers the Pearson SRF BTec Level 4 Professional Award in Coaching for Driver Development along with other client-centred courses to driver trainers. She scored 51 out of 51 in her ADI Standards Check.

Susan can be contacted at sue@tri-coachingpartnership.co.uk

Note

While every effort has been made to ensure that the book is as up to date as possible, continual changes take place in the driver training industry and with legislation. This means that some changes may have occurred since going to print. To keep yourself completely up to date, we recommend that you sign up for regular email updates from the DVSA on the DVSA's website at www.gov.uk. You will also benefit from joining one or more of the national associations as well as your local group.

Introduction

Practical Teaching Skills for Driving Instructors was originally published in 1993 as a follow-up and supplement to *The Driving Instructor's Handbook* in response to many requests from Approved Driving Instructors (ADIs) and trainee instructors who felt that there was a need for more training material that would set out, in a practical and straightforward way, the most effective teaching practices. The emphasis has always been on presenting the most up-to-date methods of teaching, learning, coaching and refresher training for ADIs and trainee instructors. For reasons of continuity, the title of the book has not been altered, but over the years the contents have been regularly revised and updated to reflect the changes that have taken place in the industry. There is now an emphasis on client-centred learning, coaching skills and techniques, the Standards Check, professional development and generally how to improve your practical driver training skills.

The Driving Instructor's Handbook deals with the ADI exams – what you must do to pass and how to go about it. *Practical Teaching Skills for Driving Instructors* is more about why we (as professional driver trainers) and our pupils need to do things in a particular way and how different methods and skills are interactive in the learning process for both instructor and trainee. The book offers a variety of suggestions on how to be an effective driver trainer and is intended to stimulate instructors to improve and extend their practical skills.

As instructors we use a wide variety of *practical teaching skills* in our everyday work. Most of these skills will have been acquired and developed in many other areas of experience, for example at school, in college, or in a previous working environment. Skills and techniques that have been transferred from these previous situations are known as 'transferable personal skills'. This term is used to define the skills that are personal to us and that are capable of being used in different situations.

For example, a pedestrian who is about to cross a busy main road uses skills in judging the speed and distance of oncoming traffic. When 'transferred' to the new environment of driving, these skills become very useful in traffic situations, such as when waiting to emerge from a junction or crossing the path of approaching traffic. The skills are similar, but the environment is different. Another example might involve the use of bicycle gears – a combination of decision making together with the physical skill of hand and foot coordination. This type of skill can be directly transferred to driving a car.

To teach learner drivers how to cope with today's driving conditions we need to develop these individual transferable skills and our practical teaching skills. This will ensure that effective learning takes place.

As driver trainers we are probably the only teachers whose 'classrooms' are travelling at relatively high speeds along busy roads. In this environment your control of the situation and your effectiveness as an instructor are vital factors with regard to the safety of your pupils, yourself and other road users. For these reasons the book is designed to help existing qualified instructors in preparing for the ADI Standards Check, as well as new instructors preparing for their ADI exams.

Communication and coaching skills

Most of the practical teaching skills dealt with in this book are dependent on effective communication and coaching skills. Instructors who can communicate and coach effectively are more likely to succeed in transferring their own knowledge, understanding, skills and attitudes to their pupils.

Knowledge of *The Highway Code* and the ability to drive with a high degree of expertise are not in themselves enough for teaching somebody else how to drive.

As a professional driver trainer, you should be aiming to teach your pupils 'safe driving for life' and not just training them to pass the test. As part of the qualifying process you are required to demonstrate not only your knowledge and driving ability, but also your communication skills and instructional techniques. In particular, your client-centred learning skills are tested by the Driver and Vehicle Standards Agency (DVSA) in the Standards Check, which all ADIs have to undergo at regular intervals.

This book focuses on showing you how to improve your teaching, coaching and communication skills so that you are better equipped to teach 'safe driving for life', whether you are a potential or a qualified ADI. The use of these skills in preparation for the ADI exams is dealt with in detail in *The Driving Instructor's Handbook*.

Being a successful driving instructor relies not only on the traditional interpersonal skills, but also on being able to:

- use and interpret body language;
- sell ideas and concepts;
- solve problems;
- identify, analyse and correct faults; and
- make immediate decisions with safety in mind.

Learning skills

To qualify as an instructor, you need to have these skills. You also need to acquire learning and study skills and a basic understanding of role play.

As an ADI, you can communicate in a variety of ways to suit the perceived needs of each individual pupil. You will be involved with selling, whether it is 'selling' yourself or your services to potential pupils or 'selling' ideas and concepts to existing pupils.

These skills are included because it's important to master them in order to develop as an effective driver trainer. This book will show you how to improve your effectiveness by developing all the important practical teaching skills.

As already indicated, practical teaching skills and other transferable personal skills are not necessarily developed overnight. The need to practise these skills while you are giving lessons is just as vital as driving practice is to your pupils. To be able to learn from each encounter with a new pupil and to structure a self-development programme you must know how studying, learning and teaching can be made effective.

Teaching and learning

Developing the skills contained in this book is essential at this level of training; it is also totally compatible with the criteria for approval for the Official Register of Driving Instructor Training (ORDIT; for details see *The Driving Instructor's Handbook*). But there is no real substitute for practical, hands-on training and practice. You cannot learn how to drive from a book, neither can you learn how to teach someone from a book; the best way to learn how to teach is to teach! The development of practical teaching skills is a continuous and lifetime process, with each new encounter offering you the opportunity to improve your skills.

Learning occurs in a variety of ways; however, as in most things, a systematic approach is invariably more effective than one that is haphazard. Trial and error in using skills will give some insight into those that are the most effective in different situations and with different types of pupil.

Reflecting on your successes and failures will also assist you in developing your practical teaching skills.

Formal training and structured learning, both in-class and in-car, are invaluable to instructors wishing to develop their own skills. This is even more relevant when developing active learning strategies, such as role-playing exercises and fault assessment skills. Formal training for the ADI test allows you to practise new skills in a safe and controlled setting before trying them out on learners or trainees in the real world. Experience gained while watching and listening to demonstrations given by your tutor will be invaluable when you have to demonstrate skills to your pupils.

Training should be a continuous circle of learning:

Trainees learn from their tutors / pupils learn from their instructors / instructors learn from their pupils / information feeds back to the tutors, and so on.

The challenge for you is to adopt a frame of mind that welcomes each learning strategy, particularly those that require a more active approach.

The key element in teaching driving (and for learning how to drive) is controlled practice.

When teaching your pupils how to drive you should take every opportunity that arises to practise the skills contained in this book. Some skills training, however, can be seen to be slightly threatening to both learners and instructors. When you are analysing someone's behaviour it is important not to cause embarrassment or offend. Because of this, teaching a practical skill must be done in a sensitive way. You should accept this from the outset. If you adopt too strict an approach, your learners are unlikely to enjoy the experience and may feel reluctant to participate. Sensitivity must be shown to all your learners and this in itself is an important transferable skill.

Remember that criticism can, on its own, be very demotivating. Encouragement is needed and praise when deserved will bring about more improvement than any amount of criticism.

Instructor qualities

To become a professional and effective driver trainer, you need to be more than a good driver who enjoys motoring. The job is about people and using your interpersonal skills effectively. You will, of course, need to have the appropriate technical knowledge and skills required to pass the ADI exams and to work on a day-to-day basis with pupils from all age groups and backgrounds. But as well as this specific expertise, the instructor requires certain personal qualities. You need to have:

- a calm and approachable manner and the ability to communicate with pupils at all levels;
- an awareness of the need for the safety of all road users, including yourself, your pupils and other people, particularly vulnerable road users such as the elderly and the very young;
- the ability to communicate ideas and instructions concisely and clearly;
- the flexibility to adapt to the specific needs of each individual pupil;
- the ability to motivate and encourage pupils, using a variety of client-centred techniques;
- the motivation to work unsociable hours, often in the evenings or weekends; and
- the ability to concentrate for lengthy periods of time and to observe closely the pupil's actions.

These qualities are expressed by the DVSA as:

- good people skills;
- patience and understanding;
- a thorough knowledge of the theory and practice of driving;
- an ability to use various teaching and coaching skills;
- an awareness of changes in the statutory regulations that govern the content and conduct of driving tests as well as driving instruction;
- the ability to provide a professional service to people from diverse backgrounds;
- business sense.

The DVSA's 'Guide to the ADI register' emphasises that you will be expected to show:

- a high regard for all aspects of road safety;
- a high standard of driving and instructional ability;
- a professional approach to your customers;
- a responsible attitude towards your pupils and the profession; and
- that you are a 'fit and proper person'.

In deciding whether you are 'fit and proper' the DVSA will check to see if you have:

- had any motoring or non-motoring cautions or convictions;
- any court proceedings pending against you; or
- any penalty points on your licence.

To enhance your personal driving skills and ensure that you are driving in line with modern techniques, you need to be aware of the qualities required by the good driver as described in *The Official DVSA Guide to Driving: The essential skills*. To supplement these skills you will need similar attributes to become an effective driver trainer.

Responsibility

As a professional driver trainer you will have certain responsibilities, including:

- showing proper concern for the safety of your passengers, other road users and yourself;
- an awareness of the need to drive in an economic and environmentally friendly manner; and
- being aware of the need to maintain the safety and well-being of your pupils, particularly in the early stages of their training.

As a driver: you should always show proper concern for the safety of yourself, your passengers and all other road users. You should also be aware of the need to drive economically and in an environmentally friendly manner.

As an instructor: you should always consider the safety and well-being of your pupils, particularly those in the early stages of learning. Avoid taking them into situations they are unable to cope with. Remember: you are responsible for their safety.

Concentration

Your concentration levels need to be maintained throughout the working day. You have a responsibility regarding safety for yourself, your pupils and for other road users.

As a driver: you must concentrate at all times. Any distraction from the driving task can have disastrous effects in today's heavily congested roads and with fast-moving traffic.

As an instructor: when you are supervising inexperienced drivers, your concentration is even more important. You will read the road further ahead, taking into account any developing situations so that you can keep your pupils safe, relaxed and eager to learn.

Anticipation

As an experienced driver, you will already appreciate that predicting what might happen as well as what is actually happening is an important element of driving. As an instructor, you will need to be even more aware of potential hazards in good time so that your pupil can prepare for them. Make sure you plan ahead as far as possible and anticipate potential hazards so that you can allow plenty of time for your instructions and for the pupil to respond appropriately.

You must recognise the needs of each individual pupil and anticipate how each of them might respond to changing situations.

As a driver: the ability to predict what might happen is an important part of the skills needed to avoid danger. You need to be aware of any possible hazards in time to deal with them safely.

As an instructor: anticipation is even more important. You will be sitting in the passenger seat beside someone much less able at the controls of your car. You will recognise the needs of each individual and anticipate how different pupils respond to changing situations. Plan as far ahead as possible and anticipate any potential hazards. This will allow time for you to give either positive instructions or prompts, so that your pupil will be able to take any action necessary to avoid problems.

Awareness

New drivers need to be taught to a high standard, with hazard awareness playing an important part in their development. Teach your pupils to:

- handle the vehicle sympathetically and in an environmentally friendly way;
- drive with courtesy and consideration;
- look and plan well ahead, anticipating what might happen;
- take early action to avoid problems;
- compensate for other drivers' mistakes; and
- understand what they are doing and why they are doing it.

Modern driving techniques are becoming relatively easier through advances in technology and design, making cars much more efficient and safe. However, road and traffic conditions are becoming more and more complex and congested. In order to keep your clients safe, you need to be aware of the major causes of road accidents including:

- other drivers' ignorance of, or total disregard for, the rules of the road;
- lack of concentration and poor response to developing situations;
- carelessness;
- driving while under the influence of drink or drugs;
- driving when feeling unwell;
- driving with deficient eyesight;
- some drivers' willingness to take risks;
- using vehicles that are not roadworthy;
- driving while under the stress of the modern need to rush everywhere;
- using mobile phones or other in-car equipment.

Patience

An efficient and effective instructor shows patience and tolerance towards other road users. Displaying a positive attitude will set a good example to your pupils and help with their driver development. From a professional point of view, demonstrating tolerance and patience, not only with the pupil but also towards other road users, will help build your pupils' confidence in you and your ability as a trainer.

As a driver: always show patience and restraint with other drivers when they make mistakes. Not everyone is as thoughtful as you!

As an instructor: displaying a positive attitude to your pupils will not only set a good example to them but, if you have your name on your car, it will also be good advertising.

Remember, we all had to learn to drive, and some find it more difficult than others! If you lose patience with a pupil it will only make matters worse. Most people are aware when they have made a mistake anyway, so be patient and always willing to give more help – even when you have explained things several times before.

Demonstrating tolerance will also go a long way in building up your pupils' confidence and also their belief in you. Hopefully your tolerant attitude will rub off on them!

Confidence

As a conscientious and efficient driver, you will be displaying confidence at all times. By planning well ahead and anticipating potential hazards, the confident driver avoids the need to make hurried and potentially unsafe decisions.

As an instructor, it is important that you are confident in your own ability both as a driver and in the skills required to help you build your pupils' own confidence.

With your driver training, make sure you avoid any road or traffic situations that your pupils are not ready for so that you help them gradually build up confidence in their own ability.

As a driver: the conscientious and efficient driver displays confidence at all times. This confidence results from being totally 'at one' with the vehicle. You should always be travelling at a speed to suit the road, weather and traffic conditions, with an appropriate gear engaged and in the correct position on the road. Planning well ahead and anticipating hazards, the confident driver can avoid the need to make any last-minute, rushed, and usually unsafe, decisions.

As an instructor: not only do you need to be confident yourself, but you will also need the skills required to help develop your pupils' confidence. To do this, you will need to ensure that the routes you select for teaching each aspect of the syllabus are matched to each individual's ability. Avoiding those situations pupils are not ready for will help you gradually build up their skills and confidence.

Knowledge

As a professional driver trainer, you should have a sound knowledge of the rules and regulations in *The Highway Code* and *The Official DVSA Guide to Driving*. Additionally, you will have the ability to pass on this knowledge so that your pupils are able to apply the same principles to their own driving.

Make sure you keep up to date with any changes to the rules, regulations or legislation so that you are able to:

- handle your vehicle sympathetically and in an eco-friendly manner;
- apply modern coaching techniques;
- maintain a safe learning environment;
- offer advice to pupils on driver licencing requirements, basic mechanical principles and the rules for safe driving on all types of road; and
- answer pupils' questions confidently and competently.

As a driver: not only do you need a sound knowledge of the rules and regulations contained in *The Highway Code* and *The Official DVSA Guide to Driving*, but you also need to be able to apply them in all situations.

As an instructor: you will need to pass on this knowledge so that the drivers you teach will also be able to apply the same principles for driving safely. As well as enhancing your driving skills, having a sound knowledge and understanding will help in your preparations to become an effective instructor.

Communication

As a driver, you communicate your intentions to other road users in a variety of different ways. Similarly, as an instructor, your instruction skills will involve communicating effectively and in different ways with the wide variety of types of pupil you will be dealing with. Adapt the terminology you use so that all of your pupils understand exactly what you mean.

As a driver: you have to continually communicate your intentions to other road users. Methods of signalling these intentions include:

- using indicators and arm signals;
- brake lights;
- early positioning on the road;
- reversing lights;
- horn and flashing headlights;
- hazard warning flashers;
- eye contact.

As an instructor: you have various ways of communicating effectively with a wide variety of pupils. You may sometimes have to adapt the terminology you use so that each individual pupil understands exactly what you mean.

Not only will you teach your pupils how to apply the relevant procedures and driving techniques, you will also need to explain why these procedures should be followed. This 'why' reasoning should lead to a better understanding that will result in safer drivers.

There are various ways in which you can communicate with your pupils, including:

- establishing the level of understanding of the individual pupil;
- finding the most appropriate method and style of communication;
- explaining new principles in a clear and straightforward way;
- using visual aids so that the pupil can 'see' what you mean;
- giving practical demonstrations of any complicated procedures;
- developing confidence and success by talking the pupil through any new procedures;
- giving your directional instructions clearly and in good time so that the pupil has time to respond safely;
- giving encouragement through positive feedback and praise where deserved;
- finding out whether the pupil has fully understood your instructions by asking appropriate questions;
- encouraging the pupil to ask questions if you feel that he or she does not understand.

Chapter 1 explains how and why people learn. In developing your own practical teaching skills and transferable skills yourself, you will recognise that training will not necessarily be easy and will often require a high degree of self-motivation and discipline. This is all part of your own learning process and will give you a better understanding of how your learners feel when they are struggling to master new skills.

You will learn how to evaluate your own strengths and weaknesses, which is all part of the learning process.

When you reflect on these strengths and weaknesses you can start to modify your teaching and coaching skills. This will promote more efficient learning through the establishment of effective relationship skills.

Remember – there is no such thing as a bad learner. Some pupils merely find it more difficult than others to acquire new skills or to absorb new information. Some people will have natural coordination skills, while others need to work to achieve them. Your explanations may need to be given in a slightly different way, or you may need to adapt your teaching methods to suit the pupil.

To bring out the best in pupils the skill of the good instructor is in knowing when to:

- *explain; discuss; demonstrate; instruct; repeat; analyse; correct; assess; question; praise; encourage.*

Being able to use all these skills, and knowing when to use each one, ensures that more effective learning takes place.

Your learners will learn from any mistakes they make during a lesson. Similarly, you can learn from your own instructional mistakes or weaknesses that may have led to that error. At the end of each lesson you could ask yourself:

- 'How much effective learning has taken place?'
- 'Could I have done any more to help my pupil achieve the objectives that we set at the start of the lesson?'

Only by continually evaluating your own performance will you be able to improve and develop your practical teaching skills.

Chapter 2 deals with communication skills, including verbal and non-verbal communication, effective questioning, active listening skills, body language and written communication.

All these skills are important as effective communication with our pupils is a key element in the learning process.

One important area that is covered involves the skill of effective listening and making sure that the dialogue between you and the pupil is genuinely two-way.

The final section in this chapter relates to feedback and how this is relevant to the process of individual learning.

Coaching and client-centred skills are covered in **Chapter 3**. The chapter includes a comparison of different teaching and coaching methods, as well as the qualities and skills required to be an effective coach. Two important sections cover the way we can modify behaviour by using the 'GROW' model and an emphasis on how attitudes, beliefs and values can affect the pupil.

Client-centred learning is, of course, vitally important to ensure that the learner gains a lifetime skill rather than simply achieving short-term learning in order to pass the driving test.

Chapters 4 and 5 are about how you can effectively structure a lesson and a training programme for your pupils by using your client-centred learning and coaching skills.

These chapters cover the basic requirements for organising the training of your pupils in a structured way. They also include the essential elements of how to involve the pupils in the learning process. There are suggestions on how to use different teaching and learning strategies, as well as ideas on how to format and structure specific lessons.

Some of the main topics in these chapters include:

- pupil involvement;

- levels of instruction;

- adapting to the pupil's individual needs;

- route planning and utilisation; and

- how to measure and record progress.

Chapter 6 includes a complete breakdown of the National Standard for Driver Training, with the addition of several highlighted notes and significant points.

The National Standard has been produced by the DVSA as a means of defining the precise role and function of the instructor. In both the Part 3 qualifying exam and the Standards Check the assessment is made against the criteria set out in the Standards.

In **Chapter 7** we introduce a model for goal setting and risk management. This section includes an explanation of over- and under-instructing, as well as several examples of setting the goal and managing the risks.

Chapter 8 deals with the ADI Standards Check and how you can use your coaching and client-centred skills effectively to obtain the best possible grading.

As well as an overview of the format of the Standards Check, the criteria required and the revised grading system, there are also sections on preparation and presentation.

The Standards Check is now much more performance-based. It is based on the requirements of the National Standards and focuses on whether the pupil has gained real benefit from the lesson. Each of the 17 'competences' is covered in some detail, including the main sections of 'lesson planning', 'risk assessment' and 'learning strategies'.

The chapter also includes practical examples of the individual competences for various types of lesson and levels of learning.

In **Chapter 9** we cover a wide range of subjects and topics that are relevant to 'continuing professional development'. The chapter includes: personal skills, business skills and customer care, your own driving, and opportunities for expanding or diversifying your business.

The two appendices include information about other appropriate reading materials and useful contact details.

By using this book in a practical manner and in conjunction with your practical training or refresher training you can learn how to improve your practical teaching, coaching and client-centred skills. This will benefit your pupils, your own personal development and assist you in achieving the best possible grading on your Standards Check.

Remember that learning is a continuous process!

01
How people learn

Whether you are a trainee instructor or an experienced ADI, you can always develop and improve your practical teaching skills by understanding:

- why people learn to drive;
- what motivates pupils;
- how learning takes place; and
- the factors involved in barriers to learning.

Your pupils may be learning for a variety of reasons, including:

- social, domestic or leisure pursuits;
- business and employment requirements;
- personal satisfaction; or
- the need for independent mobility.

Once they have passed the test your pupils will understand or appreciate how the other benefits gained will improve or enhance their quality of life by giving them:

- greater freedom and mobility;
- improved confidence and status;
- better employment or promotion potential; and
- increased earning power.

When these benefits are considered, together with the fact that a driving licence is effectively valid for life, driving lessons can be regarded as extremely good value for money. These benefits can be outlined to the pupil right from the start of their lessons and in the context of the amount of training required for acquiring a life skill.

The main objective and motivation for most learners is to pass their test and obtain a full driving licence at the earliest opportunity, with the minimum of effort and at the least possible cost. In recent years, most young people have started their driver training as soon as they are old enough, but there are now some indications that a significant number of 17-year-olds are delaying their training and putting off lessons until they are slightly older. Some 10 years ago, about 50 per cent of all 17- to 21-year-olds held a full driving licence, but that figure has now dropped to about 26 per cent. The cost of learning, combined with the escalating costs of insurance for young drivers, may be influencing their decision.

The cost of insurance is one of the inhibiting factors for a young and inexperienced driver. New drivers in the 17–21 age group are six times more likely to be involved in a road traffic accident than any other group of drivers. For this reason, insurance premiums are increased significantly for newly qualified young drivers. However, several insurance companies offer substantial discounts for drivers who have a black box fitted. With a black box policy your driving is monitored using a telematics box installed in your car, so by driving sensibly you could enjoy cheaper cover.

Structured training

The main benefits of a properly structured programme of training with a professional trainer such as you will include:

- a good relationship that allows learning to be fun and engaging;
- a potential saving in time and possible wasted effort;
- a higher level of knowledge, understanding, attitude and skill;
- a better chance of passing the 'L' test and accomplishing safe driving for life.

To ensure your customers achieve these benefits you need an understanding of how adults learn. Only through this understanding will you be able to structure a programme of learning to suit the individual needs of each of your pupils.

During your normal working day you will find that your lessons involve using several different methods and strategies. This is part of what 'coaching' is all about – 'using all facilities and methods at our disposal'. Coaching and the principles relating to 'Goals for Driver Education' (GDE) are both dealt with in detail in Chapter 3.

Private practice

Although some people still learn to drive with friends or relatives it has been shown that more than 95 per cent of all learners taking the driving test have had some professional instruction.

Sometimes they have their initial instruction with a professional to acquire the basic skills but, more commonly, they acquire the basic skills and then come to the professional just before the 'L' test saying, 'I just want to make sure I'm doing everything right!'

Of course, in the latter case it is rather like 'shutting the stable door after the horse has bolted'. It is in this sort of situation that you will have a selling job to do. This may be in the form of selling more lessons, if there is enough time and money available. Alternatively, the pupil may need to be persuaded to postpone the test to give them more time to improve and practise the correct procedures.

Unless the friend or relative carrying out the teaching has some form of instructional background, and is a reasonably good driver, it is a distinct disadvantage if the learner has received no lessons at all from a professional instructor. On the other hand, private practice of the right kind can be very helpful, particularly if it is carried out with your support.

Consider inviting a parent to sit in the back of the driving lesson so that they can see how their son or daughter is getting on. You can then guide their private practice.

Motivation

Finding out why your pupil wants to learn to drive is as relevant to you as it is to them. People learn more effectively if they have clearly defined goals to aim for. If you understand some of the personal factors governing the pupil's motivation, it helps you to structure an appropriate programme of lessons for their individual needs. Some people may indicate that they want to pass their driving test as quickly as possible. This isn't a motive for learning to drive and you will need to explore this further. There are several reasons why people might want to learn to drive:

- Independence – they may feel trapped and that they must rely on friends or relatives to run them around; they may be fed up with using public transport to get to work every day.

- Employment – they may be out of work and recognise that a driving licence will increase their employment opportunities because it will increase their ability to travel further to get to work. Or, they may be looking for work doing deliveries, for example.

- Self-esteem – they believe it will boost their self-confidence, or help them establish or keep friends.

- Mobility – they may want or need to drive their family or friends around. Or, they may live out in the country and getting around is very difficult when you must rely on public transport.

- Illness – a partner or family member becoming ill sometimes makes it necessary for people to learn to drive.

- Expectation – it is expected that they will learn to drive – either by their peers or their parents, for example. Everyone else can drive and they should also.

Holding a conversation with someone at the beginning of their driving lessons with you is very beneficial to draw out from them why they want to learn to drive. You will be able to remind them of their reasons if they are feeling despondent about their progress during their lessons or questioning why they are bothering. Keeping your pupils motivated is crucial to their learning.

The learning process

Learning is individual

All learners start from their own position of knowledge and have their own personal set of experiences to draw upon. When new pupils come to you they will each have a whole lifetime of individual previous experiences behind them that will give them a completely different starting point from other new pupils. They may have driving experience and they may already have had some driving lessons; they may have ridden a push bike or a motorcycle; they probably have been a passenger in both the front seat of the car as well as the back seat; they probably have been on buses and in taxis; they most certainly will have been a pedestrian; they may have been involved in a crash or know someone who has. In terms of their experiences unrelated to driving, they may have loved or hated school; they may find it easy or difficult to socialise and make friends; they might find learning difficult or easy. All these things set them apart from the next person and mean that, as a driver trainer, you should take your lead from them as to what their starting point is.

Learning is contextual

The context in which learners learn and operate affects how and what they understand. This is to do with giving meaning to the learning. For example, sitting inside the car isn't the only meaningful place to learn to drive. Because learning to drive involves far more than operating the controls of the vehicle, some of the learning could be done outside of the car. It is sometimes helpful to stand on a bridge and watch the traffic and discuss how it is behaving; or to watch a video of different traffic situations at home; or to be in a classroom situation with other people also learning to drive. If we make assumptions about the context needed for our pupils to learn most effectively, we could be restricting their ability to learn. Changing the environment can sometimes greatly enhance the learning.

Another aspect of the context is to do with the personal comfort of the pupil. You may have noticed that you sometimes feel the cold more than your pupils because they are struggling to learn something and it causes their body temperature to rise. Encouraging them to open the window or turn down the temperature is part of them taking responsibility and helps prepare them for driving on their own once they have passed their test. Also, recognising that your pupil needs to get out of the car and have a quick leg stretch is part of taking into consideration the learning context. Having a packet of mints available or a bottle of water is likely to help maximise their learning.

Learning is relational

In order to make sense and achieve a deep understanding of material and experiences, learners need to relate new information to existing knowledge and experiences. It is helpful to recap on what has already been covered in a previous lesson if it is going to be relevant to today's lesson because your pupil can then link the new piece of information to the old. Asking your pupil, rather than telling them, reinforces the learning that has already taken place. If your pupil actually puts the previous learning into practice this really helps. For example, you are going to move onto emerging from junctions. Encouraging the pupil to drive around a block of left and right turns concentrating on approaching to turn left or right into minor roads for 10 minutes first will make the world of difference to how well they learn.

Learning is developmental

Having made sense of new information and integrated it into an existing framework of understanding, learners can then make informed choices about what to do next and how to develop their understanding. Learning is most effective when people take responsibility for their own development. Even though you know what needs to be covered for your pupils to be able to drive safely and pass the driving test, it is helpful to them if they can choose what they want to do next. This develops their ability to evaluate their progress to date and judge what would be most appropriate for them to learn next given their current skills. You would find it helpful to structure this kind of conversation using GROW (Goals, Reality, Options, Way Forward) and this is covered in more detail in Chapter 3. When they are driving independently having passed the driving test, you will have helped develop decision-making and judgement skills, critical to safe driving.

Learning is experiential

This means we learn from experience, experimentation and self-discovery.

When you trained to become a driving instructor you probably focused most on explaining with a briefing how to do something, possibly offering a demonstration and then going out and practising a new topic by talking

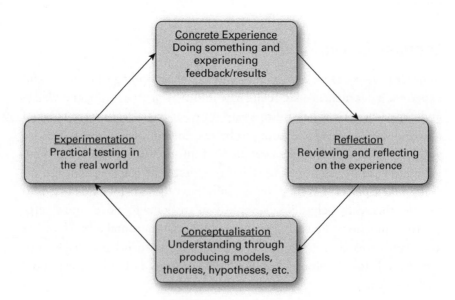

your pupil through what they needed to do in order to be successful. This is just one way of teaching a topic and may not be the most effective way for all your pupils to learn all of the time, especially when you consider the process of learning as detailed in the four points above (individual, contextual, relational and developmental). In 1984 David Kolb developed a theory of learning, which cycles through four stages. Kolb's theory of learning gives us an insight into several different starting points when teaching a new topic to your pupils or wishing to develop their existing set of skills.

1 Concrete experience

Some pupils are activists in their learning, which means that they need to have a go at something first before discussing it. To start with a briefing can be a waste of time because the information you are giving to them doesn't make any sense.

2 Reflection

Having had a go at something and experienced the results, pupils can then review and reflect on their experience by considering what went well, what didn't go so well and what needs improving. As a starting point this might mean the pupil visualises having a go at something and reflects on how they think it might go; or, the pupil could watch you demonstrating first and then discuss it; or, observe a traffic situation and consider how they would behave in a similar situation.

3 Conceptualisation

Once the pupil has had a go at something and reflected on the experience, they need to consider what to do next to either improve or develop. Here, they will need to consider several different options and, possibly, have a go at some of these in order to determine which is the most successful for themselves. As a starting point, you might, for example, introduce a manoeuvre and then ask how they think they would do this. They might draw a diagram or simply describe what they would need to do in order to carry out the manoeuvre safely. You should encourage them to come up with several different alternatives for themselves.

4 Experimentation

Now the pupil is ready to have another go at one of the options considered in the conceptualisation stage. There may be a 'double loop' here where the pupil experiments and returns to stage 3 to develop another theory or model before looping back up to stage 4 and experimenting again.

Kolb's learning theory links closely to the GROW model (for details see Chapter 3). One thing worth remembering is that most people benefit from a range of methods and teaching styles and will learn most effectively if you vary the techniques you use.

The importance of sight

In the learning process, sight is the most important of the senses. When teaching others to drive you can use this sense in various ways to improve the quality of the learning taking place.

Whether giving a demonstration, pointing out actual driving situations or using visual aids, any teaching that involves a pupil's sense of sight will be most effective in fixing new information in their mind.

The following diagram shows the proportions in which our senses gather information. The diagram shows the effectiveness of sight in the learning process compared to simply explaining the numbers.

In driving, both hearing and touch can have an important role. For example, as well as seeing things, when listening and feeling as the noise of the engine changes and the clutch is raised to the 'biting point', pupils will be developing the awareness and perception that go with these senses.

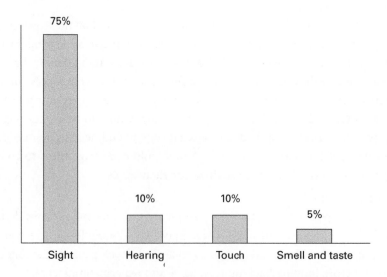

The proportions in which our senses gather information

THE DISTANCE between A and B appears to be longer than that between B and C. The illusion occurs because the space between A and B is measured out in evenly spaced dots, filling the area for the eye. The distance between B and C can only be guessed at because there are no intermediate points.

Awareness

Awareness is usually defined as knowing and understanding what is going on around you. In driving, awareness involves not only the perception and interpretation of one's own vehicle speed, position and direction of travel, but also the recognition of other hazards in time to take the necessary safe action.

Perception and awareness are the first steps towards performing a skill such as driving. Awareness is dependent on the interpretation and meaning the brain attaches to the information it receives from the senses. This involves not only looking with the eyes but also using the mind and calling upon existing knowledge from previous experience to 'see' with the mind.

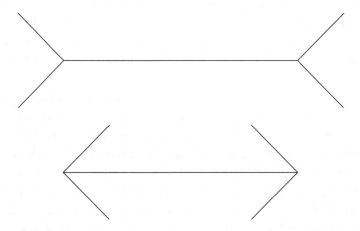

THE LENGTHS of the two horizontal lines appear unequal because of the directional arrows at the ends. Where the arrows branch outward, the line seems to be stretched out beyond its actual length. Where they branch in, the line seems to be strictly enclosed and shortened. Both of the lines are exactly the same length.

What the eyes see is not always the same as what is perceived by the brain. Optical illusions offer evidence of this. They may be caused by distortion through perspective or by a lack of intermediate visual keys that help the viewer to gauge distance accurately.

This visual distortion, plus a weakness in a driver's ability to judge correctly the width of the vehicle they are driving, or that of approaching vehicles, can have very serious consequences.

What students perceive while learning not only depends on the individuality of their senses but also on how each person has learnt to see and interpret things.

Transfer of learning

This happens when a pupil uses skills that have been acquired in previous experiences and in different environments. Examples include problem solving, decision making and prioritising.

All of these are part of everyday life. You will often be able to relate or transfer your pupil's existing skills to help in driving.

Incoming sensations are instantly compared with existing knowledge stored in the memory from previous experiences. The compatibility of these memories can either help or hinder learning of any new material. Where the new information is compatible with existing knowledge and thoughts, the established memories will be reinforced. For example, somebody learning to play tennis who is already a good squash player may find the learning less difficult because both sports are very similar. This is usually referred to as *positive transfer of learning*.

Sometimes previous knowledge can be a hindrance to learning. An example of this could be someone who decides to learn to drive a car and has been used to riding a motorcycle in scrambling trials, an activity where success depends on the frequent taking of risks. Put this rider behind the wheel of a car on the road and the difference in the steering, the width and length of the vehicle and the differing speed norms required may all hinder the learning process. This can be regarded as *negative transfer*. In this case, the learner is likely to be going for gaps that may be narrow, approaching hazards much too fast and struggling to master the steering at the same time.

It will take time for learners to establish the many thousands of memory connections needed to be able to drive safely, along with patience and understanding on your part.

Other basic requirements that are necessary for learning to take place are perception, attention, activity and involvement.

Perception

The senses vary from pupil to pupil and so does their perception. When you are driving along a wet road you will think that you 'see' a three-dimensional scene of slippery tarmac. What you actually see (the image in the eye) is neither slippery nor three-dimensional. This can only mean that you create in your mind a 'model' of what is there. You see the road as being 'wet' or 'slippery' because of the previous experience of such things you have 'fixed' in your mind.

A good example of this would be the lights of an oncoming vehicle on a dark country road at night. The amount of sensory information is very limited, but with your experience you should not have a problem interpreting it. You cannot see the vehicle, but you know that it is there! You will build an image of the type and size of vehicle to which the lights belong and decide whether any defensive action is required.

Drawing on your own experience, you will need to help your pupils to 'fix' such things in their minds. This can be done by using question and answer routines regarding road surface, weather conditions, etc.

The diagram on the next page gives an illustration of how the mind sometimes 'sees' things that may not really be there. The central triangle in each of the figures is an illusion. Although we see the edges as sharp and clear, they are not there. There is no actual brightness difference across the edges; the triangle must therefore be constructed in the mind of the observer.

In the early stages of learning to drive some pupils will have difficulty in judging the width and length of the car they are driving, and the speed, distance and size of oncoming traffic. At night the problem for the inexperienced driver may be made worse by an optical illusion called 'irradiation'. This is a physiological phenomenon that occurs when the eye focuses on neighbouring bright and dark areas.

Although both squares in the diagram opposite are identical in size the image of the white square will, to most people, appear larger. Light-coloured cars can therefore, in some situations, appear to be larger and closer than dark-coloured cars of identical size.

Because illusions of this nature could have dangerous repercussions for your pupils, you should encourage them to take some of their lessons at night so that you are there to give guidance and help in resolving any problems that may occur.

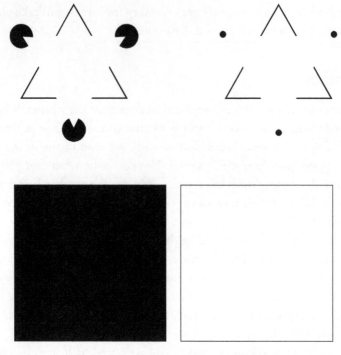

Optical illusion caused by irradiation

Attention

It is often quite difficult to maintain a pupil's attention for a length of time without either a break or a change of activity. If you are involved in intensive courses, you need to take this into account and arrange the programme accordingly. Equally, you will need to consider your pupils' attention span, whether your lessons are 50 minutes, 1 hour, 1½ hours, or 2 hours in length. Breaking the learning into small manageable chunks is going to be far more effective than giving a briefing at the start of the lesson and allowing the pupil to drive for the rest of the lesson without a break. Repeating routes and circuits that take just a few minutes to complete, with time for reflection and development, will ensure that goals are achieved and that learning takes place. If you bear Kolb's learning theory in mind then you will appreciate that the time to reflect and come up with new ways of doing things is as important as the practice.

You should watch for non-verbal signals from the pupil that may indicate boredom, impatience or fatigue (see the section on body language in Chapter 2).

Activity and involvement

An essential requirement of any effective training is that the pupil must be actively involved in the learning. Avoid very long briefings or detailed explanations that do not require any active involvement on the part of the pupil.

The more active and involved your pupils are in the learning experience, the more they will normally learn and remember. Activity, however, should not be thought of as only physical. Learning to drive obviously involves a lot of physical activity but it is often the mental involvement that initiates the physical response to a situation. Effective instructors will help their learners to think and reason things out for themselves, leading them to the desired conclusion.

Use questions to test your pupils' understanding of what they are doing and why it is important, and then through physically carrying out the task learning will take place. This practical involvement validates the teaching and can be done in various ways.

Old-style methods of instruction often involve very little intellectual activity on the part of the learner. Typical examples include teaching the answers to questions without confirming the pupil's real understanding, instructing without any explanation or pupil involvement, or telling the pupil to do something without explaining why or finding out if the pupil knows or understands what is being taught. This teaching method is very limited because it tends to promote only short-term learning.

Using a more up-to-date method that includes coaching techniques means that the teaching/learning is much more 'pupil-centred' than 'instructor-led'. This approach leads to a higher level of individual participation, with pupils taking more responsibility for their own learning.

Memorising

This is sometimes called *rote learning* or *parrot-fashion learning*, and is the method by which many of us learnt our times tables at school. Rote learning is rather limited in that it does not necessarily provide an understanding of the subject.

For example, a learner could memorise the overall stopping distances of a vehicle and be able to tell you, 'The stopping distance if you are travelling at 30 miles per hour on a dry road would be 23 metres'. The learner should then be asked to point out something that is 23 metres away! Even when pupils can do this reasonably accurately, it is still necessary to test their ability to keep a safe distance from the car in front when driving at 30 miles per hour.

> *Knowledge in itself does not guarantee an understanding, or the ability to use the knowledge and link it with the skill of leaving sufficient distance between vehicles. Knowledge is often, therefore, just the starting point.*
>
> *An efficient instructor or coach uses a skilful question and answer technique to verify that the pupil understands the topic and to test their ability to put that knowledge into practice.*

This is sometimes known as *validation*: it involves proving that something has been understood by demonstrating the ability to carry it out.

Memory is vital for those learning to drive as there is no point in learning something if it is forgotten in a short time. The ability of your pupils to retain information and knowledge, and their capacity for forgetting what they have already learnt, will vary enormously from person to person. Engaging with the pupil and varying the methods you use to communicate with them is very important because it will make the learning more fun and therefore more memorable.

Developing long-term memory

The first stage is to put the information in a form that can be more easily remembered by:

- breaking it down into its key components;
- using mnemonics – for example, M S M, P S L, L A D;
- painting pictures – 'What would happen if...?';
- using word associations like 'ease the clutch', 'squeeze the gas' and 'creep and peep';
- using visual keys – for example, 'round signs give orders, triangular signs give warnings', 'think of the thickness of a coin'.

When you have translated the information into a more memorable form, you could write it down and ask your pupils to memorise it by rote. You could then check whether they have remembered it by asking questions at the beginning of the next lesson. If they have not learnt it, do not lose heart. Explain that it can be difficult to learn and encourage them to do some more studying. Repetition is a very good way of fixing information in the brain, but care should be taken to ensure that your repetition does not sound like 'nagging'.

You should encourage your pupils to study *The Highway Code*, *The Official Guide to Learning to Drive* and *The Official DVSA Guide to Driving: The essential skills*. You will then need to confirm that this has been done by testing their knowledge. This can be achieved by setting simple multiple-choice questions that could be given as homework, thus helping them both to maintain interest in between their driving lessons and to prepare for the theory test.

There are some very good CDs and DVDs you could lend to your pupils for home use. This should also help to maintain their interest. If you do this, you must ensure that you are not infringing any copyright restrictions.

Understanding

An effective way of finding out whether your pupils understand something is to ask them to explain it to you: 'What are the reasons for looking round over your shoulder before moving off?' 'What must you do when you get to your turning point before you begin to reverse into a parking space?' And 'What is the reason for this?' 'What might happen?'

Understanding something means knowing its meaning, whether it is a statement of fact, a concept, or a principle. When a pupil is learning to do something, it is important that, to begin with, the key steps are understood, and then practice takes place until mastery has been achieved. Rote learning will be of little help to the pupil here and you need to use a technique that involves learning by understanding.

This method involves using mental processes as well as physical ones. It relies on the principle that the whole is greater than the sum of the parts. The easiest way to illustrate this is to use the analogy of a piece of music. Many of us often remember a catchy tune, to such an extent that we cannot get it out of our heads. It would be much more difficult, however, to remember just a few notes, and almost impossible to remember just one note, as this would depend on having perfect pitch.

When teaching pupils how to approach junctions, you need to outline the complete manoeuvre and then break this down into its component parts. First of all, they need to understand the *mirrors-signal-manoeuvre* routine and then be able to break down the manoeuvre part into the *position-speed-look* and *look-assess-decide* routines.

Not only do pupils need to understand the when, where, how and why elements involved in these sequences, but they also need to practise carrying them out until a reasonable degree of safety is achieved. No matter how well pupils understand and can carry out any component parts of the junction routine, unless they can approach and emerge safely, very little will have been achieved.

So, the next teaching technique is to go back to whichever component part needs improving to get the learner to carry out the complete manoeuvre effectively. This may involve you in giving more explanation, possibly a demonstration and certainly more practice in order to improve performance. All these principles are dependent on the pupils' understanding.

> *There is little point in getting to the practice stage if pupils do not understand what is expected of them.*

The starting point in teaching understanding is to 1) ask questions, and 2) solve problems.

Asking questions to check knowledge and understanding

When deciding how to get information across to your learners you should ask yourself 'where, when and how do we need to do that?' You will then need to ask the pupils the same questions or discuss the reasons. Effective instructors will probably use a mixture of asking and telling to make lessons more varied. When using a question and answer routine, avoid making it sound like an interrogation as this will only annoy or demoralise, and you may lose the pupil!

Relate any new information to what pupils already know (teaching from the known to the unknown). This will allow them to build up a store of understanding. It is of little use for your pupils to know how and when to do something if they do not understand why it is important.

We have all had pupils come to us from other instructors, or those who have been taught by friends or relatives, who are making mistakes and do not understand why what they are doing is wrong. For example, you may get pupils who signal every time they move off when there are no other road users in sight. When you ask, 'Was that signal necessary or useful?' the reply might be: 'I've been told that you must always signal before you move off.' It is obvious from this response that there is no understanding of what signals should be used for, or how and when to use them. The pupil's response can be followed up by supplementary questions such as 'Did anyone benefit from your signal?', which will lead to a useful discussion on the subject.

> *Your job is to explain why it is important to assess each situation on its own merits, and then decide if a signal is required. You could confirm this by asking, 'Who were you signalling to?' or, 'What if... ?'*

Open-ended questions that encourage active and creative participation, insight and contemplation will bring about better understanding by the pupil rather than closed questions that only require a yes or no response.

Solving problems

Learning how to solve problems for themselves will help your pupils to understand things and therefore take responsibility for their driving once they have passed the driving test.

Solving problems usually relies on learners being able to transfer to new situations any knowledge and understanding already stored in their long-term memory. This should assist them in working out different possible solutions to a particular problem. They can then evaluate these solutions and decide which is the most appropriate for the problem concerned. This is a valuable skill when they are driving on their own and will develop their ability to work out for themselves how to prevent risky and dangerous driving situations from occurring.

> To encourage your pupils to solve problems successfully, you will need to pose the appropriate questions, which will enable a solution to be arrived at. Once the problem has been solved, it is easier to understand why it occurred in the first place and how to prevent it in the future.

The technique of problem solving is particularly useful when analysing the driving errors made by learners, whether they are in the car (errors of control) or outside (errors of road procedure). An example of this would be a learner driver turning left and swinging wide after the corner. The cause of the error might be obvious to the instructor, but not so obvious to the learner, who may perceive several possible reasons. Perhaps the steering was started too late, there was a misjudgement of the amount of lock needed, or the corner was approached at too high a speed, meaning that there was insufficient time to steer accurately enough to maintain the correct position.

Having recognised the fault, the effective instructor would help the pupil to analyse the fault by using a discussion to arrive at the cause of it. The first question could be: 'Do you think you swung wide after that last corner?' After a series of supplementary questions such as, 'How can we avoid that situation on another occasion?' and, 'What, in particular, might we do differently?' followed by a discussion, the pupil should eventually arrive at an answer that works for them.

Having arrived at a possible solution it would be helpful to take the pupil round the block to have another attempt at turning the same corner. You might agree to give the pupil a 'talk-through', particularly on when to start braking and how much to brake, in order to ensure that the corner is negotiated more accurately. When success is achieved, the pupil should then be allowed to deal with similar corners unassisted, thus validating their understanding and skill.

This all sounds logical when you put it down on paper. However, it is sometimes surprising how some instructors would, first of all, fail to pinpoint accurately the cause of the error (not just the effect), and then not be able to assist the pupil in working out a solution to the problem, or to put the solution into practice.

Skills training

In learning to drive it is the practical application of the knowledge, understanding and attitudes gained that is most important. Whatever the situation, when learning to do something there are three basic steps:

1 *Determine the purpose* – what we need to do and why it needs to be done in a particular way.

2 *Identify the procedures involved* – the different alternatives of how it might be done.

3 *Practise the task* – do.

1. Determine the purpose

Learners must have a clear understanding of the reason for needing to be able to do whatever it is that you are teaching them. When teaching people how to drive the reasons why things are done in a certain way are invariably to do with:

- safety;
- convenience;
- efficiency;
- simplicity;
- economy.

One example that covers all of the above would involve the use of brakes to slow the car rather than the gears:

- *Safety*: both hands are on the steering wheel when the weight of the car is thrown forward; the brake lights come on to warn following drivers.

- *Convenience*: there is less to do if you slow the car with the brakes rather than using only the gears.

- *Efficiency*: the car is being slowed by all four wheels rather than just two.

- *Simplicity*: it is easier to change gear at the lower speed.

- *Economy*: brake pads and discs are much less expensive to replace than clutches and gearboxes.

2. Identify the procedures

The most efficient way for a learner to understand how to do something is to break the skill down into manageable chunks or stages. This can be done by following a few basic guidelines:

- *Known to unknown*. Start with what the pupil knows, understands and can do, before moving on to new skills and procedures.

- *Simple to complex*. Setting intermediate targets and moving gradually to more complex tasks will help the pupil through the learning process.

- *Basic rules to the variations*. Once the basic rules for a particular procedure have been mastered, the pupil will find it easier to deal with the variations.

- *Concrete observations to abstract reasoning*. Organising a structured learning process is much less difficult if the learner can start with the more obvious facts before attempting to cope with more complicated or abstract matters.

For more detail on structuring the learning process, see *The Driving Instructor's Handbook*.

3. Practise the task

What I hear, I forget.
What I see, I remember.
What I do, I understand.

Remember that it is the doing that will give pupils the greatest understanding. In each driving lesson you must therefore give your pupil time to practise the skills that have been learnt.

Although some car driving routines could be taught initially by *rote* (for example, the M S M, P S L and L A D routines), putting them into practice requires an understanding that allows the pupil to make connections with any previously established principles. For example, once your pupil has carried out a basic manoeuvre using the criteria of control, observation and accuracy, it will be relatively easy for them to follow the same pattern in a similar, but slightly more complicated manoeuvre.

As an instructor you will be mixing learning methods to suit the needs of each individual pupil, combined with the all-important practice. The skill of the teacher is to find a mix that works and to be prepared to change to a different mixture if necessary.

The key to good instruction is the flexibility of the instructor to be able to work out what is best for the pupil and adapt the teaching to suit.

Defensive driving

You can contribute positively to reducing the risk of accidents by teaching your pupils defensive driving techniques and attitudes. The development of a defensive attitude is as important as skill development. It is good to be able to get out of trouble when a potentially dangerous situation arises, but it is much more effective and sensible to avoid getting into trouble in the first place! The theory of defensive driving relies on the fact that human behaviour is generally motivated most powerfully by a desire to preserve one's own safety.

Defensive driving develops this concept by instilling in drivers an attitude designed to do just that, coupled with the advanced observation of potential accident situations. It may be defined as 'driving in such a way as to prevent accidents, in spite of adverse conditions and the incorrect action of others'. The need for teaching defensive driving skills is emphasised by the DVSA's use of 'hazard-perception' testing in the theory 'L' test.

An accident has been described as 'an unforeseen and unexpected event', but in many cases potential road accidents can be foreseen and avoided. In most cases, when accidents happen, they are caused by driver error. Everyone then asks who was to blame. Of far more value to driver education is to consider: 'Was it preventable?' A preventable accident is one where the driver – not necessarily at fault – could reasonably have taken some action to prevent it happening.

Some of the main factors involved in road accidents include:

- the driver;
- the vehicle;
- road conditions;
- visibility;
- weather conditions; and
- time of day.

In this section we will be concentrating on the driver and how we can instil into our learners a 'defensive attitude', although *The Driving Instructor's Handbook* gives more detail on hazard awareness, reducing risk and the theory of defensive driving.

Human actions that may contribute to accident situations include:

- committing a traffic offence;
- abuse of the vehicle;
- impatience;
- discourtesy;
- lack of attention.

The defensive driver will consider all the main factors in the first list. This involves making a continuous and conscious effort to:

- recognise each hazard in advance;
- undertand the defensive attitude needed; and
- apply the skill required to take preventive action in enough time.

Encourage your pupils to drive with full concentration to avoid potential accidents caused by other drivers and road users.

> Constant awareness is required so that, no matter what they do, other road users will be unlikely to be involved in an accident with drivers you have trained.

Teach your pupils how to avoid confrontation with other drivers and how to keep a cushion of safe space around their vehicle. This includes advice about drivers who follow too closely.

Encourage your pupils to continually ask themselves, 'What if... ?' In this way they will improve their anticipation skills and be able to take defensive action before a situation develops into an accident.

Teach them to consider using the horn to let others know they are there; just a gentle tap on the horn can sometimes prevent an accident. It is far better for your pupils to sound the horn to alert another person than not to sound it and have to carry out an emergency stop, especially if there is a vehicle close behind.

As well as thinking defensively, develop positive attitudes towards:

- vehicle maintenance and safety;
- traffic law (for example safe use of speed, traffic signs and road markings, parking restrictions, drink/drive laws, dangerous driving implications);
- the more vulnerable groups of road users;
- reduced-risk driving strategies;
- further education and training for advanced/defensive driving;
- learning and studying.

Overcoming barriers

Pupils all learn at different rates. Your training will need to be structured to take this into consideration and allow for the fact that some of them will experience barriers to learning. These barriers may affect the learners' studies for their theory tests, the rate at which they learn to drive or a combination of both.

There are many barriers to learning that you will need to help your pupils overcome. As a rule, the older the student, the greater the barriers tend to be. Learning is the bringing about of more or less permanent changes in knowledge, understanding, skills and attitudes. Adults in general find that learning new skills and developing fresh attitudes are more difficult than gaining knowledge and understanding. Barriers to their learning may have to be overcome in any of these areas.

In adult learning the most frequently encountered barrier is previous learning.

Previous learning

Consider how you got on at school and which lesson or activity you enjoyed the most – was it Maths, English, Sport, Science, Cookery, Woodwork, History, Art, Music or French? In your class you will not all have got the same amount of information from all of your lessons. All of us will have taken something different from each of the lessons because each of us processes information through different channels. Most people are able to process information through several channels – visual (seeing), auditory (hearing) and kinaesthetic (feeling). However, a significant minority process information strongly through just one and possibly two channels, to the exclusion of the other channels of communication. In schools it is expected that most information will be learnt through reading and writing and yet this does not meet with the learning needs of a large proportion of the population. The result is that lots of people go through school without feeling they learnt very much at all, and, possibly, blaming themselves for this because they didn't concentrate or pay enough attention. This creates a barrier to their future learning.

Similarly, in driver training, it is important to vary the means of communication to ensure that each customer is learning to the best of their ability. This means that the traditional form of 'Explain, Demonstrate, Practice' is not always the most effective way to learn. Identifying how someone learns best (by asking them) and then choosing together what to do will ensure that learning takes place at a deep and long-lasting level because it has been specifically adapted to suit the individual learning needs of the client. Together, you could choose to let them have a go; get out of the car and look at the road layout; talk them through a situation; swap seats and encourage them to talk you through a situation; draw a mind map; draw a diagram; use a pre-printed diagram; or give a demonstration; or experiment with any other idea the customer might suggest.

Lack of motivation

This is also a barrier to learning. Each learner will have different reasons for wanting to learn to drive and helping them identify those at the start of their driving lessons will help keep them motivated. When they are despondent with their progress, asking them to remind you why they wanted to learn to drive can re-inspire them and re-focus them on their goals.

Difficulties with reading and writing

Difficulties with reading and writing can be a barrier to learning how to drive. However, if you are prepared to adapt your teaching to suit the needs of your pupil you will usually find ways of overcoming these problems.

Very often, people who struggle to read or write make up for these inabilities by being very practical and dextrous and frequently pick up driving with little or no instruction at all!

You will need to use visual aids, discussion and demonstration to get your message across. It would also be useful to involve the pupil's family in assisting with study and learning. Help may be needed, particularly with *The Highway Code* and other essential reading materials.

Dyslexia (word blindness)

The inability to recognise certain words or letters is known as 'dyslexia'. Neither its cause nor its effects are easily explained. Partially genetic, it can be described as a disorganisation of the language area of the brain which, in turn, produces problems connecting sounds with visual symbols. The end result is more readily understood. A person who is dyslexic may experience some learning difficulties with reading, writing and arithmetic.

Ignorance of dyslexia in the past has meant that many people who suffered from the condition were regarded as stupid or unintelligent. However, there is no link between dyslexia and intelligence.

Dyslexia should not present a problem if you are prepared to vary your instruction to suit the needs of the pupil. Use visual aids as well as giving help in recognising and acting on traffic signs. More help may be needed when learning *Highway Code* rules and driving principles.

You should also try to encourage the pupil's family to help with the study. Interactive computer programs are now available to help people with dyslexia overcome some of the problems.

Colour blindness

This is likely to cause problems only when dealing with the different types of traffic light, controlled situations such as junctions and pedestrian and level crossings. Rather than focusing on the colours, you will need to base your explanation on the positioning and sequence of the lights and what each of them means.

Language difficulties

If the pupil's understanding of English is very poor, this can be a barrier to learning and, in extreme cases, the learner might need the help of an interpreter. Provided the pupil has some knowledge of English, the use of visual aids, demonstrations and getting to know what the limitations are, will help you to overcome these difficulties.

It is important, right from the start, for you to encourage pupils to say if there is anything they have not understood. If there is someone in the family who speaks better English than the pupil, it may be useful to have a debriefing with him or her present. This should enable you to clarify specific requests to the pupil and also allow the pupil to convey any queries to you.

Hearing difficulties

There are about 50,000 people in the UK who were either born without any hearing or who lost it during early childhood. There are several thousand others who have become profoundly deaf in adult life, well after they have learnt to speak, read and write. By the time they reach the age of 17 and are thinking about learning to drive, those with severe hearing problems may have had most of their education in specialist schools or units. Some will have speech, but this may be difficult to follow, especially for anyone who is not used to dealing with this type of disability. They will probably use sign language and may also be able to lip-read.

With understanding and patience from an effective instructor, people with hearing difficulties should be able to assimilate all that is necessary to learn to drive.

Although not being able to hear will undoubtedly be a barrier to learning, an understanding of the pupil's special problems will quickly enable you to overcome them.

People who cannot hear do not regard themselves as being disabled. In fact, deafness is not classed as a driver disability, so no restrictions are placed on the full licence.

It is particularly important for people with hearing difficulties, and those with no useful hearing at all, to disclose this fact in the 'Disabilities and special circumstances' box in the DVSA application form for the driving test (DL26). This will ensure that the examiner will be prepared to modify the method of delivery of instructions to suit the candidate's particular needs.

Test candidates who have neither hearing nor speech are allowed a special interpreter. When no interpreter is to be present, you must find time to talk to the examiner well before the date of the test so that you can explain which method has been used to give directions and instructions during training. The examiner can then give directions and instructions that are compatible. This will mean that the pupil on test is much more likely to be relaxed.

Most instructors are rarely asked to teach pupils who have hearing problems and some are reluctant to take this type of pupil. This is mainly because there is a widespread lack of understanding of the problems of people with hearing difficulties and the ways in which they are able to communicate. For many instructors the task may seem too daunting. As a result, people without hearing often find difficulty in obtaining expert tuition and tend to rely on parents and friends – people who may be good at communicating with deaf people but who are not necessarily able to teach safe driving for life. Driving instructors who are specialists in communication, have good practical teaching skills and who understand the effects of not being able to hear are better equipped to teach than friends and relatives.

After adapting your practical teaching skills for people with hearing difficulties, you will find the experience both rewarding and enriching. The problem for you will be to learn the best way to transfer your knowledge, skills, understanding and attitude to these pupils.

It is not necessary for you to learn the British sign language used by people with hearing problems, but you must use simple straightforward words that have only one meaning, avoiding those that might be ambiguous. As lip-reading depends as much on the clarity of the speaker's lip movements as on the ability of the pupil, it is essential that you speak slowly and distinctly, and move your lips to form each word. Face-to-face conversation while stationary becomes more important than with a hearing pupil. Don't shout – the pupil cannot hear what you are saying!

With impaired hearing, sight and touch become a great deal sharper and this helps pupils to overcome the disadvantage of not being able to hear. They are likely to be much more aware of what is happening on the road ahead and will quickly master how to assess risk.

People without hearing also develop great sensitivity of feeling over the normal course of living in silence. Consequently, they often acquire clutch control and coordination with the accelerator fairly easily. People with hearing problems normally have better powers of concentration than learners with normal hearing.

Communication between you and pupils with any hearing difficulty, whether this is with visual aids or by signing, should be reinforced with demonstrations.

When teaching people who have a hearing problem it is vital that a method of communication acceptable to both of you is established at the beginning of the first lesson.

Pre-prepared cards covering what, how, when and why can be used, although the 'why' card needs to be used very carefully to avoid being seen to be confrontational or threatening. The cards can be used to reinforce the key points of any manoeuvre or exercise with drawings of pedestrians, cyclists and cars, indicating the involvement of other road users. A magnetic board can be useful to recreate situations quickly and easily.

When giving directions, a simple form of sign language can be used provided you both agree and understand the signs to be used. These signs, because they are being used while the vehicle is moving along the road, will not be the same as those used in the British sign language. This must be explained to, and fully understood by, the pupil. For example, putting a thumb up will mean 'good', whereas putting a thumb down will mean 'incorrect'.

As a large amount of learning will take place through the eyes, the task of teaching people with hearing difficulties becomes easier with the use of visual aids and demonstrations. Visual aids are not only invaluable, they are essential (see the section in Chapter 4 on visual aids). Face-to-face conversation, simple language and written notes should cover all the other needs of most pupils.

Because you will not be able to use an effective question and answer technique while on the move, diagrams will be invaluable when teaching pupils with hearing difficulties. More time will need to be spent parked somewhere safe so that non-verbal instruction can take place.

Theory training

The DVSA CDs and DVDs on *The Highway Code* and *The Official Theory Test* will be useful for pupils to study in between lessons. Questions can be devised in written form to test their understanding of the rules. Always have a writing pad handy so that any questions and answers can be written down.

If any problems arise, you will benefit from talking to the parents or relatives of pupils and getting in touch with any local associations for deaf people, or The British Deaf Association, 356 Holloway Road, London, N7 6PA, Tel: 07795 410724, Website: www.bda.org.uk.

Other barriers to learning

Mere discomfort can be a barrier to learning. You need to be able to recognise whether or not your pupils are comfortable. Discomfort can have many causes, ranging from toothache to sitting in an incorrect position, or being told, 'You must keep your heel on the floor when using the clutch' when the pupil's feet are too small or legs too long to do this comfortably.

Allowances may have to be made for very tall people – they will need the seat as far back as possible with the back rake adjusted to give more leg room. If the tuition vehicle is very small, it may even be necessary for you to advise them to take lessons with another instructor who has a larger car with more headroom.

Pupils of small stature may be assisted by securing cushions underneath and behind them, and pedal extensions may be needed for those with short legs or small feet. Your terminology may also need to be adjusted to allow for pupils not being able to keep their heel down when controlling the clutch.

If a pupil is not driving as well as usual, there may be some simple explanation. For example, was the driving seat adjusted properly on entering the vehicle, or was the pupil in too much of a hurry to 'get going'? Make sure any necessary adjustments and procedures are carried out correctly otherwise you may both be at a loss as to the cause of the problems and the lesson may be wasted.

If the pupil is having an uncharacteristically bad lesson, it may be due to something as simple as wearing different shoes, or as complicated as having problems at home. Ask tactfully if you think a pupil may not be feeling well. The lesson may be completely wasted if a minor illness is causing a distraction. You could even be aiding and abetting an offence if the pupil is taking medication that affects driving.

Other barriers to learning to drive can be related to the use of alcohol which, as well as being illegal when driving, can cause a false sense of confidence and impetuous risk-taking. If you think a pupil has been drinking, ask tactfully and abort the lesson if necessary. On no account let pupils take the test if they have been drinking.

Anxiety, emotion and stress can all affect concentration. If a pupil's driving is not up to the usual standard and they have recently had personal problems, it may be advisable to postpone the lesson.

We are all affected by the ageing process. For those who decide to learn to drive later on in life the going can be difficult. You should explain that it will be more difficult to learn and to remember new procedures. Things may be more easily forgotten and concentration more difficult to sustain. Problems may be even greater for older pupils who have decided to learn to drive because they have lost a partner or close relative. You will need lots of patience and understanding if you are to help these pupils attain their goal.

Continually assess your own effectiveness by asking yourself:

- Do I discuss the benefits of learning to drive in order to motivate my pupil?
- Do I agree the lesson structure with my pupil to make it easier for the pupil to memorise, understand and do things?
- Do I hold conversations to help my pupil develop or modify their attitudes towards driving and other road users?
- Do I discuss with my pupil how to develop their studying skills, setting them enough 'between-lesson' tasks?
- Do I help pupils to overcome any barriers to learning they may have?

Physical disabilities

A physical disability need not necessarily be a barrier to learning to drive, but it is a subject that requires special skills from the instructor. These are dealt with in much more detail in *The Driving Instructor's Handbook*, with an overview in this section.

There are thousands of people with disabilities, some quite severe, who have passed the driving test. Many have proved their skill by also passing an advanced test. Teaching people with disabilities can be very rewarding as such pupils usually have a considerable amount of motivation to learn and will often put in more effort than their able-bodied peers. If you are involved with people with any kind of disability, the practical teaching skills in this book will be particularly relevant in helping you to improve the quality of learning taking place. You will need to pay special attention to the following:

- *Flexibility* – being able to adapt your usual teaching methods to suit the perceived needs of the pupil. Assess each pupil's individual requirements and adapt your teaching methods accordingly.
- *Lesson planning* – being prepared to build in rest breaks and taking care not to spend too long on manoeuvres that may put physical strain on the pupil.
- *Body language* – watching carefully for signs of strain or tiredness. Some people tire very easily as the day progresses, so arrange the lessons to suit the individual pupil's needs.
- *Feedback* – offering feedback only on things that are controllable. Make allowances for limited mobility. Encourage feedback from the pupil.

The above points are essential when teaching all types of pupil whether they have learning difficulties, barriers to learning, physical disabilities or are able-bodied.

Pupils who have quite severe disabilities should be advised to have an assessment from a specialist at one of the mobility centres around the country. A list of these is included in *The Driving Instructor's Handbook*. If it is considered that the pupil will be able to learn successfully, he or she will be advised on how an appropriate vehicle could be adapted to suit the particular requirements.

If you wish to specialise in this kind of work, we recommend that you attend a course for instructors in teaching people with disabilities. Courses are conducted at various centres around the country, including special courses for ADIs at QEF Mobility Services at Carshalton. Full details of all available courses and centres can be found in *The Driving Instructor's Handbook*.

02
Communication

In this chapter we deal with the practical teaching skills of communication that help bring about learning. These skills include verbal, non-verbal and listening skills, all of which are covered in detail.

According to DVSA criteria, to become an efficient instructor and to pass the ADI exams you need to be:

- *Articulate.* This doesn't mean that you need to be a fluent public speaker, but it does mean that you should use language that is clear to your pupils and that can be easily understood by them.

- *Enthusiastic.* Always endeavour to create a supportive learning environment by showing enthusiasm for the work and for your pupils' efforts.

- *Encouraging.* Give encouragement to the pupil when deserved, but balance this with criticism when required. Any criticism should be constructive and related to the requirements of the particular task or situation. Remember that pupils need to be encouraged to take on responsibility for their own learning and not be passively receiving instruction and information.

- *Friendly.* The way you approach the teaching of your pupils should be in a friendly but professional manner, creating a relaxed atmosphere in which learning can take place and in which the pupil can gain confidence.

- *Patient.* As with your own driving, show patience and tolerance, both with other road users and with your own pupils when they make mistakes or are not as efficient as you would like them to be.

- *Confident.* Have confidence in your ability as a driver and as an instructor, but also develop the skill to help your pupils build confidence in their own driving.

In addition to these qualities you also need to be a good listener, perceptive, aware and attentive, as outlined in Chapter 3.

Communication is a two-way process between you and your trainees. This means listening to the pupils and observing their actions, as well as talking. Make sure that any communication from you to your pupils is at a level that is easily understood by them.

As an instructor you will need to develop different ways of communicating effectively with your pupils. You will often have to vary and adapt your methods and terminology to suit the needs of individual pupils, so that each of them clearly understands your message or instructions.

As an effective driver trainer, you need to use a wide variety of methods to communicate with the trainee, including:

- establishing an appropriate level of understanding for each pupil;
- explaining any new principles in a clear and straightforward manner;
- using visual aids where appropriate to give the pupil a clearer picture of what is required;
- considering whether a demonstration would be effective for a particularly complex procedure or manoeuvre;
- offering to 'talk through' any new procedures or routines to develop the pupil's confidence;
- giving any directional instructions clearly and in good time, allowing the pupil plenty of time to make decisions and respond accordingly;
- using positive feedback and praise where appropriate, to encourage and motivate the pupil;
- using questions to ensure that the pupil has a thorough understanding of the task;
- encouraging pupils to ask questions and allowing enough time for them to respond.

Whatever means of communication you use, make sure that both you and the pupil agree about what is required and be ready to modify your methods to suit the needs of the individual.

Use each lesson with a pupil as an opportunity to practise your communication skills. At the end of each lesson, you should analyse your own performance with a view to improving your ability and skills. Reflect by asking yourself:

- 'Have I spent sufficient time looking at and listening to my pupil?'
- 'Have I misinterpreted or not seen any silent signals?'
- 'Have I missed the pupil's control faults or observational errors by not watching carefully enough?'

- 'Has my own body language been positive?'
- 'Have I encouraged or discouraged the pupil by the way in which I reacted to their actions or responses to my questions?'
- 'Could I have communicated more effectively with the pupil during the lesson?'

These points are dealt with in more detail later in this chapter.

Driving instruction has, traditionally, been just that – instructing. This implies telling pupils what to do and expecting them to do it. The problem with this method is that the instructor will usually tell pupils how to do things in the way that he or she – the instructor – was taught originally. This leads to a situation where old procedures and conventional wisdoms are passed on and perpetuated without much consideration for new methods or best practices and without allowing for the personal attributes of the individual pupil. As a result, there is too much dependence on the instructor and this is maintained all the way through the training. In this situation the instructor gives advice and if the pupil is not able to do it there is a tendency to blame the instructor. To give pupils more responsibility to make their own decisions we need to use more effective coaching methods.

Coaching is much more about extending and developing the individual pupil's knowledge and skills and establishing an effective working relationship. The effective coach does this by raising awareness and responsibility in the pupil. Effective coaching involves much more use of active listening and detailed questioning by the instructor as coach and the active involvement of the pupil or student.

Instruction

Instructing mainly involves telling the pupil what to do and how to do it. This has the effect of personal and long-standing individual methods being passed on to the pupil and perpetuated without considering any new methods or practices. The pupil has no real involvement in the learning process and takes very little responsibility for any decision making. One of the problems with instructing is that we are generally not very good at learning by being told things because we do not remember them particularly well; we are usually much better when we actually do something.

Instructing is based on a hierarchy: 'I'm the expert, this is what you have to do.' With this method the emphasis is on the skill and expertise of the instructor being 'pushed' onto the pupil. The result is that the pupil is not sufficiently involved, other than practising what has been taught, and will generally be content to be told what to do in order to achieve a licence. This, of course, does very little to encourage any longer-term learning and often results in the pupil simply learning enough to pass the test rather than generating a life skill.

Coaching

The skill of the effective coach is in extending and developing an individual's knowledge and skills by raising awareness and responsibility in the pupil.

Coaching involves selling ideas and concepts to the pupil and transferring responsibility; it should be an equal partnership between pupil and instructor. In this respect, the objective is not to demonstrate how much the instructor or coach can do or how skilful they are, but to bring out the best in the pupil. It is generally better to let the pupil do what comes naturally, with steering for example, and then gradually guide the pupil along the right lines.

Coaching has many benefits, particularly relating to retained and long-term learning. The instructor is no longer seen as the 'expert' in the traditional way – the coaching relationship is much more an equal partnership. Coaching puts learners in an active role and encourages them to identify their own goals and objectives, both in the long and short term. This is done by creating a situation where the coach finds out and establishes the prior knowledge and experience of the pupil and builds on it.

Coaching (as opposed to instructing) can help to achieve a better performance because of the greater participation, willingness and satisfaction on the part of the trainee.

Coach or instructor?

With 'old-style' instructing, pupils feel that the instructor is in control and that they are indirectly encouraged to take a passive role, simply following instructions. This is why, when instructors ask probing questions as part of the teaching/learning process, they often find that the pupil is reluctant to answer or to be involved in detailed discussion. The pupil's expectation is that the information will be provided. To overcome this situation, it is important to establish the relationship between coach and pupil from the first lesson. This relationship should ideally be an equal partnership, with the instructor (coach) encouraging pupils to set their own goals and to take more active responsibility in the learning process.

As instructors we are used to giving instructions, usually in rote form: 'This is what you do in this situation', 'M S M' and so on. As coaches, we need to move more towards taking what the pupil knows and understands and building on that, using questions such as 'How do you think...?', 'What if...?', 'Why not try...?' To apply coaching techniques effectively to the driving situation, think in terms of the pupil's potential and not simply the actual performance at any one time.

Coaching involves coaxing, questioning, motivating and listening. The most important of these is listening – not just listening but attending to exactly what is being said. The instructor (coach) should listen to, and pay attention to, the pupil always and make sure that he or she is being given the coach's full attention.

There are two major benefits of coaching. The first is improved performance. Coaching brings out the best in individual pupils – instructing does not necessarily do this effectively. The second concerns life skills. Coaching, with more emphasis on the active involvement of the pupil, is more likely to provide the pupil with longer-lasting skills ('safe driving for life'). Instructing is more to do with passing a series of tests.

Neutral and non-judgemental communication

As instructors we can sometimes find ourselves concentrating too much on fault-finding and correction, with an emphasis on pupils' errors and in giving direct criticism. This can create tension and make the pupil defensive. To overcome this, the effective coach/instructor/trainer should be neutral and non-judgemental with pupils.

Try to balance the positives and negatives by offering information on the good points before dealing with any weaknesses. Rather than criticising the pupil, try to direct attention to the specific situation. Where possible avoid direct criticism (unless it is necessary) by using non-judgemental questions such as 'What happened...?' or 'What do you think caused...?'

Neutral communication means ensuring that what we are saying is not being misinterpreted by our pupils. This comes back to self-awareness, which is the key to being aware of others and being able to empathise with them. Too often, what we say is misinterpreted by our pupils because of our tone of voice or the words we have chosen to use. Being in rapport with our pupils is about understanding how they learn, the kind of risks they are likely to take, and adapting the way we choose to communicate with them to ensure our message is received as it was intended. If we are going to adopt a uniform approach in the car with our pupils, then we are not using neutral communication. A 'one size fits all' approach is not going to raise awareness and build responsibility in the learner driver.

Non-judgemental communication means avoiding criticism or blame, which can result in defensiveness and make the learner close up. It can be a challenge to understand how to avoid criticism within the context of driving instruction because of the focus we put on faults. However, if we aim to raise the learners' self-awareness, then we broaden the context to identify their strengths, limitations and development needs. It is important for learners to understand how their personality impacts on the way they control the car; and to recognise how they will cope with distractions, passengers and unfamiliar driving situations, such as night, bends and motorways once they are qualified. Adopting a uniquely fault-based approach does not encourage learners to take responsibility for the whole of their driving because they sit back and allow themselves to rely on us for guidance and feedback.

With non-judgemental communication we ask pupils what they think happened, and how they think it could be improved; we focus on the specific situation and we look for the positives first.

Coaching and instruction

It is sometimes said that coaching and instruction do not mix effectively and efficiently because instructing involves telling the pupil what to do, whereas coaching deals much more with asking and discussing. However, in the context of driver training a mixture of the two methods is often necessary. For example, on the move in heavy traffic it may well be necessary for the instructor to take an active role to prevent potentially dangerous situations from developing. Here it is usually better to use only key words rather than a detailed instruction. This instructional intervention would, however, be followed by a period of coaching while stationary and a structured discussion about the particular situation. Even while on the move there is scope for effective coaching to take place. This can be done by using appropriate questions without distracting the pupil from the main task, or by getting the pupil to indicate developing hazards and then use this for subsequent discussion.

We may also find it useful to start the series of lessons with coaching methods to establish a partnership before moving on to instruction on specific routine matters. More instruction 'on the move' might follow but with an emphasis on coaching techniques once the skills have become more established.

All of the above can be regarded as 'coaching' because coaching is generally seen as being 'appropriate for the circumstances' and 'ensuring that the learner is put in an active role wherever possible'.

Coaching means discovering the individual's possibilities and developing them in a supportive and challenging way. Coaching therefore means communication not by telling, but by asking and involving the pupil actively in the learning process.

Verbal communication

As an instructor you should use speech effectively and in such a way that your pupils will hear and understand what it is that you need them to hear. For example, even though you may be frustrated or exasperated, you may not want your tone of voice to convey this to your pupil. There are, however, certain times when for safety reasons you must get your point across reasonably forcefully. The elements of speech that help you to communicate effectively include:

- tone of voice;
- use of emphasis;
- content;
- use of figurative language;
- use of humour;
- speed of speaking;
- use of pronunciation;
- pitch of your voice; and
- use of implied speech.

The tone of your voice

When you speak to your pupils it is important to put them at ease and to maintain their interest and attention. If they are not paying attention, it is doubtful whether they will learn anything at all.

Your tone of voice conveys your emotions and feelings, such as annoyance and pleasure, and supports the content of what you are saying. As the tone of voice often conveys the true meaning of your message, it is important that you sound friendly and relaxed even though you may be feeling the opposite!

Consider the following question: 'What made you decide to slow down?' If you pose this question in a harsh tone of voice, you will sound as though you are telling the pupil off. If you ask the same question with a soft tone of voice, you are showing interest in the pupil's actions. Practise asking the question in different ways and attempt to convey different meanings.

When teaching, you need to consider the tone of your voice to ensure that your meaning is clear and to add variety to your delivery. This is essential if you are going to retain the pupil's interest and attention. If you restrict yourself to only one tone, your delivery will become monotonous and it is likely that the pupil will lose interest.

The use of emphasis

By putting greater stress on certain words, you can alter the meaning of a sentence. For example:

- '*What* are you looking for?'
- 'What *are* you looking for?'
- 'What are *you* looking for?'
- 'What are you *looking* for?'
- 'What are you looking *for*?'

Practise asking this question out loud and put the emphasis on the word in italics. In the first question, you are asking about the action of looking itself. In the second you imply disbelief that the pupil is bothering to look at all. The third sentence queries whether it is the pupil who should be looking – perhaps somebody else should be looking! In the fourth example you are questioning the action – perhaps there is no point in looking at this moment. In the last question you are probing the pupil's understanding of what needs to be seen as a result of looking.

Now say each of the questions again, continuing to emphasise the word in italics, but try to vary your voice to express concern, anger and amazement. As well as saying the words in a particular way you can sometimes stress a particular consonant or vowel to accentuate your meaning, for example, 'Slooowly let the clutch come up.'

People who are practised and skilled speakers, such as politicians or lawyers, often use emphasis to considerable effect not only to help the listener to understand the message but also to indicate hidden meanings. Sometimes it is only when a speech is heard rather than read that you understand what message is being conveyed.

The content of speech

As well as the tone and emphasis you use when speaking, the words themselves are vital if you wish to be effective in communicating.

The use of an unambiguous vocabulary is vital when teaching people how to drive. You should always try to match the words you are using to the level of understanding and ability of the pupil. The skilled trainer will be able to put trainees at their ease by talking to them at an appropriate level. There is no point in using long and complicated words when teaching somebody who cannot understand them. The best advice is to keep it simple as this is more likely to bring about learning.

Getting to know your pupils will help you to use suitable words and phrases that they will readily understand. One common criticism of less able instructors is that they tend to use inappropriate phraseology that is not easily understood. The use of jargon should be avoided where possible. If it is necessary, make sure that the expressions have been explained to the pupil.

When dealing with the controls of the car it is best to explain to the pupil not only what the control does and how it is used, but also the words that you are going to use when dealing with it. This will avoid your trainee becoming confused, with possibly dangerous results. For example, if you are going to call the accelerator the 'gas pedal', don't confuse the pupil by then referring to the 'throttle'.

While communicating with pupils, you should avoid talking about race, religion, sex or politics. Remarks of this nature may be offensive to the person in question and, even if they are not, they will devalue whatever else you may be saying, causing the pupil to 'switch off'.

The use of figurative language

Try to make the content of your message interesting: there is nothing worse than boring your pupil. You can avoid doing this in several ways by using figurative language. For example:

- *Metaphors*: used to imply a similarity between things or situations that are not necessarily associated – for example, 'crawling along at a snail's pace'.
- *Similes*: figurative comparisons using terms such as 'like' or 'as'. An example would be to say that a bad driver was 'driving like a lunatic'.

- *Hyperbole*: the use of deliberate over-exaggeration – for example, 'That gap is big enough to get a bus through'. (Be careful to avoid sarcasm.)

- *Analogies*: comparisons made to show a similarity in situations or ideas – for example, 'If you have time to walk across, then you will have time to drive across!'

- *Personal experiences (or anecdotes)*: these allow you to compare situations happening now with those that might have happened before. For example, if you had a pupil who tried to emerge unsafely, you might use examples from your own driving experiences to illustrate the point.

By using these figures of speech you will make your lessons more interesting and the messages less likely to be forgotten. Take care not to overuse them to the extent that the intended content of your message is diluted or lost.

The use of humour

Instructors who are humorous often maintain their pupils' attention and interest very effectively, but humour does not work for every pupil or every instructor. If you try unsuccessfully to be funny you could lose your credibility. We all know someone who, when telling a joke, invariably forgets the punch line. You should not tell jokes during the lesson time as this will annoy most pupils, and in no circumstances should you tell racist, sexist, religious or dubious jokes.

Some instructors can be extremely amusing without telling jokes. They can put a message across using wit but, again, not every pupil will respond well to witty remarks and some may take offence, especially if they do not realise that you are trying to be witty. You can often bring a smile to your pupil's face without trying too hard, simply by being alert and responding to a possibly difficult situation with a humorous remark. For example, you might be waiting at traffic lights that turn to green and your pupil does not move – you could gently ask, 'What colour are we waiting for?' You should avoid using sarcasm, however, as it adds nothing to the learning process and could cost you a pupil.

The speed of speaking

The speed at which you speak can help to maintain the interest of your pupils. You can create anticipation by increasing the speed of speech as you build up to an important point. You can also use silence or pauses to allow things to sink in before you continue. If you pause while you are talking you can indicate a sense of deliberateness to give emphasis to certain key points. For example: 'Mirrors (pause), signal (pause), manoeuvre'.

You can also use pauses to give you time to think before delivering your next piece of information, but such pauses should not be excessive or you will lose your pupil's attention completely. Try not to fill in the pauses with 'ums' and 'ahs' as this will irritate your pupil and detract from what you are saying.

Slowing down the speed at which you say a single word can be useful in indicating the speed of action required. For example, 'Squeeeeze the gas' or, 'Geeently brake'.

Pronunciation

It is important that as an 'expert' you pronounce the words you use correctly. Your pupils will expect you to be fully conversant with the subject you are talking about and if you mispronounce your words too often you could damage your credibility, distract your listeners from what you are saying and reduce their attention. If you come across new words when reading books on driving and intend using them but are unsure of their pronunciation, it is best to refer to a dictionary for guidance.

Pitch

Pitch is a combination of the tone you use and the loudness of the sound you make. Considerable emphasis can be given to the instruction or direction you are giving by varying the pitch of your voice. Pitch is particularly useful when you wish to convey urgency, caution or importance either to what you are saying or the way you wish your pupil to react to the words you are using.

Take care not to over-exaggerate the pitch of your voice because it can be a distraction to your pupil. Your speech should be a comfortable variation of harsh and soft tones and of loudness and quietness.

Speaking loudly will not always get the attention or response you want. You only have to think of British tourists abroad trying to communicate with somebody who does not speak English. In vain they end up almost shouting, 'Do you speak English?'!

Pitch is useful when using keyword prompts, particularly those that require urgent action such as 'wait', 'hold back', or 'stop'.

Implied speech

Speech can be used to convey your feelings and especially your attitude to a given situation. The dictionary meaning of the words you are using is not as important as what they imply. It is not only the words being used but also the way in which they are delivered that gets the message across.

Implied speech will sometimes be used to break the ice. For example, if you ask, 'How are you today?' it not only puts the pupil at ease but also gives you some feedback, which might be useful when structuring the lesson content. If the pupil is feeling good, then perhaps you will agree to set the goal for the lesson high. If the pupil is not feeling good, then perhaps their sights will be lowered to maybe consolidating an existing skill.

When meeting people for the first time, we often talk about the weather or the journey we have had to get to the meeting. The person opening the conversation might genuinely not be interested in these things but is really saying, 'I wish to communicate with you, please respond.'

All these elements of speech can be developed. Whether teaching in the car, in the classroom or speaking to larger groups at meetings and conferences, it may be useful either to record or, better still (because you can also see what visual impact you are having), video the proceedings with a view to assessing and improving your performance.

There are certain speech distractions that should be eliminated where possible. The most common is the frequent use of speech mannerisms such as, 'OK', 'right', 'you know', 'I mean', 'well then'. This trait gives the impression of nervousness or a lack of confidence, neither of which will help to put the pupil at ease or inspire trust. Also, the use of the word 'right' to mean 'correct' could be misleading and dangerous.

Talking plays a great part in teaching people how to drive and you should take every opportunity to further develop your speaking skills. Remember that, when speaking, you are not only giving a verbal message but also conveying your feelings and attitudes. By varying your speech, you can drastically change your listener's interpretation of what you are saying, whether you are talking on a one-to-one basis, or to small or large groups.

Other common mistakes that speakers make which, particularly when they are talking to groups, can cause their listeners to become bored and lose concentration, are repeating things and getting too technical for the audience.

Telephone conversations form a valuable part of your life, given that the initial contact with a potential customer is often made on the phone. Much of what has been said about speech also applies here. The problem is that you are unable to read the body language of the person you are speaking to.

If you cannot see the gestures and facial expressions of the other party, you lose some insight into what they are thinking while they are speaking.

Communicating is not just talking but should be a two-way exchange of ideas and information. You will therefore need to develop your listening skills.

Developing the communication skills of speaking and listening will help you in presenting a driving lesson. Similar rules will apply to presentations to larger groups, but in the next section we will concentrate on listening skills and the one-to-one lesson.

Listening skills

We will learn more about our learners' needs by asking questions and listening to what they say than we will by talking to them.

As indicated in the section on coaching, the effective trainer listens very carefully to the pupils' responses and attends all the time to exactly what is being said. Just as important, pupils should be made aware that they have your full attention.

You need to pay particular attention to anything that your pupils say voluntarily and try to look at them when they are talking so that you can pick up the silent signals as well. These non-verbal messages will often reinforce the verbal message and help you to understand what people are really feeling. This may often be at variance with what they are saying. You can then use questions like, 'You don't seem too happy with that. Is there anything that you don't understand?'

When people are listening, they tend to show their interest and attention both verbally and non-verbally. They will nod their heads, lean forward and say things like, 'Yes, I see', 'That's true', 'I absolutely agree' and 'Hear, hear'. On the other hand, if they are not listening, they do not look at you, they yawn, or they do not respond. Any of these responses will indicate to you that they are bored with the proceedings and that you need to alter your approach to this part of the lesson.

You can develop your listening skills in the following ways:

- 'Listen' with your eyes as well as your ears. By looking at the speaker you will not only hear the words but detect the silent signals that help you to understand the true meaning of what the person is saying.

- Ask questions. If anything is unclear, do not be afraid to ask for it to be clarified, and if you disagree with the point being made, then say so, but give your reasons why.

- Use open-ended questions to test pupils' understanding of anything you have explained to them and seek their views and opinions on what you are saying. When they respond, hear them out. Do not interrupt – wait until they have finished speaking before replying.

Let's look at five different levels of listening:

1 The lowest level of listening is where you are planning what to say instead of listening to what your pupil is saying. This is the most irritating level of listening because the pupil can tell that you are not listening. For example:

Instructor: 'Hi, how are you today?'

Pupil: 'Oh, feeling stressed. You know how it is…'

Instructor: 'Good, good. Today we are going to work on roundabouts.'

In this example you clearly focus only on your own agenda. Often it can be difficult to make the switch into client-centred learning because we get caught up in our long-held beliefs that this is how we were trained and therefore this is what we must do on each lesson. We have a set format to follow, which we know will get our customers ready for their test, and it is difficult for us to hear anything else. But, in a client-centred relationship, how the client is feeling is critical to their ability to learn and their ability to drive.

2 The next level of listening is where you give a reply that is about yourself and not about the pupil. This is probably how the majority of conventional conversations are conducted. For example:

Instructor: 'Hi, how are you today?'

Pupil: 'Oh, feeling stressed. You know how it is…'

Instructor: 'You think you're stressed! There's so much going on in my life at the moment you wouldn't believe. My son… blah, blah, blah.'

If you were sitting with a group of friends chatting, then this would be an okay way of holding a conversation because communication in groups tends to meander and then make its way back to the beginning so someone would eventually ask the original person why they are feeling stressed. In a client-centred relationship the client is the important person in the conversation. How they are thinking and feeling will affect their ability to control the vehicle and also will potentially create barriers to their ability to learn. As driving instructors, it is important that we actively listen and stay on the client's agenda because learning to drive is about so much more than dealing with faults. We are not giving value for money and allowing learning to take place if we jump in and tell our own stories.

3   This level of listening is about giving advice that is still more about you, the instructor, than your pupil, and can be close to the lowest level of listening in the irritation stakes if the pupil is looking for a sympathetic ear rather than direction. For example:

Instructor: 'Hi, how are you today?'

Pupil: 'Oh, feeling stressed. You know how it is...'

Instructor: 'Well, let's get these roundabouts sorted and then things will look a lot brighter', or, 'Cheer up, it might never happen.'

In a client-centred relationship the word 'stressed' is like a golden nugget because it gives us an opportunity to explore with the client how their emotional state impacts on the way they handle the vehicle and how this could be an issue once they are driving unsupervised. It is important to listen to the words that clients are using and the way they use them, rather than to assume we have the answers and know how they are thinking and feeling; or, worse still, to dismiss what they are saying and move straight back onto our agenda.

4   The fourth level of listening is getting into active listening (see more on active listening in Chapter 3) and is moving onto the pupil's agenda. It is about listening and inviting more. People often work things out while they are talking and a prompt from the coach/instructor may help the flow. For example:

Instructor: 'Hi, how are you today?

Pupil: 'Oh, feeling stressed. You know how it is...'

Instructor: 'What are you feeling stressed about?'

How easy is that? All that needs to be done is repeat the words the client used and you will find yourself right on their agenda. Often people get confused about coaching because they think they have to come up with complicated questions and spend their time planning their questions rather than listening. Repeating back allows both ADI and client to check meaning. The client hears the words they used and might respond: 'I didn't actually mean stressed ... I meant ...'. The ADI has focused on the words that were used and, in doing so, has not had the opportunity to wander off on a different track and has demonstrated to the client that what they are saying is valued.

5 The highest level of listening is all about listening behind and between the words; listening to the silences; using one's intuition. For example:

Instructor: 'Hi, how are you today?'

Pupil: 'Oh, feeling stressed. You know how it is...'

Instructor: 'What are you feeling stressed about?'

Pupil: 'I have to book my theory test and I never seem to find the time to do it.'

Instructor: 'What's getting in the way?'

Pupil: 'Oh, I don't know. I'm busy or someone else is on my laptop when I want to be. I don't seem to be able to stop long enough to work out how and when to do it.'

Instructor: 'Is there anything else that's stopping you?'

Pupil: 'Actually, I keep putting it off because I don't want to book it.'

Instructor: 'And why don't you want to book it?'

Pupil: 'Because I'm afraid I'll fail it.'

What started off looking like a time-management issue ends up being about self-esteem. If the pupil's self-esteem affects their ability to make decisions and gets in the way of their progress, then that is going to have a serious impact on both their learning and their driving.

One powerful listening technique is silence. Sometimes we take a lack of response from the pupil as meaning they don't want to talk, when in reality they are still preparing what they want to say. If we sit and wait we will often be surprised by how much they will share with us.

Briefings and explanations

Although 'briefings' and 'explanations' are not strictly communication skills, they are included because they are examples of situations where good and effective communication skills are vitally important.

You will often need to give your pupils briefings in which you explain what is likely to be covered during the lesson to come. These briefings will usually include a discussion with the trainee about the goals for the lesson, and a short summary of the key points of what is to be covered. The briefing will usually be followed by a more detailed explanation of how to do whatever is being taught, when to do it and, particularly, why it is important for the content to be dealt with in a certain way. Be careful not to 'overload' the pupil. Information should be divided into the following categories:

- must know;
- should know;
- could know.

You should be able to identify the 'key points' of the message and then concentrate on making sure that the pupil understands the 'must know' elements. Further information from the 'should know' and 'could know' categories may be given in response to discussion with the trainee or questions from them and can be added at a later stage. This can often be done 'on the move' as and when situations develop that require this further information to be given or discussed.

Making sure that pupils know and understand everything that they need to know can be achieved by:

- breaking the information down into its component parts;
- using mnemonics or acronyms to make routines more memorable, for example, M S M or P S L (see Chapter 4);
- using word associations like 'creep and peep';
- using visual keys like 'Think of the thickness of a coin';
- slowing or quickening the speed of your speech to match that at which you want the action to be carried out;
- using pauses after important points have been made;
- using effective questioning techniques after each key point has been made to confirm the pupil's understanding of what has been said; and
- using visual aids where appropriate and, if the subject is technical, giving handouts for pupils to refer to after the lesson.

At the end of each lesson that has contained a briefing or full explanation, assess your own performance. Ask yourself, 'Has the pupil understood all the key points that I have explained?'

Problems can arise during lessons if your instructions and directions are not given in a clear and unmistakable manner. You need to take account of all the previous points made about verbal communication, but you should also take special note of the following:

- Use language that will be readily understood by the pupil to avoid any confusion.

- Avoid ambiguous words that might be misinterpreted by the pupil. For example, 'right' meaning 'OK' or 'correct' could cause the pupil to think you want them to turn right. 'Top', meaning top gear, could be misheard as 'stop', especially on a hot day with all the windows down and noise from traffic.

- When on the move give the instruction and directions early enough for the pupil to do whatever is necessary without rushing.

- Match the level of the instruction to the ability of the pupil. A novice will need almost total instruction in what to do, whereas a trained pupil may only need the occasional 'keyword' prompt.

- Use the alert–direct–identify routine. For example: 'I would like you to... (alert) ... take the next road on the left please (direct). It's just around the bend' (identify).

Remember to take into account that less-experienced pupils will take longer to react to the instruction or direction. An instruction given too late is likely to result in the pupil:

- missing out important observations;
- losing control with feet or hands;
- assessing situations incorrectly;
- making poor decisions;
- losing confidence.

When teaching a pupil who is at an advanced stage, you can transfer the responsibility of working out where the various junctions and hazards are by not giving too much help.

A very good way of transferring responsibility and finding out whether the pupil is ready to drive unaccompanied would be to ask, 10 minutes before the end of the lesson, 'Do you think you could find your way back home/to college/to work from here on your own?' If the answer is yes, then let the pupil drive back without any instructions or directions being given.

Once the pupil is nearly at driving test standard you should make sure that you use phraseology similar to that of the examiner as a way of preparing for the test situation. It is extremely important that you 'sit in' on driving tests regularly so that you can reaffirm your understanding of how an examiner gives directional instructions and their timing.

One of the most common criticisms of ADIs is that of over-instruction. This happens because the instructor does not know when to 'drop out'. Are you guilty of 'over-instructing'? If so, what are you going to do about it?

At the end of each lesson ask yourself:

- Were the instructions and directions given to my pupil in a clear and unmistakable manner?
- Did the timing of the directions given allow the pupil to do all the things necessary to deal with situations?
- Was there any ambiguity in the instructions and directions given?

Body language

Whenever we communicate with others, we use body language – it is unavoidable and instinctive. Speech and the development of language began about 500,000 years ago but it is probable that body language has been used for at least 1 million years.

Because body language is so deeply ingrained in us, it is difficult to disguise. Even when you are not speaking you are sending messages to others, sometimes without even being aware of it. Your physical appearance, posture, gestures, gaze and facial expressions indicate to others your moods and feelings.

It is important for you as an instructor to be able to use positive body language and to interpret the body language of your learners. Because the body language of your learners may give you more information about their mood and receptiveness than what they are saying, being able to interpret accurately these silent signals will assist you in deciding whether to modify your delivery, back off, or even change the activity entirely. For example, should the face of your pupil show frustration when failing to master a reversing exercise, you may decide to switch to something that is less demanding to boost the pupil's confidence rather than destroy it.

The ability to interpret body language will also enable you to tell whether there is any difference between what the pupil is saying and what they really think. The driving instructor needs to develop a high degree of perceptual sensitivity to read accurately the silent signals being sent by pupils.

Body language is particularly important in interviewing, negotiating, selling and buying situations. Although the general rules regarding body language will apply at meetings, in the classroom or during social encounters, when you are giving driving lessons your skills will need to be adapted to take account of the fact that, on the move, you can only see the side of your pupil's face. (We do not encourage our pupils to look at us while they are driving!) Of course, while stationary you will often be able to see their eyes as well.

If you want to be able to use your own body language in a positive way and be able to read that of others, you need to recognise its constituents. There are seven main constituents, some of which are more relevant to driving instruction than others:

1 facial expressions;

2 gaze;

3 posture;

4 gestures;

5 proximity;

6 touch; and

7 personal appearance.

When teaching in the car, you will need to spend much time not only reading the road ahead but looking at the face, eyes, hands and feet of the pupil. Although the hands and feet will tell you how well the controls are being used, the face and eyes will not only show where pupils are looking but also what they may be thinking or feeling.

1. Facial expressions

In driving instruction, facial expressions are most useful. The face is highly expressive (even in profile) and can convey one's innermost feelings. Think of the expression on the face of someone who has just failed the driving test and then compare it with that of someone who has just passed!

The face is a very spontaneous communicator of messages and will generally convey the feelings of its owner in a uniform way. The face is, therefore, a reliable indicator of happiness or despair, pain or pleasure. Consequently, when teaching, you should ensure that your facial expressions do not contradict what you are saying – if they do, it will have a disturbing effect on your pupils.

2. Gaze

When explaining things to your pupil, or debriefing at the side of the road, or in a classroom situation, you will normally have eye-to-eye contact.

The eyes can tell you a great deal about what people may be feeling but, with skill and practice, your eyes can tell others what you want them to think you are feeling. Poker players and salespeople use this technique to good effect, sometimes with high stakes to play for.

A strong gaze usually shows that you are being attentive and concentrating on what the other person is saying. However, in some cultures it can be impolite to stare. When people become embarrassed they will often break eye contact and look away.

Breaking eye contact may show that you have made an error or cannot answer a question, while a reluctance to look at someone at all may show your dislike or distrust of that person. However, establishing strong eye contact will show that you have a genuine desire to communicate and it will be seen by your pupils as an invitation to speak. It is a cultural expectation that people look at each other when communicating. If you are reluctant to look someone in the face when talking to them, or continually shift your eyes around, you will not inspire trust.

Your emotions, attitudes and honesty, as portrayed by your eye contact, make gaze an important constituent of your body language. Aggressive stares and shifty looks should be avoided. You should try to develop a strong gaze, with an occasional blink or look away, which will make people feel more comfortable and receptive.

3. Posture

In the confined space of a motor car, when your feet and hands are occupied, posture is not quite as revealing as in a classroom situation where how you stand or sit and the position of your arms and legs will reflect your feelings and attitudes to others. A normal seating position, which allows pupils to reach the foot and hand controls comfortably, will of course determine the 'angles' of their legs and arms.

You can display a warmth and liking for someone by leaning towards them slightly, with your arms relaxed. In contrast you can show your disgust at their actions by turning away and looking out of the window. Be careful not to hover over the dual controls with your feet as this will unnerve pupils and destroy their self-confidence. Try to avoid continually looking round to check the blind spots on the move for the same reason. Careful and subtle use of your dual mirrors will achieve the same objective without worrying the pupil.

In meetings or in the classroom, your posture becomes much more important. An erect posture will indicate a sense of pride, confidence and self-discipline, while stooping shoulders and head down may be interpreted as being slovenly or lacking in confidence. Your impressions of others and their impressions of you will be influenced by posture and gait. When walking across the room you should therefore adopt a confident, purposeful walk, which will indicate self-assurance and personal dynamism.

When giving presentations, you can use posture and body movements to help to bring your story to life, supporting any verbal message and thus maintaining the interest of those who are watching and listening.

4. Gestures

Gestures may be used instead of words in certain circumstances. If you are trying to communicate with someone who has hearing difficulties, or who does not speak English, gestures will help you to communicate. Your hands can be used to demonstrate how the clutch plates come together, for example.

A nod of the head or a wave of the hand are friendly, passive signals that may be given to other instructors or road users to acknowledge a courtesy, whereas a shaking of the fist conveys aggression. Sometimes your gestures will be involuntary. For example, scratching your head or chin may signal that you are uneasy or concerned about what your pupil is doing. Driving instructors who constantly fidget or wave their arms about will give their pupils the impression that they are nervous or worried. This will do little to build up pupils' confidence! Gesticulations of this nature, or pen waving while going along the road, will also distract the pupil from concentrating on the road and could be dangerous.

To control your gestures, you need to be aware of them, especially those that may be distracting to others. If you give presentations at meetings or in the classroom, a videotape of your performance will be invaluable in helping you to recognise those gestures that are weak and those that are effective in emphasising and reinforcing your verbal messages. If you are uncomfortable using deliberately planned gestures, rehearsal and practice will allow you to deliver them in such a way that they appear to be spontaneous and natural rather than forced and awkward.

5. Proximity (personal space)

You should be aware that each pupil needs a certain amount of personal space (a 'space bubble'). Encroaching on this personal space may make the pupil feel uncomfortable and could even cause them to change to a different driving instructor.

Make sure that this space is not so great that your teaching loses its effectiveness. The diagram on the next page shows the different environments and situations and the amount of space required. You will see that the driving instructor is in the privileged position of being allowed to get closer than almost everybody else, with the exception perhaps of the family doctor!

The amount of personal space required sometimes depends on the cultural background of the person. In many Mediterranean countries and in Norway, for example, people feel comfortable almost rubbing shoulders. For most British people this would be quite unacceptable.

You will need to be very sensitive to the needs of each individual pupil in this respect and generally should avoid getting too close wherever possible. This can be difficult in a small car, especially if both you and the pupil are quite large!

In the classroom, distance can be a barrier to communication, as can speaking from behind a desk or up on a rostrum. Avoid being seen as authoritarian and try to establish an informal atmosphere. For instance, it can sometimes be more effective to sit on the edge of the desk than behind it.

6. Touch

Formal touches are important when meeting someone for the first time, like a new pupil. A firm (but not crushing) handshake will indicate self-confidence, which is especially important with new customers. A limp handshake implies weakness and it would be better not to give one at all.

At the end of a lesson a handshake is not always necessary and a wave or pat on the back might be more effective. These can also be nice gestures when the pupil passes the driving test.

You must be extremely careful not to touch pupils in the car unless it is for reasons of safety. Touching pupils may make them feel uncomfortable or threatened and cause them to distrust your motives. Pupils often change instructors because unnecessary physical contact upsets them. On the other hand, in some cultures people continually touch each other during conversation.

If a pupil has just received some distressing news you might feel tempted to give them a hug but, generally, a sympathetic ear is just as effective and certainly less likely to be misinterpreted as a social advance.

ENVIRONMENT		SPACE REQUIRED
In the car		About 20–25 cm
With close friends and relatives, spouses and children		About ½ metre
Social functions		About ½ metre to 1 metre
In the classroom, with strangers or at business meetings		Public space of between 120 cm and 3 metres
When giving a lecture or talking at a conference		Lecturer space of at least 3 metres

The space bubble

7. Personal appearance

When you are a driving instructor, from the moment you leave home to the moment you return back at the end of the day, you are under scrutiny from the public, particularly if you have your name on the car! Your appearance, dress and grooming may create an initial impression that is very difficult to change.

When considering body language, your personal appearance, your hair and the clothes that you wear are of great importance because you may well have more control over them than your facial features and posture. There is little we can do to change our shape, features and size, but much can be done to improve our appearance, the suitability of our clothes and the general impression that we convey.

When teaching people to drive, you do of course have to take account of the weather conditions and, while it might not be necessary to wear a three-piece suit, you can still dress casually but smartly. In the summer and winter you will need to dress for comfort, but never forget that your appearance can influence your impact on people and can help to create a favourable or an unfavourable impression.

Propriety of dress is particularly important for the female instructor to help overcome possible problems with male pupils who might see revealing clothes, together with the natural caring attitude of the teacher, as an invitation to develop social relationships.

Pupils' body language

All the constituents of body language that we have discussed in the previous section may combine to present a positive image to those you meet. It is equally important that you recognise the silent or implied signals your pupils give out. We have chosen common signs that your pupils may give you to indicate the way they feel. Getting to know your pupils better will assist you in accurately interpreting their body language. The following rules generally apply.

Pupils who are willing to listen:

- sit with their head on one side;
- look directly at you;
- rest their chin on the palm of their hand;
- nod in agreement;
- say things like, 'I see.'

Pupils who are pleased:

- smile;
- use strong eye contact;
- can't stop talking;
- use humour in their speech;
- are polite and courteous.

Pupils who are anxious to ask a question:

- lift a hand or finger;
- shift their sitting position;
- fidget with their ear or chin;
- look intently at you with their head on one side.

Pupils who are annoyed with themselves:

- shake their heads;
- tightly cross their arms;
- hit the steering wheel;
- exhale loudly;
- frown.

Pupils who have had a fright:

- cover their eyes with their hands;
- open their mouth and put their head back;
- bite their bottom lip;
- become red in the face;
- inhale sharply.

Pupils who are disappointed:

- frown or scowl;
- drop their shoulders and let their head drop forwards;
- let their arms fall into their lap;
- droop their mouth.

Pupils who are nervous:

- talk incessantly about nothing;
- tighten their grip on the steering wheel;
- lick their lips;
- bite their nails or chew their fingers.

Looking at your pupils will not only allow you to see and interpret their body language, but also assist you in identifying faults being made that involve their feet, hands and eyes. If you do not see the fault, how can you suggest a remedy for it?

Feedback

Listening to what the client has to say about their driving experiences is the most vital part of feedback, as this is what tells you whether and to what extent they are learning. Driving is a task which involves a high level of reflection and self-evaluation if it is to be carried out safely. The process of feedback develops the student driver so that they can evaluate and reflect upon their driving when they are unsupervised. If a newly qualified driver is involved in a 'near-miss' incident and has been coached to develop self-evaluation skills, they will be able to reflect on this incident and determine how to prevent a similar one occurring in the future.

What sort of questions could you ask in order to elicit feedback from the learner on their own performance? Questions around scaling are effective because they encourage the learner to take responsibility for their own learning. You could ask, for example, 'On a scale of zero to 10 how confident did you feel when we were reversing around the corner, where zero is horrendously nervous and 10 is super confident?' or 'On a scale of zero to 10 how well do you think you controlled the speed of the car when we were reversing around the corner, where zero is very badly and 10 is brilliantly well?' It doesn't matter what number they give when scaling themselves because you are helping them to monitor their own progress so that they can take and remain in control and go on to establish new goals.

During a feedback session, scaling questions could be followed up with questions that look for evidence because evidence objectifies the feedback and ensures that it is constructive and can be built upon. The next question might be 'What evidence have you got for giving yourself that number?' You might need to use additional questions at this point to help your learner find the evidence that made them give themselves whatever mark they did. For example, when considering how well they controlled the speed, you might need to ask them what kind of gradient they were on to get them to consider whether they needed clutch or brake control. Alternatively, you could ask them what they need to do with the clutch to slow the car down; or, where was their right foot when controlling the speed of the car – on the gas or on the brake? These questions encourage the learner to recall precisely what their feet were doing in order to control the speed of the car and this raises their self-awareness and builds their self-evaluation skills.

Follow-up questions could be around development and goal setting. This is all still part of the feedback process where you are coaching the learner to take responsibility for their learning. You could ask, 'What would you need to do to move up the scale one point?' (If they gave themselves a 10 from the outset, then the question might be, 'What would you need to do to maintain a 10?') The previous questions were around recalling what they did. Now you are asking them to visualise what they could do. If they say 'I don't know', you could refer back to the evidence they used to give themselves the score in the first place because within that evidence will probably lie the information about how to improve.

Other questions could be:

- 'What help do you need from me to move up the scale one point?'
- 'When would you like to have another go?'
- 'How long is it going to take you?' and
- 'How will you know when you have got there?'

This pupil-centred approach to feedback ensures that newly qualified drivers remain safer than if they had simply been taught to pass the driving test.

The reason they remain safer is because they have practised giving themselves feedback on their own performance and this has developed their ability to self-evaluate and take responsibility for their driving.

Communication should always be two-way. Make sure that the pupil is actively involved and that you respond to the pupil rather than dictating. Most importantly, use your active listening skills.

03
Client-centred learning and coaching

Most people nowadays receive information in a completely passive way from a TV or computer, rather than taking an active part in the learning process. In the driver training context, they often expect to remain in the passive role and be taught 'how to pass the test'. Coaching and client-centred learning skills take the pupil out of this passive role and encourage awareness and responsibility so that they are able to make safe decisions when driving on their own.

According to many experts, 'Coaching is a learner-centred method that develops awareness and responsibility with an equal relationship between coach and learner.' For example, with a complete novice you could establish how they learnt best and then use the most appropriate method to teach them. Rather than giving a lesson with an explanation covering the cockpit drill and all the controls of the vehicle you might agree to let the pupil try the controls on their own. Alternatively, the pupil might prefer to watch you demonstrate before having a go themselves. In this way we are using coaching right from the start of our pupils' training process and actively involving them in taking on responsibility for their own learning.

Many experienced instructors ('driver trainers') do this anyway – but they have not necessarily called it 'coaching'.

The process of coaching involves:

- active listening;
- effective questioning;
- neutral and non-judgemental communication;
- giving and gaining feedback; and
- reflecting back.

Coaching skills include the use of the 'GROW' principle (goal, reality, options, way forward), which is explained in more detail later in this chapter. Most instructors will know about the principle, but will have probably used slightly different wording. For example, in *The Driving Instructor's Handbook* and in previous editions of *Practical Teaching Skills for Driving Instructors* we have used expressions such as:

- agree and set the objectives;

- set the baseline;

- establish prior knowledge and understanding;

- move from the known to the unknown and from the simple to the more complex;

- the different methods available to achieve the objective;

- what we might we need to do to achieve the objective.

Coaching or instructing

Traditional methods of instruction are short term – they tend to help the learner to pass a test, but do not do a great deal for longer-term learning. Coaching focuses more on active learning which then fosters ongoing learning and prepares the learner for solo driving and more post-test learning.

Instructing is often seen as being quicker in the short term, but this kind of teaching only prepares the pupil for passing the test and does little to encourage any ongoing awareness or responsibility for the learning. Coaching, however, has the advantage that the learner is involved in the learning process. This means that there is more chance of them being prepared for longer-term learning, and better able to make safer decisions when driving.

Some coaching experts feel that coaching and instructing do not mix. They stress that giving basic instruction has the effect of lowering the level of awareness and responsibility in the learner. An 'instructor' is, in effect, saying to the pupil, 'I'm the expert, do as I say'. The overall effect is that any learning that takes place is minimal and short term. Others in the coaching industry, however, feel that there is sometimes a need to give basic instruction – especially in the early stages of novice driver training. What is clear is that there is a need for instruction in safety-critical situations. In other words, if the learner is unaware of a hazardous situation that is developing, the instructor must take appropriate action. This could be in the form of a question, 'Have you noticed that the lights have changed to red?' or a direct instruction, 'Brake. The lights have changed to red', or using the dual controls. Taking control like this affects the coaching relationship because the pupil was no longer taking responsibility for the driving task at that point. However, it was necessary for safty reasons.

'Coaching means using all methods and facilities at our disposal.'

This means that in a coaching environment we can use explanations, demonstrations, instruction, direct intervention where appropriate or necessary but, at the same time, using all the recognised coaching techniques such as questioning, active listening, reflecting back and giving feedback.

However, starting with coaching methods as early as possible makes it much easier to encourage the pupil to take responsibility for their learning and also makes it easier for you, the instructor, to address the higher levels of the GDE matrix right from the start. (The 'Goals for Driver Education' are dealt with in detail later in the chapter.)

To summarise:

- *Instructing* is mainly about telling. 'I'm the expert; this is what you have to do.' Giving too much training or instruction lowers awareness.

- *Coaching* is mainly asking. In particular, asking questions that the instructor (coach) does not know the answer to. The teacher/trainer/instructor becomes much more of a 'facilitator of the learning process'.

- *Mentoring* includes offering some advice based on the mentor's expertise or experience.

- *Coaching* encourages awareness and responsibility for the task.

- *Coaching* means using 'active listening' and 'effective questioning' as well as discussing, reflecting, offering feedback.

- An effective coach will always follow the pupil's agenda.

- All training, instructing, coaching, mentoring must be pupil-centred (following the pupil's agenda and the agreed topics and goals or objectives). That is, responding to the pupil's individual needs rather than 'following the set syllabus' and relying on what the instructor wants to impart.

- As a result of using coaching methods we will be drawing the information or skill out of the pupil rather than 'pushing the information in'.

Principles of coaching

The main principles behind the concept of coaching include:

- The coach and the trainee have an equal relationship. The coach is no longer seen as the 'expert' as in instructing.

- Coaching raises awareness and responsibility in the pupil.

- Coaching means that the pupil or trainee is in a much more active role in the learning process.

- Coaching increases the pupil's awareness of individual goals, aspirations, attitude and emotions as well as improving skills and knowledge.

- Coaching builds on the learner's prior knowledge and previous experiences.

- An effective coach communicates with the pupil in a neutral and non-judgemental way.

- Coaching involves the use of effective questioning, active listening, giving and gaining feedback, and reflecting back.

- Coaching is not just about using question and answer techniques – it is also about using methods that are appropriate for the individual circumstances, making sure that the pupil is actively involved in the learning.

Benefits of coaching

Coaching enhances the way we learn naturally. We learn many things without instruction – walking, running, throwing, catching, talking – and must take on awareness and responsibility to do each of these tasks. One example that is often used by coaching experts to illustrate the benefit of using coaching methods involves trying to instruct someone to stand up from a lying down position as if they have never done this before.

Main benefits of coaching:

- Better self-awareness and self-reflection.

- Increased long-term individual performance.

- Higher motivation and commitment.

- Clarity in purpose and meaning.

- Greater responsibility for individual learning.

Coaching promotes:

- self-directed learning;
- personal growth; and
- improved longer-term performance.

As driving instructors (or 'driver trainers'), and particularly as instructor trainers, we should be able to apply the overall framework of the 'GROW' technique and use the core coaching skills of questioning, listening, summarising and offering feedback.

Coaching can include the use of other forms of intervention such as a command in a real emergency situation or an explanation of how something works or a particular procedure, but we should revert to coaching as soon as possible.

Coaching builds awareness (particularly self-awareness) and responsibility in the pupil from the earliest stages of learning.

Because it is difficult to accurately replicate the potentially risky circumstances that young or inexperienced drivers may be faced with it is sometimes necessary to use imagination exercises.

For example:

- 'What particular dangers or risks do you think there might be when you are driving on your own after passing your test?'
- 'If you were out for the evening with a group of mates and...'
- 'What would be significant about that situation?'
- 'Your car is full of passengers who might have had a few drinks and you are under pressure to get somewhere...'
- 'What could you do...?'
- 'What else could you do to alter the situation?'
- 'Would that effectively control the situation?'
- 'Are there any other...?'

Coaching skills

Rapport

We have previously looked at how people learn differently and how learning is most effective if instructors adapt the way they teach to suit the way the customer learns. In this next section we consider the effect the relationship has on the learning potential of the customer – that is, the rapport between the instructor and the pupil. We also look at the difference between a traditional 'instructor-led' relationship and a coaching 'client-centred' relationship.

From a business point of view most instructors understand that it is entirely down to them to 'get on' with all their customers individually. If a pupil expresses a view that you, personally, do not agree with it will not be good for business to show disagreement or disapproval. We need to be non-judgemental. As driving instructors we would all recognise that this is fundamental to our business success – to get on with our customers. This can be done in two ways: from an instructor-led point of view or from a client-centred perspective.

What does it mean to get on with our customers from an instructor-led point of view? Many instructors have great personalities and in the car they come across as larger-than-life characters. They would tell you that all their lessons are a great laugh and their pupils love them. They tell jokes, tease and banter and expect their customers to behave in a certain way so that they will be able to take and pass their test. Their pupils learn to drive and probably get to grips with the controls of the car and driving in different road, weather and traffic conditions in reasonable amounts of time. But they go away with little or no understanding of the higher-level goals in driver education. They will probably not understand how their personality, views, values and opinions affect the choices and decisions they make when driving independently with friends in the car. They may not realise how susceptible they are (or are not) to the effects of fatigue, or to peer pressure; how risky they are (or are not) and what their potential likelihood is (or is not) of driving under the influence of alcohol or drugs.

The driving instructor may cover the effects of alcohol and drugs or the risks of distractions inside and outside of the car, but if the driving lessons have all been about the instructor putting on a show to get the pupil to have a good time, then the teaching has all been one-sided. Some people will take on board the information and will process it effectively – these people probably share the same learning styles as the instructor.

Rapport is a key element in creating a learning environment where the customer feels safe enough to express how they really think and feel about things – things that are not always related to driving. This is important for them to develop an understanding of the inextricable link between behaviour, thoughts and feelings. How they think and feel affects the choices and decisions they make – always. They might not be clear what they think about things or how they feel about things. Often this is because their attitudes to driving, drink, drugs, sex, religion, road safety, seat belts, speeding etc are the result of a lifetime of influences from friends, family, the media, people they look up to. For example, being told 'you are stupid', or 'you will never make anything of yourself', or 'you are selfish' will affect the way we see ourselves and the world in a very different way from if we had been told 'you are going places', 'the world is your oyster', 'you are really bright'.

As driving instructors, we need to build a different relationship with each of our customers because each one has a different set of experiences, which will affect the quality of their learning. Some will really respond well to banter, joke telling and levity. Others will much prefer a studious silence without constant interjections. And most will be somewhere in the middle. However, the point is that until you are with your customer on their driving lesson you cannot decide how to communicate best with them so that they learn about how thoughts and feelings govern behaviour.

It is important in a client-centred relationship that the customer is treated as an equal and knows that their views and opinions are a crucial part of the learning process. The instructor's job is to be non-judgemental. As a result, the customer can work on developing their self-evaluation skills so that when they are out driving on their own they know how to recognise a near-miss, reflect on it, and put strategies in place to avoid it happening again.

How is client-centred rapport established? Mainly through non-verbal communication techniques, with the instructor taking their cue from the customer. It is necessary that effective learning takes place and for this to happen the instructor needs to use non-verbal communication techniques to relate on an equal basis and establish trust.

Eye contact: This doesn't mean staring into someone's eyes but it is about looking at the person when they are talking rather than looking down at some notes or straight ahead out of the windscreen. It helps establish equality and makes the person feel valued.

Body language: Ensure that your body language is open. When parked at the side of the road turn and face the customer.

Nodding, smiling: Nodding and smiling are part of active listening. These non-verbal communication techniques encourage the customer to open up further because they know they are being listened to.

Matching: Listening to the words that someone uses and adopting those types of words really helps build rapport. If you have an aural learner they may say things like: 'I hear what you're saying', 'That sounds like a plan', 'That rings a bell'. A visual learner might say: 'I see what you mean', 'That looks okay', 'I see what you are saying'. A kinaesthetic learner might say: 'That feels good to me', 'I get your drift', 'I'll give it a go'. By matching the words they use you are breaking down a potential processing barrier. If you don't adapt the language you use to suit the language of your learner, they have to work through and around your learning style before they can even get to theirs – many people give up on the way.

Matching tone of voice and speed of speech can also be very effective in establishing both rapport and an excellent learning situation.

Rapport is an essential coaching skill in a client-centred relationship because it puts the responsibility for learning on the learner (customer). This will accelerate their learning because rapport will ensure that barriers to learning are broken down. The instructor, by using their non-verbal communication techniques, will establish a relationship that is non-judgemental and equal. This means that the person learning will become more self-aware; that is, of how their individual and personal thoughts and feelings affect their behaviour.

Communication skills

To become an effective coach in driver or instructor training, you need to have excellent communication skills as outlined in Chapter 2, but specifically you need:

- to be observant and an active listener;
- to use non-judgemental verbal communication;
- to have self-confidence, so as to avoid slipping unnecessarily into an instructional or directive approach; and
- an open and honest working relationship with the pupil.

Listening, questioning, clarifying, reflecting back, giving feedback are all essential skills for the coach (within a framework of goals, strategies and actions).

Awareness and responsibility

Building awareness and responsibility in the pupil is at the heart of good coaching. The effective instructor/coach should be able to raise this sense of awareness and responsibility in the pupil mainly by using effective questions. These will not only be based on 'What can you see?' but will be more probing in terms of feelings and attitudes.

The pupil needs to have awareness of what is happening around them and also self-awareness, in terms of 'What do I feel?', 'How do I control this situation?' If the pupil is not fully aware of both of these aspects, there will be a tendency for the situation to control the pupil rather than the other way round.

A good coach can build awareness mainly through effective questioning, using appropriate questions such as 'What can you see?', 'What do you feel is happening?', 'How do you feel about...?' This line of questioning ensures that pupils are gaining feedback from what is happening around them and what they might do to control the situation.

If the learner feels that the instructor is controlling the training by using too much basic instruction they will feel encouraged to adopt a passive role. If the pupil/coach relationship is more of an equal partnership the pupil is likely to be more relaxed and ready to take on responsibility for their individual learning.

Ideally pupils should be encouraged to take responsibility from the start of their training. This does not necessarily mean that pupils have to make the decisions about any major traffic or safety issues at an early stage, but that they should feel responsible for their own learning.

A sense of responsibility for their own learning can be developed in learners at an early stage in the learning process. This transfer of responsibility is much more effective if pupils are involved in making decisions and identifying goals and objectives in partnership with the instructor/coach from the start of training.

Effective questioning

Just because you ask questions does not mean you are coaching. The use of effective questions is an important aspect of driving instruction because it involves the learner in the process and allows the instructor to check that learning is taking place. Coaching questions are very different from traditional instructing-type questions and this next section explores these differences.

We have previously considered the importance of rapport in a client-centred relationship and how active listening is all about listening behind and between the words, looking at body language, and helping the speaker explore their thoughts and feelings. By using a combination of skills such as building rapport and active listening, we can establish a balance between instruction and coaching – a balance that is critical in keeping the car safe. There are various questioning techniques that can be employed to help strike this balance but before we look at these techniques, we should look at the use of coaching questions.

Coaching questions are effective questions that target the thoughts and feelings that motivate behaviour. Questions such as 'What were you thinking as you approached that roundabout?' or 'How did you feel as you drove along that road?' are excellent conversation openers to use when parked up at the side of the road. It is important to ensure there is no negative tone attached to these questions so they should not be used when you know your customer has just made a mess of whatever they were doing. The questions need to be asked in a way that is neutral and non-judgemental. You don't know what answer the customer is going to give but you are curious and want to explore with them what they were thinking or how they were feeling. This is so that they can understand how these thoughts and feelings link to their behaviour. In fact, the questions can be even more open than the above example because, by mentioning the roundabout or the road they have just driven along, we are potentially restricting and guiding the pupil's response. 'What have you been thinking about?' or 'Describe your thoughts to me' or 'How did that feel?' or 'What were you feeling?' are examples of wide open questions. If the rapport is good the client will have no problem in telling you that they were thinking about what they were going to be having for tea or how they are looking forward to going out at the weekend. These kinds of response open up a discussion about distractions and how distractions can interfere with the decisions we need to make when driving. This becomes a good example of how thoughts and feelings motivate behaviour.

Now let's look at the different types of questioning techniques we can use to maintain a client-centred approach:

1 Goal questions

This type of question is used to help the client in setting the goal and also to check what support is required from you to facilitate them achieving this. These questions would often be asked at the start of a lesson but could also be asked in the middle of a lesson where one goal has already been achieved and another one is being set. Normally, they would be used at the side of the road because they are useful in making sure the customer is in control of their own learning process.

Example questions might be:

- What would you like to achieve today?
- How do you learn best?
- How do you want to do this?
- What skills do you already have that will help you achieve this today?
- What support do you need from me?
- Where would you like to practise?
- How much time do you want to spend practising?
- Do you need me to do anything?
- Would you like a demonstration?
- How will you know when you have succeeded?
- How will you measure your success?

2 Closed questions

Closed questions are good for checking knowledge and facts. They have just one correct answer. For example, 'What is the speed limit on this road?' These questions can be asked on the move because they are not generally too distracting. They also work well at the side of the road if the customer is a little reticent in opening up – by asking a couple of closed questions you help establish rapport.

One of the benefits of the goal-setting questions is that you will have established what level of support the customer requires during any practice. If the customer wishes to have a go on their own this doesn't mean you would step in and ask them questions to check where they are looking and what they intend to do. You would allow them to drive in silence. However, if the customer is, for example, practising raising their awareness of hazards then you might have agreed to ask them closed questions that draw their attention to particular hazards as they drive on their chosen route.

3 Safety-critical questions

Sometimes it will be necessary to step in and say something to keep the car safe even though you have agreed that the customer is going to practise something on their own in silence. You would ideally explain this before the car starts moving but if you haven't it is still crucial that you recognise the time to intervene with instruction. If you can do this in the form of a question, all well and good. However, it really doesn't matter when there is a risk of danger. Whether you ask a question or not you will still be instructing in this situation and will have taken the responsibility back from the customer for the driving task.

Examples of the type of safety-critical questions you might use are:

- Do you need to brake for this car emerging?
- Are you going to steer round this cyclist?
- Will you be stopping at this pedestrian crossing?

All these questions have an instruction in them and the response expected is in the form of an action rather than anything verbal. It would also be appropriate in these situations to have the dual brake covered or to be ready to go for the steering wheel.

The good thing about asking a question in these types of situations rather than giving an instruction is that you are endeavouring to keep the responsibility sitting with the customer. They still must decide how to respond to your question. Afterwards, it is important to discuss the situation at the side of the road. Remember, though, that timing is critical and if you have no time to ask a question then don't!

4 Open questions

Open questions have more than one correct answer. A question that can be answered with Yes or No is an open question. It could also be answered with 'Maybe', 'Sometimes', 'That depends', for example, so there are several alternative responses. Usually, the instructor does not know what answer the customer is going to give. These types of questions are asked to start a conversation where the customer is given the opportunity to explore their thoughts, values, opinions about something related to driving. The more open the question can be the better; however, sometimes a question that just gets a yes or no response is good because it then helps move the conversation forwards.

Example questions might be: 'What do you think about the speed limit on this road?' or 'What are your views on alcohol and driving?'

5 Task-specific questions

These questions are part of an exercise that has been agreed with the customer. They could be to do with reading the road ahead where you agree that you are going to ask questions about the signs and road markings. For example, What is the next warning sign? What is the speed limit on this road?

Another type of exercise is about distractions where you might say to the customer that you are deliberately going to ask them questions that are unrelated to driving and that you will discuss with them afterwards how easily (or not) they were able to maintain their focus on the driving task. For example:

- Have you got a holiday booked this year?
- What are you going to do this weekend?
- How did you get on at college this week?

The most important thing about the use of questions is to recognise the outcome that each type of question is likely to produce. It is very easy to ask questions and struggle with this and therefore assume that coaching doesn't work. Some people do not like being asked questions and often this is because the questioner has bombarded them with questions rather than considering the rapport and using their listening skills. Client-centred questions need to be asked for a reason and the reason is to accelerate the learning of the customer by raising their self-awareness, building their responsibility and developing their self-evaluation skills.

To summarise

- Start with questions that link the current situation with any previous experiences: 'With your previous instructor did you...?'
- Start broadly, with a general question: 'What are your main concerns to-day?' and then move on to more detailed questions as a result of the pupil's responses.

- Use 'open' questions: 'What...', 'When...', 'Where...', but be careful with the use of 'Why...', as this can often be seen as over-critical or too personal.

- Ask only one question at a time and listen very carefully to the answer before asking any follow-up questions.

Very often the most important questions are those that the instructor/coach does not know the answer to. For example, 'How do you/did you feel about...', 'What do you understand by...', 'What do you think would happen if...?' and so on.

Questions – a few reminders

The effective instructor/coach should be able to raise awareness and responsibility in the pupil mainly using effective questions. These will not only be based on 'What can you see?' but will be more probing in terms of feelings and attitudes.

Closed questions (those with only one correct response) should be used sparingly. Questions that the instructor/coach does not know the answer to are usually the most effective in raising the pupil's awareness and responsibility.

Questioning technique involves: listening; probing; reflecting; discussing; feedback.

A typical Q&A routine:

Pupil: 'I'm not sure what to do about...'.

a) Mentor: 'What I would do is...'. (The reply is all about the speaker and is not particularly helpful to the questioner.) This kind of approach would usually be used by a parent or an amateur instructor.

b) Instructor: 'What you should do is ...' (The answer is still mainly about the speaker and, as a result, the pupil does not feel particularly involved.) This is the type of answer used in 'traditional' instructing methods.

c) Coach: 'What are you not sure about?'

Pupil: 'How to...'
Coach: 'What would you...?'
Pupil: 'Well, I would...'
Coach: 'What do you think you might...?'
Pupil: 'I'd...'
Coach: 'What effect do you think...?'

(Note that the pupil now sees that this discussion is all about their own situation and feels more involved.)

Some basic coaching-type questions

- 'What is your main concern today? Any other concerns? Do we need to go over any of those again?'
- 'What do you feel you need to do next?'
- 'What do you feel we need to do to change...? How do you think we can best achieve that?'
- 'Have you done this manoeuvre/exercise/routine before? How did it go?'
- 'What do you need to know to do...? Anything else?'
- 'What, in particular, do you need to watch out for/be aware of in this situation? What other road users do you need to be aware of?'
- 'What can you see/feel/hear? How do you feel about...?'
- 'Is there anything more we can/could do to...?'
- 'How will you deal with...? Are there any alternatives?'
- 'Where are you looking? Are there any other areas where you might need to look/be aware of?'
- 'How did you feel in that situation where...? What did you actually do? Anything else?'
- 'How did you think that went? Overall, what did you do well?'
- 'What could you do another time to change...?'
- 'What could you do that would make it easier/safer...?'

As previously indicated, all of these questions assist in raising awareness but they also allow pupils to express themselves with their feelings. The coach's supplementary questions should then follow on from the pupil's responses. This means that 'active listening' (see also the section in Chapter 2 on Listening Skills) is an important skill for the trainer/coach. Sometimes the more difficult part is knowing when to keep quiet and allow the pupil time to consider a response.

Most of the time our listening consists of 'apparent listening'. It may appear that we are listening, but we are not actually concentrating fully on the content and meaning of what is being said. What we should be doing is using 'active' or 'effective' listening.

The ability to listen 'actively' is a key feature of any good communication and is essential in the process of coaching. As we can think much faster than we can talk, this speed of thought can be used to advantage in coaching. The available time can be used to consider what the pupil has said, make sure in your own mind that you have fully understood, and consider what further questions or responses might be needed.

The effective coach is able to concentrate effectively and efficiently on what the pupil says, possibly over a lengthy period of time. There is always the temptation to only half listen, or to assume when the pupil is only part way through their response. In the same way, it is tempting to start formulating the next question or response too early and to risk missing the main point of the pupil's response. Active listening is a skill that can be acquired, but only with planning and practice.

When listening to the pupil and judging their response to your questions, make sure you look directly at the pupil and use friendly facial gestures. This is particularly important when dealing with pupils who are reluctant to answer or who have difficulty in expressing themselves.

During the questioning and listening process it is sometimes worth summarising what the pupil has said. Telling the pupil what you think they have said can show that you have taken notice of any concerns and will usually assist in continuing the discussion in an appropriate way.

The effective coach listens to the pupil's reply not only to check for accuracy, but also for any indication of uncertainty or a lack of confidence. The need is to listen carefully and to make an immediate interpretation of the meaning. In doing this, the coach/instructor will be able to decide on the next question or series of questions to put.

Active listening – a few reminders

One often-repeated quote – 'When you talk, you are only repeating what you already know. If you listen, you may learn something new.'

A few basic principles for listening:

- Listen more than you talk. Wait until the other person has finished – don't interrupt or finish the sentence for them.

- Even if the speaker pauses, still wait in case they have more to say. Even if you think you have understood what is being said, avoid cutting off the person who is speaking.

- Use gestures or nods to allow the speaker to continue.

- Maintain eye contact – show that you are actively involved in what is being said.

- Concentrate on getting the whole picture rather than just some of the information.

- 'Listen' with your eyes – be ready to pick up any non-verbal signals.

- Don't let the other person's mannerisms distract you from the actual content.

- Show the speaker that you are concentrating on what is being said by avoiding any unnecessary distractions on your part.

Pupil feedback

So far we have looked at Rapport, Questioning and Listening skills in terms of delivering client-centred learning as opposed to instructor-led teaching. In this section we look at feedback from the pupil. Developing feedback skills in your customers is the key to safe driving. This is the most important skill; the whole point of building rapport, actively listening and asking effective questions is to develop the clients' ability to feed back to themselves how they are getting on.

With client-centred learning, feedback is used to raise the client's self-awareness of their strengths, limitations and development needs. It's also about how their thoughts and feelings impact on their behaviour. For this to be effective the instructor needs to be able to develop the client's ability to set their own benchmark, against which they can measure their performance. This process takes more or less time depending on the level of independent thinking the client is capable of. For example, when someone asks you, 'Would you like tea or coffee?' what is your response? Some people will say, 'Whatever is easiest for you'. This is often a conditioned and polite response but it betrays the fact that some people find it difficult to make choices. Being able to make choices, recognising consequences and understanding the impact that choice will have on you, as an individual, is the result of effective self-evaluation skills – the ability to give oneself feedback.

When you ask your client how something went, the response may well be, 'I'm not sure'. This is not necessarily the time to dive in and give your opinion on how it went. It cannot be stressed enough how important it is to develop self-evaluation skills through the process of feedback. A newly qualified driver's inability to self-evaluate leads to errors of judgement. Developing in your clients the ability to consider how their driving is coming along, and giving them the skills to do so once they have passed their driving test, will enable them to recognise and reflect, in order to take steps to prevent further errors.

If someone blasts their horn at you how do you feel? Some people will feel a surge of rage, which will consume them for moments, and during those moments they could make decisions that are fuelled by their anger. In extreme cases, these decisions result in examples of road rage. Other people feel immediately embarrassed and assume they have done something wrong. This embarrassment is also consuming and may lead to decisions that are less than safe, such as sudden braking or swerving without checking the mirrors. Still others may feel fear, again resulting in unsafe actions. Do you know how you respond? Do your customers know how they will respond? Do they understand how their feelings affect their thought processes and therefore their actions? Understanding how our emotional state motivates our behaviour is the first step to anticipating the likely consequences of the choices and decisions we make. Knowing how to manage our emotions so that the choices we make are safe is the result of feedback and self-evaluation.

Making mistakes while learning to drive provides an ideal context to develop self-evaluation skills. With traditional, instructor-led driver training we focus on the core competencies of fault identification, fault analysis and fault remedy. By dealing with faults and through repetitive practice we bring people's driving up to a satisfactory level so that they can take and pass the practical test. On a behavioural level this works very well but it doesn't take into consideration the fact that our thoughts and feelings drive our behaviour. A learner driver behaves in a certain way because they will be rewarded by their instructor and allowed to go for their driving test. However, this behaviour will not necessarily remain in place and when put under different pressures – driving unsupervised – the now newly qualified driver will drive in a certain way according to their beliefs and motivation – and not because their driving instructor told them to.

So how can we develop self-evaluation skills in our clients? Let's take a brief look at Reflection and Scaling.

Reflection is arguably the most important process we can use because it reinforces learning and helps it to become long-lasting. It is through reflection that we can learn from our mistakes and move forwards. Some people reflect formally by writing everything down and keeping reflective diaries; others just spend a few moments thinking about what happened and breaking the whole thing down in their minds. An important part of reflection is to consider how you were feeling and what you were thinking because both feelings and thoughts play a part in the behaviour that is displayed. Developing these skills of reflection in your clients is about encouraging them to think about a piece of their driving and looking at what happened. They may need to draw a diagram or go back and look at the scene; they may need to drive the same route again or they might benefit if you drive. Ask them what they were thinking at that precise moment and then ask them what they were feeling. These questions help them analyse their actions and encourage them to take responsibility and put strategies in place to develop.

Great reflective questions for developing feedback skills are:

- What just happened?
- What were you thinking?
- How were you feeling?
- What do you need to do next time to develop?
- What help do you need from me?
- How will you know when you have succeeded?

Scaling is a means of reflection and a powerful feedback tool because it develops self-evaluation skills. It keeps the responsibility for the learning process sitting firmly with the person doing the learning, rather than the person doing the teaching. It doesn't matter what the scale is. It can be a ladder drawn on a page or a set of steps; it can be a numerical scale from 0 to 10 or 1 to 5; it can be a ruler held in your hand or theirs. The important thing is that the limits are defined. For example:

> 'On a scale of 0 to 10, where 10 is very good and 0 is rubbish, where would you put yourself regarding the bay parking you just did?'

The answer they give also does not matter – there is no need for you to comment. The next question is about their evidence for putting themselves at this point – encourage them to look for positive evidence. Even if they gave themselves a one they have at least got off the ground so you can ask:

> 'What was good enough to make you give yourself a one?'

The next questions are:

- 'So where would you like to be?'
- 'How will you get there?'
- 'Do you need any support from me?'
- 'How will you feel when you have got there?'

These questions keep the responsibility sitting with the client and you are just there to facilitate the process. Practised often enough, scaling becomes a feedback technique they can take away and apply in their driving once they have passed the driving test.

Scaling can be used very effectively on feelings:

- 'How tired/confident/stressed/focused are you on a scale of nought to 10?'

- 'Describe a situation where you are at a much better point on the scale.'

- 'What do you need to do to get there?'

- 'How can I help you?'

Scaling also works very well when giving feedback on the use of the controls, for example: 'On a scale of nought to 10 where 10 is amazingly smooth and nought is horrendous where would you put yourself with the last gear change?'; 'Okay, so you say you are a three, next time aim for a four.'

As far as client-centred learning and coaching are concerned it is not constructive or helpful to constantly be throwing away words like 'Excellent', 'Well done', 'That's great'. These do nothing to develop self-evaluation skills in your clients and often silence is far more powerful. They need to know how to congratulate themselves on their strengths and to also be able to identify their weaknesses and have the skills to develop and improve. Your job is to help them set a benchmark by which they can measure themselves. At times it is necessary to give praise, especially with someone who is not very good at evaluating their own performance, because this helps them set their own benchmark. You should, however, cut back on the praise you use as soon as you notice the time is right because you are restricting their self-evaluation processes by constantly chipping in with your opinion. Easing them into the process of self-evaluation so that they can take full responsibility once they have passed their driving test will help keep them safe for life.

Using a question and answer routine is only one way of giving and obtaining feedback. When teaching learner drivers you should give feedback on what they are doing well and what may need improving. Just as important is finding out from pupils how well they think they are doing. They might think they are doing brilliantly when they are really struggling. Alternatively, pupils might think they need extra tuition on a particular topic, whereas you might think this is unnecessary. Every pupil will benefit from extra lessons, so never discourage them from booking more if they feel they need them.

Many driving instructors do not understand feedback and instead give constant criticism, which only destroys what confidence pupils may have and leaves them feeling dejected and wanting to give up. Many potentially good drivers give up because they do not receive support and encouragement from their instructors. Invariably these pupils will start learning again, if they really need to drive. However, they nearly always go to a different instructor. Never forget that if you are not fulfilling the needs of your pupils, there are plenty more instructors for them to choose from.

Several guidelines can be followed when giving feedback to your pupils:

- Feedback should always focus on what actually happened rather than on what should or might have happened.

- Suggest that pupils comment on their own performance before giving feedback. They will often be more self-critical than you expect.

- Make sure that you balance pupils' strengths and weaknesses.

- Concentrate on areas where you know that the pupil is capable of improvement; don't dwell on points that you know they are not able to alter. This is most important when pupils are aware that they have limitations.

- Be helpful rather than sounding judgemental. For example, rather than saying, 'You will fail your test if you do that', you could try, 'Your passengers will have a much more comfortable ride if you do this.'

- Try to 'round off' any feedback by stressing the good points.

- Above all, feedback should be seen by pupils as being constructive and positive.

Hopefully these guidelines will help you to give feedback in a 'human' way, as this will build the confidence of your pupils.

After each lesson, reflect on any feedback you have given. Decide whether you could have improved the way in which you presented the feedback to your pupil. Think carefully about how your pupil reacted to the feedback. Did you give the student an accurate indication of their performance or did you just criticise their driving?

Modifying behaviours in driving

GROW is a four-stage problem-solving model that focuses on behaviour. It stands for Goal, Reality, Options and Way Forward.

Goal – What do you want to happen?

- Agreed in partnership with the pupil.
- Pupil takes more responsibility and 'ownership'.
- Must be challenging and measurable, but also achievable.
- Difference between the topic of a lesson and the outcome.
- May be a bite-sized part of a lesson.
- First agree the topic, then establish the goal.
- Must be realistic, and will come from the pupil after discussion.
- Agreed, with small chunks of achievable progress. Sets the goal (or objective) so that the pupil can finish the session/part of lesson with a measurable result.

Reality – What is actually happening now? Where are we now?

- A realistic assessment of the current situation.
- Using open-ended questions can clarify to pupils exactly where they are.
- Reality needs to be clarified, agreed, fully understood and accepted.

Options – What could we do to make it happen? What are the alternatives?

- Coach helps the pupil to generate the options and explore how to move forward.
- Coach's role is to assist pupils in exploring for themselves the different options.

Way forward – What will we do to achieve the agreed goal? What is the most efficient strategy?

- Provides clarity on which of the options are most appropriate for the trainee and the goal and the level of certainty.
- Confidence in taking the agreed option forward.
- Job of the coach is to ensure that the pupil has made a complete assessment of what needs to be done, and that the pupil takes on responsibility for the outcome ('ownership').

Goals

What do we want to achieve?

Identifying and agreeing goals

Setting goals or objectives is an important principle in coaching. Rather than imposing a strict programme of goals on the pupil, the coach helps the learner to identify their own goals at each stage of learning and then to realise them.

In driver training there are clearly some predetermined limits for the objectives – laws and regulations for example – but it is important for the instructor and pupil to mutually agree the goals and that those goals meet the needs of the pupil. For example, there is little point in the instructor having a fixed idea for the content of a lesson if the pupil is concerned about an aspect of the previous lesson. In this situation the pupil would feel uncomfortable about moving on to the next part of the syllabus without resolving the outstanding issues. The instructor should be able to recognise this and initiate a discussion and listen to the concerns and needs of the pupil in order to move the learning process forward.

This way of working may need to be relatively formal in the early stages of training, particularly as the pupil will not necessarily know or understand what goals or objectives are important to them. However, as the series of lessons continues the pupil should be encouraged to identify their own goals or objectives and to work in partnership with the instructor. In practice, this often means that the pupil's perceived goal is to do what needs to be known and done to pass the driving test. To get the pupil to focus on the necessary attributes of awareness, responsibility, attitude and generally preparing for driving after passing the test can be more difficult, but can be achieved by using the appropriate coaching techniques.

If after a lesson the pupil is not comfortable about a particular aspect, the instructor cannot agree or set the goals for the next part of the lesson. There will inevitably be interference caused by the pupil's anxiety about the concern or doubt. This needs to be addressed before deciding on the next goal or objective.

As previously indicated, most young people are used to having instructions given to them. As a result, the pupil's idea of setting goals may revolve around 'passing the test' and 'getting a licence'. The job of the effective coach is to guide the discussion towards agreeing on appropriate goals for each part of the training programme. To do this you need to be able to lead the discussion and encourage the learner to identify their own individual goals.

In order to clarify and define the goal and help the pupil (or 'coachee') achieve an agreed objective, the instructor (or 'coach') might ask:

- What would you like to get from today's lesson?
- Which particular area would you like to develop today?
- What must happen today for you to get some benefit from the lesson?
- When you have done it, what will that enable you to do in the future?

Reality – Where are we now?

Prior knowledge and experience

We need to know and understand a lot about the pupil's existing knowledge and prior experience before we can start on agreeing appropriate goals and effective objectives. Effective coaching does not start from scratch or by assuming that the pupil is completely inexperienced.

All our learners will have had some previous non-driving experiences that will be useful in linking to the process of learning to drive. They will have been pedestrians; will almost certainly have been passengers with parents and other people; they will probably have ridden a bicycle and may have used a moped; and they could have had off-road driving experience. These experiences can, and should, be linked to the new learning experience.

In order to explore the reality of the current situation the coach might ask:

- What do you know so far?
- What is the potential gain/loss?
- What barriers could there be to achieving this?

Options – What are our alternative strategies?

Deciding on our options

- What are our options for making changes?
- What could we do to make them happen?
- What are our alternatives?
- Are we able to change or modify our strategy or method as appropriate or as required by the particular situation?
- It is sometimes helpful to split this section into two parts; firstly to generate a list of options and secondly to take each option and evaluate it.
- What options have you considered so far?

- What other options are there?
- How/why might these options work/not work?
- What might be the consequences of each one?
- Let's rank the options.

Way forward – How are we going to achieve our goals?

- What will we do to achieve the agreed goal?
- What is the most efficient strategy for us to achieve the goal?

The final part of the GROW model is to establish and agree a Way Forward. One way to do this is to ask the pupil for their thoughts on summarising a plan:

- Could you summarise for me the actions you are going to take?
- How will you make this happen?
- What are you going to take away from this session?
- What do you need from me to achieve this?

Used effectively in driver training the GROW model can raise self-awareness and develop responsibility, making our newly qualified drivers safer in the long term.

Goals for Driver Education (GDE)

A brief overview

The Goals for Driver Education are summarised in a framework or matrix, consisting of four levels and three columns. Levels one and two are addressed in traditional driver training and are sufficient to prepare someone to pass their driving test.

Level 1 is all about the vehicle – its controls and how to use them, maintenance, vehicle regulations. Level 2 is about driving the vehicle in traffic, dealing with different road and weather conditions as well as different amounts of traffic, forward planning, hazard management, and the effects of driving on the environment. Levels 3 and 4 are not addressed in traditional driver training. Level 3 focuses on the how, why, where and when of driving in recognition of the fact that driving involves choice and

GDE matrix

(Goals for Driver Education)
(Hatakka, Keskinen, Glad, Gregersen, Hernetkoski, 2002)

Level	Knowledge and skill	Risk-increasing aspects	Self-assessment
4. Goals for life and skills for living	Lifestyle, age, group, culture, social position etc, vs driving behaviour	Sensation seeking Risk acceptance Group norms Peer pressure	Introspective competence Own preconditions Impulse control
3. Goals and context of driving	Modal choice Choice of time Role of motives Route planning	Alcohol, fatigue Low friction Rush hours Young passengers	Own motives influencing choices Self-critical thinking
2. Driving in traffic	Traffic rules Co-operation Hazard perception Automatisation	Disobeying rules Close-following Low friction Vulnerable road users.	Calibration of driving skills Own driving style
1. Vehicle control	Car functioning Protection systems Vehicle control Physical laws	No seatbelts Breakdown of vehicle systems Worn-out tyres	Calibration of car-control skills

decision. While learning to drive the learner is often robbed of any opportunity to make decisions for themselves. Even choosing what they want to do on their driving lesson is a step in the right direction towards taking ownership and control of the driving task. Level 3 also includes other influences that affect the decisions the driver must make, such as passengers, distractions and the effects of alcohol and drugs.

Level 4 acknowledges how the personality, values, opinions and beliefs of the driver influence the way they handle the vehicle, drive in traffic and choose when, how and where to drive every time. Depending on the personality of the driver, they will respond in different ways to the effects of peer pressure, for example. If they are tired this can affect the way they handle the vehicle and the decisions they make. One person might be fine with three or four mates in the car having a good time, while another might find it impossible to concentrate and feel quite stressed in this situation. Understanding how they might respond in different situations gives them the ability to make choices about their safety.

The three columns of the Goals for Driver Education matrix show the competencies the driver needs to be able to apply across the levels. These are, for each level:

Level	Knowledge and skills	Risk-increasing factors	Self-evaluation
Level 4 The person	Who am I? What goals and ambitions do I have? What skills do I have? What views and opinions do I hold? What do I enjoy most about driving? Why do I want to learn to drive?	What type of personality do I have and what are the risk-increasing factors of being a thrill seeker, or aggressive, or anxious and nervous? What are the risks for me when I've passed my test?	How well do I manage myself? Am I able to reflect? Do I understand consequences to actions? How will I cope with driving once I've passed my test?
Level 3 The journey	What do I need to know about planning my journey? What mode of transport should I use? What is the best time of day to travel? What roads should I avoid? What do I need to know about distractions, passengers, alcohol and drugs?	What risks are involved with drinking and driving, speeding, being distracted, using my mobile phone and driving, driving when tired, driving my mates?	How good am I at navigating and route planning? How does tiredness affect my concentration? What strengths do I have in dealing with peer pressure? What are my weaknesses?
Level 2 The road	What do I need to know to drive in traffic, negotiate busy junctions, forward plan, read the road ahead, anticipate hazards, as well as driving in different weather conditions and at night?	What are the risks of driving at night, or in adverse weather conditions? What could go wrong if I don't look properly or forward plan?	How good am I at dealing with other traffic; what strengths do I have and what weaknesses?
Level 1 The vehicle	What do I need to know to operate the controls smoothly, move away and stop, complete manoeuvres, deal with basic junctions; as well as maintain my vehicle and carry out basic checks?	What if I didn't wear my seatbelt, or check my tyres, or carry out basic checks; what if I brake harshly, or accelerate fiercely, or steer sharply – what could go wrong?	How good am I operating the controls? What weaknesses do I have? How well do I choose the correct gear or time my gear changes?

- the knowledge and skills the driver needs;

- awareness of the risk-increasing factors; and

- the ability to self-evaluate.

Traditionally, the bottom left-hand corner of the matrix is covered – levels one and two and the first two competencies.

Another version of the GDE matrix is shown above, populated with the kind of questions you could ask your pupils to help address the goals for driver education.

With grateful thanks to Martin Lewis, Cranbrook Driver Training for this interpretation of the GDE matrix.

Coaching – a summary

So far, we have looked at essential coaching skills and shown how these skills, when used in client-centred learning, raise awareness and build responsibility in the individual learner.

- **Rapport**

  This is all about the relationship between you and your customer. The relationship must be equal, and the customer must trust that you will be non-judgemental. Being non-judgemental is critical in empowering the customer to be themselves. Customers must believe that they can express how they think and feel about things knowing that you will not be dismissive or defensive in your response.

  This equal relationship enables the customer to learn how the way they think and feel about things influences the choices they make. The learning environment is such that they feel comfortable exploring and experimenting with different strategies to manage their emotional state and help them make decisions that are safe for them.

  Rapport is not necessarily created through banter or even establishing common ground. It is created through non-verbal communication techniques, such as the use of eye contact, nodding, smiling and matching body language, tone of voice or use of words.

- **Listening**

  There are several levels of listening, most of which are ineffective when aiming to create a client-centred relationship. Active listening is about focusing entirely on the customer's agenda and almost seeing yourself as a blank sheet. As the coach, you have no idea where the conversation is going to go and simply facilitate the process.

There are several techniques you can use to do this, such as repeating back parts of what has been said, paraphrasing and summarising. These techniques enable the customer to check that what they have said is what they meant. Listening is very important when developing the customer's ability to set their own goals and determine for themselves how they learn.

- Questioning

  Effective questions target thoughts and feelings. They are open questions and may start with words like what, where, why or how; or explain, or tell me. Coaching or client-centred questions are very different from the use of questions in an instructor-led relationship. Coaching questions do not check knowledge and understanding. They focus on the underpinning things that motivate behaviour. They help the customer recognise how individual they are and how the decisions they make are affected by their state of mind.

- Feedback

  There are many forms of feedback. In client-centred learning the most powerful form is one that develops effective self-evaluation skills in pupils. Feedback is all about the customer identifying a set of skills, against which they can measure their performance. They need to be aware of their strengths, weaknesses and development needs and they need to understand how their emotions impact on their behaviour and their ability to rationalise. Their measure of 'good' and 'safe' will be very different from yours because they think and feel things differently from you. 'Drive like me and you will always be okay' is not helpful to an individual when all their life experiences, conditioning, peer groups and influences have developed them into human beings who do not resemble you in one tiny little way. They can 'drive like you' up to their test and pass but post-test they will always 'drive like them'. Effective feedback is about developing their ability to make choices by evaluating the potential consequences of those choices and deciding whether this is what they want or need to do.

  Consider two different emotional states: happiness and sadness. Reflect on how you feel when you are happy; where that feeling of happiness sits; how it affects the way you carry yourself; how you feel when you smile or laugh; how you relate to other people. Now consider the same points when you reflect on how you feel when you are sad. Now imagine you are sitting waiting to emerge at a busy junction in a sad state and then in a happy state. Does your emotional state affect your judgement of a safe gap? The answer is 'Yes' but the extent to which it affects your ability to make a decision depends on you and will vary from individual to individual.

For example, in order to make a safe decision to go I have to consider my emotional state and understand how it influences my thought processes and my behaviour. I will drive differently depending on how I feel and I will develop strategies to help my decision-making process based on my recognition of my emotional state. Sadness slows down my ability to make decisions. I am more hesitant. Happiness may encourage me to take more risks and I may emerge into gaps that are too small.

It is the use of essential coaching skills that empowers our trainee drivers to recognise how their thoughts, feelings and behaviour are inextricably linked.

Finally, there is one more essential coaching skill we should think about and that is the use of Intuition.

- **Intuition**

As driving instructors, we use our intuition in many ways. We recognise when our customers are feeling nervous as their shoulders tense and the grip on the steering wheel tightens or they sit forwards in their seat when the demands of the task suddenly increase. The physical tension will make them tire more quickly and affect their ability to focus on the hazards and risks outside of the car. We know instinctively when they are thinking about changing gear before they have even done so or when they have mis-interpreted our instructions and are about to signal left when they should be going right.

It is important that we use our intuition to develop coping strategies in our customers. They need to understand how their behaviour is a reflection of their thoughts and feelings. If something becomes too difficult for them to manage and we notice this in their behaviour, then we need to identify this to them so that they can work out for themselves the link between the way they are thinking and feeling and the way they are behaving.

For example, let's imagine that one of your customers struggles with busy junctions and roundabouts. Often, she will end up stalling. You notice that, on the approach to these junctions, she takes her left hand off the steering wheel and places it on the handbrake. When you pull up to discuss this you use your intuition – you know that her hand going down to the handbrake is because she feels nervous about the busy junction and wants to make sure she can stop the car. The problem with this is that she is 'thinking stop' whereas she really needs to be 'thinking go' and getting the car ready to go by slipping into first gear and holding it on the bite.

You could tell her all this and she would practise it and get it. However, she wouldn't have had the chance to reflect on her nervous state and appreciate how this emotion was governing her behaviour. So, instead, you scale her on how nervous she felt approaching these junctions and she says she rose from a 4 to a 9. You then ask where she was on the scale when her hand went down to the handbrake. After practising this for a couple of junctions she can identify that when she gets to a 9 her hand goes to the handbrake. Only once she realises that her behaviour is a direct result of her feelings is she able to rationalise her fear. She realises that her fear is producing risky behaviour – the opposite of her intention. By encouraging her to keep her hand on the wheel until she needs to change gear and getting her to 'think go' she is now able to bring her nervousness back down to 4 and keep it there. In this case, her behaviour now governs her emotions.

Intuition, therefore, is about recognising a mis-match between behaviour, thoughts and feelings. Someone might start yawning when you are giving them a briefing. Your intuition tells you that they are no longer paying attention and processing what you are saying to them – they have stopped learning and you need to change your methods.

To become good coaches and always remain client-centred, we need to develop our ability to use these five essential coaching skills. This can only be done by constant practice, reflection and evaluation and it is a long process that will not happen overnight. When you come across someone who you think cannot be coached, ask yourself whether you have been using these essential coaching skills effectively enough.

04
Structured learning

The specific requirements for presenting the lesson on the ADI exam are covered in *The Driving Instructor's Handbook*. The exam is a slightly artificial situation compared to a normal lesson in that there is a strict limit to the time available for the lesson.

With a real pupil on a normal lesson it is for you and your pupil to agree the objectives or goals and to make effective use of the time available. Your lesson plan should, of course, consider the particular needs of the individual pupil rather than simply following a set syllabus.

The most effective way to start is to think of the trainee's needs and their current level of ability, knowledge and skill. Then ask yourself a series of questions involving what, why, how, where and when. This is best done by holding a conversation with your pupil asking them a few questions, such as:

- What do you already know?
- What are you going to need to learn?
- What do you need to have included?
- How are we going to get the message across?
- Where will we need to go to carry out the lesson in an appropriate environment?
- When should we get to the main content of the lesson?
- How are we going to manage the available time?

Once you have answered the questions you should be able to organise the planning and presentation of the lesson.

In any teaching/learning situation the lesson should be properly structured and will need to be 'pupil-centred'. For you and the trainee to achieve any mutually agreed objectives or goals you will need to involve the pupil. Effective use of your coaching and communication skills will help you to achieve this.

Through discussion with the pupil, agree for each lesson what you are going to teach and why you are going to teach it, where the lesson is going to take place, how the available time is to be utilised, and how the lesson is going to be structured.

Professional driving instruction should not be a matter of driving around for a bit to see what develops. An effective instructor should:

- have a clearly defined plan of what is going to be taught;
- consider the level of ability of the pupil when agreeing the goals for the lesson;
- have an idea in advance what activities and techniques could be used to help keep the pupil interested and attentive;
- be prepared to modify the lesson plan if the need arises during the lesson;
- have specified learning goals for the student;
- vary the teaching methods to suit those goals and the characteristics of the student;
- demonstrate a range of skills when using these teaching methods and any visual or learning aids;
- carefully manage the time, structure and content of the lesson;
- adapt the lesson to suit the perceived needs of the student where necessary;
- identify, analyse and correct faults;
- identify any problem areas, taking remedial action or recommending further training where necessary;
- always take account of the safety of the student, the passenger and any other road users;
- offer feedback to the student during and at the end of the lesson, where appropriate;
- link forward to the next lesson; and
- encourage reflection to evaluate what learning has taken place.

To appreciate the variety of lesson plans that are needed, consider how you would plan a lesson for each of the potential pupils listed below – what type of routes you would choose and how you would vary your level of instruction:

- an absolute beginner;
- a partly trained pupil;
- a pupil at about 'L' test standard;

- somebody who has recently passed the 'L' test but has never driven on motorways;
- somebody who passed the 'L' test a few years ago but has not driven since;
- a full licence holder who wishes to take an advanced test;
- someone who has a full licence for cars with automatic transmission but has not driven a vehicle with manual gears;
- a company driver taking a 'defensive driving' course;
- the holder of a full foreign licence who has never driven in this country or on the left-hand side of the road;
- somebody who is just about to appear in court on a traffic offence and who needs an assessment and report;
- somebody who will need to retake the driving test as part of a court order;
- somebody who must take an extended test as part of a court order.

At the end of each driving lesson, you should ask yourself:

- Did the lesson plan help the student to achieve the objectives that were agreed at the start of the lesson?
- Did I involve the pupil in the lesson sufficiently?
- Should I have changed the lesson plan to take account of perceived problems?
- Did I give the pupil enough feedback on how well they were doing?
- Did I plan the lesson thoroughly?
- Were the routes chosen correctly?
- Was the level of instruction pitched appropriately for the pupil?
- With hindsight, was there anything I should have done differently?

Goals and goal setting

One of the most effective ways to learn to drive is through goal setting. There are several important reasons why your customers need to learn how to set goals for themselves:

Goal setting breaks learning into bite-sized chunks

Creighton Abrams famously said, 'When eating an elephant, take one bite at a time.' When your customer feels overwhelmed, it helps to look at the whole learning to drive task with all its commitments and actions as bite-size, or fun-size, goals. Remind them that they have choices about what they say 'yes' and 'no' to, and when and how they move forward. This shifts the focus away from the driving test and means that they can achieve goals without them having to be 'test standard'. What is meant by this is that we often look at our pupils' achievements and measure them against the standard expected in the driving test. This undermines what has been achieved on that occasion. If the only goal is the driving test, then think how long it can take before the customer experiences a sense of achievement.

Goal setting identifies strengths and development needs

If you know what you are good at you can choose to channel your decisions through your strong points. Lots of people have a way of talking ('I'm rubbish at that', 'I could never do that', 'I can't do it') that is a clear reflection of how they think about themselves. Their choices and decisions are all about running away from what they are bad at, rather than positively focusing on what they are good at and basing their choices on this. In learning how to set their own goals your customers will also be learning to identify what they are good at and what they are weak at; what they need to do to improve; and what improvement/success will feel like to them.

Goal setting raises self-awareness

Do your customers know how they learn best? Do they know how their emotions fuel their decisions, judgements and behaviour? Do they know what (if any) barriers to learning they are inclined to put up? Learning how to set goals for themselves will raise your customers' self-awareness in these areas. In many cases, barriers disappear as soon as someone is encouraged to determine their own goals for the lesson. They no longer feel defensive or insecure or fearful.

Goal setting builds self-responsibility

Self-responsibility is all about taking ownership of the learning process as well as the driving task. This leads to more effective decision-making skills as well as an ability to be self-determining. By setting the goal the customer is taking control of their learning. Many instructors feel understandably nervous about this aspect of goal setting in particular. Taking responsibility is an exciting, challenging and, sometimes, nerve-racking experience for the individual involved. It is not about the learner driver driving amok. You are ultimately responsible for their safety – they are learning to become responsible for their learning and together you will share the responsibility for the driving task.

Goal setting develops skills for life

Learning how to set goals leads to the development of skills for life – in particular, self-evaluation skills. Naturally, this links closely with the Goals for Driver Education Framework (GDE) where Level 4 is entitled 'Goals for life and skills for living' and is about self-evaluation or self-assessment. This is about learning how to give an accurate assessment of strengths and weaknesses in terms of judgement and decision making. For example, when you have to emerge from a busy junction, is your decision to go different depending on whether you are hungry, tired, happy, sad or angry? If you recognise that you are functioning in a particular emotional state do you have strategies to ensure your decisions are still safe and objective?

Goal setting moves towards realising full potential

In terms of Abraham Maslow's Hierarchy of Needs, widely published in 1954, human beings have five needs:

- Biological and physiological needs – air, food, drink, shelter, warmth, sex, sleep, etc.
- Safety needs – protection from elements, security, order, law, limits, stability, etc.
- Belongingness and love needs – work group, family, affection, relationships, etc.
- Esteem needs – self-esteem, achievement, mastery, independence, status, dominance, prestige, managerial responsibility, etc.
- Self-actualisation needs – realising personal potential, self-fulfilment, seeking personal growth and peak experiences.

According to Maslow, each of us is motivated by needs. Our most basic needs are inborn, having evolved over tens of thousands of years. Maslow's Hierarchy of Needs states that we must satisfy each need in turn, starting with the first, which deals with the most obvious needs for survival itself. Only when the lower-order needs of physical and emotional well-being are satisfied are we concerned with the higher-order needs of influence and personal development.

Learning how to set goals moves individuals towards being able to realise their full potential.

These points about goal setting are important in ensuring that you are giving value for money in your lessons and that learning is taking place.

When discussing and agreeing goals and objectives it is important that both the instructor and the pupil agree what they are to be, and that some record is kept of progress made. Using this system gives an immediate progress chart for each pupil and will also act as a memory prompt for you so that you will be able to remember which particular item is the next one to be covered.

By using a log book or progress report, another instructor would be able to pick up where the previous instructor has left off.

As well as giving each pupil feedback on their progress on a record or appointment card, you should also keep a master list in the car so that each pupil's progress can be monitored. Progress sheets can be filed on a clipboard in alphabetical order by surname or the information can be recorded on an iPad or tablet.

Do not lose sight of the fact that as well as giving pupils an individual 'test-related' programme of learning, we are also preparing them for a lifetime of safe driving. The requirements of the test go further than performing the set exercises. Knowledge, understanding and attitude all come into it as well as practical skill. Your course of instruction should cover all of these.

With the more traditional old-style conversations the instructor decides on the objectives for the lesson. With a client-centred approach the conversations will be very different, as shown in the following examples:

1: T-junctions

At the start of a lesson an old-style instructor might say:

'Today we are going to deal with emerging at T-junctions. Is that OK with you?'

'Fine.' (Pupil thinks: 'Oh no! I'm dreading this because I can't even deal with turning corners yet. I don't know how I'll cope with all the other traffic.')

Using a coaching dialogue:

'OK, we've got a one-hour lesson today. What do you feel we need to achieve by the end of the session?'

'Well, I don't know – that's up to you isn't it?'

'Is there anything left over from last time that you feel could be improved?'

'Well, quite a lot, I suppose.'

'Anything in particular?'

'Not sure.'

'How did you think the last lesson went?'

'Reasonably well.'

'Were you happy with the way you were turning basic corners and dealing with the limited amount of traffic that we met?'

'Yes, I think so.'

'Do you feel that you're ready to take it a little further and deal with slightly more complex junctions and a bit more traffic?'

'Possibly.'

'So, if we spend a little time in consolidating what we did last time and then move on to, say, emerging at junctions you'd feel that's what we should do?'

'Yes, I think I'll be happier with that.'

'Right, so that means that the goal for today is to be able to emerge properly at T-junctions?'

'Yes, that's fine.'

'You're happy with that goal that you've set yourself?'

'Yes.'

'Fine, let's make a start, shall we?'

(Thinks: 'I'm pleased that we're going to do it that way and that I was able to make up my own mind about how the lesson was going to be structured.')

During a lesson (ie, at the end of a particular part of the session):

2: Reversing

Old-style instructor:

'Your regular instructor has told me that today we are to deal with reversing' or, 'If you remember, last time I saw you I told you that today we would be making a start on reversing.'

'Yes, OK.'

'Right, this is what we do.'

(Thinks: 'How can I tell him that I know half this stuff he's telling me?')

Coaching style:

'Just going back to our previous lesson, do you remember what we said we would be doing today?'

'Er, I think we said reversing.'

'Oh yes, that's right. What do you know about reversing?'

'I know that it's part of the test.'

'Yes, but we don't need to worry about that yet – have you got any thoughts about what we're going to do?'

'Well, yes. And in fact, at the weekend, I had a chance to do a bit of manoeuvring in my Dad's car in the big yard at the back of the house.'

'Oh good – how did you get on?'

'Well, quite reasonable, I think.'

'You probably know quite a bit about handling the car then, so what we'll do today is build on that.'

'Good.'

'What do you think will be the big difference between what you did at home and what we're doing today?'

'Well – er – other traffic, I suppose – pedestrians, cars and so on.'

'That's right, so those are the things that we'll have to deal with in today's lesson. At the same time though, we'll check your control of the car and the accuracy of the reversing.'

'That's fine.'

'OK, so let's imagine that we've now got to park on the right-hand side of the road. Are there any rules about what we do? For example will it be safe to reverse in this area or might we be affecting other traffic?'

(Thinks: 'What a good job I was able to explain what I'd done.')

These are all examples of client-centred learning that involve:

- coaching principles;
- pupil involvement;
- use of Q&A;
- persuasion;
- most of the elements described previously in this book.

By using this style and method of teaching, your pupils will be more likely to develop self-awareness and they will be encouraged to take more responsibility for their own learning. Both of these are important elements of an effective coaching environment.

When teaching by goals and objectives you will need to ask yourself at the end of each lesson:

- Were the goals set at a realistic level for the pupil?
- Am I concentrating too much on 'getting them through the test' instead of teaching safe driving for life?

- Am I paying enough attention to knowledge, understanding and attitude, or spending too much time on skill training?
- Have I kept my pupil's progress chart or driver's record up to date?
- Have I kept my own progress chart for this pupil up to date?

Levels of instruction

In most driving lessons, you are likely to be involved in the following activities:

- teaching new skills;
- consolidating partly learnt skills;
- assessing skills already learnt or partly learnt.

Some lessons may contain a mixture of some or all of these activities. Many instructors make the mistake of trying to cram too much into one lesson to the detriment of the learning process.

As well as planning the content of the lesson to be given, you need to consider carefully the routes and areas chosen and the level of instruction required for each particular pupil.

One of the problems for instructors is knowing when to 'drop out' and transfer to the pupil the responsibility for solving problems and making decisions. The sooner your pupils start to think things out and make decisions for themselves, the sooner they will be ready to drive unaccompanied.

For many learners, the first time they ever drive 'unaccompanied' will be on the 'L' test, when the examiner is there purely as an observer.

The skilful instructor knows when to stop talking. Of course, in most driving lessons, you will need to give directions, but it would be very beneficial to the learner if you say, 'Let's see if you can drive home on your own, without me saying anything at all. You make all the decisions and pretend that I am not here.' You would, of course, be prepared to step in and prevent any safety-critical situations from occurring, either by telling them what to do or by using the dual controls.

This exercise will boost the confidence of the pupil in achieving their goals, and give you a measure of the pupil's readiness to drive unaccompanied. At the end of the 'unaccompanied drive' it will be useful to ask the pupil: 'How did you feel about driving on your own then?'

Some feedback would then need to be given to the pupil. Two very common instructional errors arise from instructors not matching the level of instruction to suit the level of ability of their pupil. This can take the form of over- or under-instruction.

Over-instruction

This often occurs when the instructor is teaching a new skill or has identified a problem area and is giving the pupil a complete 'talk-through' on a subject. The new skill will probably be mixed in with the skills that are already learnt or partly learnt.

For example, the instructor may be talking the pupil through a difficult junction, with the added problem of roadworks. When the junction has been negotiated, the pupil is asked to pull in and park somewhere convenient, so that they can discuss what happened. The instructor forgets that the pupil knows how to park unaccompanied and says: 'Gently brake to slow; clutch down; gently brake to stop; apply the handbrake; select neutral.'

The pupil may have parked a hundred times unaided, without any problem. What has happened is that the instructor, who has got so involved in the 'talk-through' mode, has forgotten when to keep quiet.

You should therefore try to restrict your prompted practice or talk-through to those aspects of driving that are new to the pupil or are as yet unaccomplished. Over-instruction is particularly common when the pupil is approaching test standard. It is as if the instructor is reluctant to 'let go of the reins'. Always remember that at this level your pupils will learn a lot more by doing it themselves, even if they get it wrong, than by listening to you telling them what to do.

Under-instruction

This is particularly common when the pupil is in the novice stage or is only partially trained. When teaching new skills it can help the pupil learn more effectively if you control the practice so that, where possible, the pupil gets it right first time. There is nothing more motivating for pupils than success, even though that success may be the result of you prompting or talking them through the task. Some pupils will learn most effectively if you talk them through each stage of the operation, skill or exercise until they develop the ability and confidence to do it for themselves.

The possibility of the need for a full talk-through is greater in the early stages of learning a particular task so as to lessen the risk of vehicle abuse and inconvenience or danger to other road users; and where it matches the particular learning style of the pupil, or they are especially nervous.

The talk-through must give the pupil enough time to interpret and execute your instructions comfortably. The speed with which each pupil will be able to do this is likely to vary. You therefore need to match the level of instruction and the timing of your delivery to the needs of the pupil.

Knowing when to drop out is important. If you leave the pupil on their own too soon, resulting in a poor execution of the task, it can be very demotivating. However, when you consider the pupil is ready to take personal responsibility, you should encourage them to do so. Some pupils will need plenty of encouragement to act and think for themselves. Others will make rapid progress when left to work on their own initiative.

Prompting is the natural progression from controlled practice and will largely depend on the ability and willingness of pupils to make decisions for themselves.

If conditions become too busy for the pupil's ability, or if potential danger is a factor, then the pupil may be reluctant to make any decisions at all. Where these situations arise, you may need to be prepared to step in and prompt when required.

The use of detailed instructions should decrease as the ability of your pupils increases, thereby transferring the responsibility from you to them for making decisions and acting on them.

In the last few lessons leading up to the driving test, it should not be necessary for you to prompt the pupil at all. If this is not the case, then you have a selling job to do. You need to either sell more lessons and the necessity for further practice or postponement of the test.

At the end of each lesson ask yourself:

- Did I match the level of the instruction given to the ability and needs of the pupil?

- Did I over-instruct on things that the pupil should need no instruction on?

- Did I leave the pupil to do things without prompting or should I have given more help?

Route planning

Route selection and planning is itself a practical teaching skill and is an essential part of lesson preparation and planning. Part of an instructor's role is to create a situation in which learning can take place, and the selection of routes is an integral element in this process.

The ideal route would be one that takes account of the character and level of ability of the pupil. It should be designed to stretch them but not be daunting.

Using training routes which are not relevant to the needs of the pupil or not appropriate to the requirements of the lesson plan can have an extremely negative effect on the training.

The confidence of some learners can be destroyed because they are taken into difficult situations that require good clutch control before they have mastered this skill. Imagine how you would feel if you were sitting at a red traffic light on your first driving lesson and you stalled the engine a couple of times!

If new drivers are unnecessarily exposed to road and traffic conditions with which they are unable to cope, it is quite likely that the amount of learning taking place will be reduced. In the most extreme case, the pupil's confidence will be severely affected, with a detrimental effect on learning or even a reversal of the learning process.

At the other end of the scale, restricting experienced learners to inappropriate basic routes will not encourage them to develop their skills.

When planning routes, you should consider some of the main requirements:

- the specific objectives for the lesson;
- the standard and ability of the pupil combined with the need to introduce or improve any skill or procedure;
- any particular weaknesses or strengths of the pupil;
- any hazards or features that you may want to include or avoid in the overall lesson plan;
- the length of time available for the lesson;
- whether any danger or inconvenience might be caused by using a particular area at a particular time;
- if any unnecessary or excessive nuisance would be caused to local residents.

Ideally, you should have a thorough knowledge of the training area and any local traffic conditions. However, as this is not always practicable or possible, you will need to take care to avoid any extreme conditions.

If, because of the road layout and the limited time available, complex situations cannot be avoided, consider whether you should drive the pupil to a more appropriate training area. In this event, use the drive to give a demonstration of any relevant points and to include a 'talk-through' of what you are doing.

Training routes and areas tend to fall into three main categories: nursery or basic, intermediate and advanced. There will not be a clear division between the three groups and there will often be a considerable overlap from one group to another. Nevertheless, it is important that you have a clear idea of the appropriate routes within your own working environment.

Nursery routes – These will normally include fairly long, straight, wide roads without too many parked vehicles and avoiding pedestrian crossings, traffic lights and roundabouts. This type of route will incorporate progressively most of the following features:

- roads that are long enough to allow for a reasonable progression through all the gears and for stopping from various speeds;
- several upward and downward gradients suitable for starting and stopping;
- left- and right-hand bends to develop speed adjustment and gear-changing skills;
- left turns from main roads to side roads;
- left turns from side roads to main roads;
- right turns into side roads and onto main roads.

Intermediate routes – These should include busier junctions and general traffic conditions. At this stage, try to avoid dual carriageways, multi-lane roads and any one-way systems. Some or all of the following features might be incorporated in the routes:

- Crossroads and junctions with 'stop' and 'give way' signs.
- Several uphill, give-way junctions.
- Traffic lights and basic roundabouts.
- Areas for manoeuvring.

Try to avoid too many complicated traffic situations – for example, right turns onto exceptionally busy main roads or complex junctions.

Advanced routes – These will incorporate most of the features of the intermediate routes and should be extended to give a wider variety of traffic and road conditions. They should include, where possible, dual carriageways, multi-lane roads and one-way systems as well as residential, urban and rural roads. A properly planned 'advanced' route will provide the opportunity to conduct mock tests without using actual test routes. You should be able to find routes that include:

- different types of pedestrian crossings;
- roads with varying speed limits;
- level crossings, dual carriageways and one-way streets;
- multi-lane roads for lane selection and lane discipline;
- rural, urban and residential roads.

Starting with nursery routes, try to introduce new elements and situations at a controlled rate, bearing in mind the needs of the individual pupil and their level of ability. Get used to what seems to be 'their own pace' – one at which the pupil feels comfortable.

There may be occasions when a mixture of all types of route may be incorporated into one lesson – for example, when making an initial assessment of a new pupil who has previous driving experience.

Ideally, you should start off with a fairly wide selection of routes. This will give you the opportunity to vary and extend them with experience. Retain a certain amount of flexibility in using the planned routes because you may, for instance, need to spend more time than anticipated on a topic that the pupil is finding more difficult than expected.

If a specific problem is identified, you may need to bring the pupil back to a particular junction in order to 're-create' a situation.

Excessive repetition of identical routes will often lead to a lack of interest or response from the pupil. This in turn will lead to slow progress in learning and may also be counterproductive. Some variation of routes is essential to the learning process and will sustain the pupil's interest and motivation. Chunking your lessons, however, by repeating short circuits that last perhaps five or six minutes can give your pupil the opportunity to drive independently towards the end of the lesson as if you weren't in the car. This gives them a sense of achievement and means they are more likely to achieve the goals agreed at the start of the lesson.

Remember that training routes are often a compromise between the ideal and the reality of local conditions in the training area. The nature of traffic conditions can vary enormously from time to time and from lesson to lesson. You may find that a carefully planned route may unexpectedly prove unsuitable and you are faced with a situation that the pupil is not ready for. Careful route planning can, however, keep these incidents to a manageable level. Be ready to extend the length of a lesson for a particular pupil if appropriate training routes are not readily available in the immediate vicinity.

At the end of each lesson, ask yourself:

- Did I choose a route that was suitable for the level of ability of the pupil and for the objectives stated?

- Did I vary the route sufficiently to sustain the interest of the pupil?

- Am I using routes that stretch the ability of the pupil but without destroying their confidence?

Fault assessment

This section deals with fault recognition, assessment and correction.

Driving faults normally fall into two separate categories: in the car (control skills) and outside the car (road procedure errors).

You will often find that 'in-car' errors will lead to errors of road procedure, lack of accuracy or failure to respond correctly to traffic situations.

You will need to use your eyes, dividing your attention between what is happening on the road ahead, what is happening behind and what your pupil is doing with their hands, feet and eyes.

Try not to: watch the pupil so intently that you miss important changes in the traffic situation ahead to which your pupil should be responding; or watch the road and traffic so intently that you miss faults that are happening in the car.

An effective way of coping with all the visual checks required is to use the M S M, P S L and L A D routines – but from an instructor's point of view. For example, when approaching a hazard, you should check that your pupil:

M – checks the rear view mirrors; look in your own mirror to confirm what is happening behind and check that your pupil acts sensibly on what is seen;

S – is signalling properly, when necessary and at the correct time;

M – carries out the manoeuvre correctly;

becomes:

P – positions the vehicle correctly for the situation;

S – slows down to a suitable speed and selects an appropriate gear when necessary;

L – is looking early enough, at the correct time, and that the observations are effective and include use of the mirrors;

becomes:

A – assesses the situation correctly;

D – makes a good decision as to how to deal with the hazard.

Continuous assessment should be sensitive to the pupil's needs and is concerned with improving performance. In the last few lessons leading up to the 'L' test, the continuous assessment should give way to 'objective' or 'mock' testing. The purpose of this is to assess the pupil's readiness to take the test and it should be matched to the requirements of the test itself.

Grading of errors

Don't think of errors as being black or white. In driving, there are many shades of grey, and the circumstances surrounding the error need to be considered. When assessing driver error, you should take into consideration the following: an error can involve varying degrees of importance; some errors are of a more serious nature and can result in more severe consequences than others.

Driver errors will generally fall into one of four categories:

1 Not marked – This is where the fault is so slight that you decide not to mention it.

2 Minor – This is where the fault does not involve a serious or dangerous situation. No other road user is potentially or actually involved.

3 Serious – A serious fault is one that involves potential risk to persons or property.

4 Dangerous – This is where the actions of the pupil cause actual danger to persons or property.

There is a need for some standardisation between the consistency of assessments made during driving lessons and those used for the driving test.

Having said this, there is no need to grade errors exactly to test criteria. Remember that we are teaching safe driving for life. Consequently, some instructors may aim for a much higher overall standard of ability than that required on the 'L' test.

This can be beneficial to their pupils. It would be true to say that most learners do not perform as well on the driving test as they do while out with their instructor on lessons. Pupils who have been trained to a higher standard should therefore stand a better chance of passing. Even if they do not drive as well on the test as on previous lessons, they are still likely to pass, provided that there are no serious or dangerous errors. In any event, the extra training before taking the test will mean that these pupils are better prepared to drive unaccompanied after passing.

To give maximum benefit you need to:

- recognise the fault;
- analyse the fault;
- correct the fault.

Fault recognition

Having recognised a fault, you should identify it as being minor, serious or dangerous. Minor faults can normally be corrected on the move. However, if a recurring pattern of minor faults is identified, you will need to spend some time on dealing with them before they become more serious.

Minor faults could include errors in coordination and inefficient or uneconomic driving style, slight inaccuracies in positioning (either travelling along the road or during the set manoeuvres) and harsh use of the controls.

Serious or dangerous faults will need to be discussed more fully. This discussion should be carried out while parked somewhere safe. Do not get into discussions at road junctions, or while pupils are trying to negotiate hazards – this will only confuse them, which could lead to even more serious faults being made.

Fault analysis

When analysing faults, you need to compare what your pupil is doing, or has done, with what you would be doing or would have done in similar circumstances.

A useful approach would be to ask the pupil: 'How do you think that drive/manoeuvre went?'

It may be that the pupil realises that a mistake has been made, in which case you could help them to analyse the fault.

You should:

- discuss what was wrong (both the cause of the error and its effect and consequences);
- discuss what should have happened;
- discuss and explain why it is important (paying particular attention to how the error could affect other road users).

Consider using a visual aid if you need to recreate a difficult situation or explain incorrect positioning on the road or illustrate how other road users were involved. Diagrams, models and magnetic boards are useful aids.

After analysing the fault, use questions to make sure that the pupil has fully understood what went wrong, what should have happened, and why it is important. This will then lead to the last, and most important, part of the routine.

Fault correction

You should be able to offer remedial action while the fault and the improvements needed are still fresh in the pupil's mind. It is of little use to say that you will come back to the fault on the next lesson as by that time the pupil will have probably forgotten what happened and what to do.

If the fault involved the way in which the pupil dealt with a particular hazard or junction, the most effective way to correct it would be to get the pupil to approach the same situation again. Depending on the fault, you may agree to talk the pupil through the situation, or just prompt on the points that need improving. The main thing is that success is achieved. If time allows, a third approach to the same situation will help to validate your instruction, this time leaving the pupil to deal with it entirely unaided. Feedback must be given when improvement has been made.

At the end of each lesson, ask yourself:

- Did I identify all the main faults made by my pupil?
- Did I correct all the minor faults on the move and stop to analyse the major faults as soon as convenient?
- Did I analyse the faults made with regard to what went wrong, what should have happened, and why it was important?
- Did I offer appropriate remedial action, bringing about improvement?

Hazard perception

Hazard perception is part of the theory test for learners and the ADI Part 1 exam. It is a subject that instructors need to be expert at – both in theory and practice.

The driving skills involved include:

- scanning the road well ahead;
- anticipating the actions and reactions of other road users;
- being aware of following traffic;
- planning an appropriate course of action;
- maintaining a safe and appropriate distance behind the vehicle in front;
- driving at a speed that is appropriate to the conditions.

However, the main element is concentration!

As an instructor, your own perception of hazards is even more important. You should also be able to develop these skills in your learner drivers by utilising a variety of practical teaching skills, but mostly by effective question and answer techniques.

A 'hazard' is usually defined as anything that might cause us to change our direction or to alter the speed of our vehicle. Some of these will be static hazards such as road junctions or bends; others might be moving hazards, such as pedestrians, cyclists, horse-riders, motorcyclists and other vehicles.

Using your Q&A techniques you should be able to help your pupils to improve their skill in recognising and dealing with all types of hazard.

The ultimate aim of your instruction will be to enable your pupils to:

- scan the road ahead and behind effectively;
- anticipate the main points of danger;
- recognise that what we can't see is often more important than what we can see;
- think about what might happen as well as what is happening;
- give themselves time and space to carry out a particular manoeuvre or to avoid a problem;
- maintain absolute control of their vehicle while carrying out correct driving procedures.

Encouraging your pupils to look well ahead, keeping their eyes moving all the time and continually looking for clues as to what might happen, can achieve this.

Demonstration

A demonstration can sometimes be useful in that pupils will be able to see a model of correct behaviour which they can then imitate. Complex tasks can be broken down into component parts that can be demonstrated before the learner practises and repeats them until mastery is achieved.

There are several advantages in giving a demonstration, including:

- you can adapt the demonstration to suit the specific needs of the pupil;
- you are there to answer any questions the pupil may wish to ask.

The demonstration must not be used to impress the learner with your own expertise. The key points in the preceding briefing or explanation should form an integral part of the demonstration by way of an abbreviated commentary.

A learner may often be genuinely unaware of a mistake. A demonstration will help to show them where they are going wrong and what is needed to correct the problem. This is especially so when the pupil's perception of safety margins, the need for 'holding back' procedures, and speed approaching hazards, is poor.

You might mention slowing down approaching a hazard and get no response from the learner if their understanding of 'slow' is different from your own. Under these circumstances a demonstration can be a valuable aid to you in persuading pupils to modify what they are doing to fit in with how you want the manoeuvre carried out.

It may be helpful to pupils if you simulate what they are doing so that they can appreciate the difference.

This technique would be particularly useful when giving feedback on the pupil's performance in the set manoeuvres.

Points to remember:

- Explain beforehand what you are going to demonstrate and give the reasons for the demonstration.
- Pitch the demonstration and the commentary given while carrying it out to the correct level for the ability of the learner.
- Make the demonstration as perfect an example as possible of what you want the pupil to do.

- Restrict the commentary to key points only and those that are necessary for that particular learner.
- Consolidate afterwards with a debriefing and controlled practice.

The demonstration should be concluded with a summary of the key points, which might then lead to a Q&A session to identify any aspects of the task that the learner still does not understand.

Demonstrations can be carried out in different ways depending on the learning style of your pupil. For example, if your pupil has told you they learn visually and process information most effectively this way, you could carry out the demonstration in silence having previously discussed what your pupil needs to look at and watch. If your pupil has an auditory learning preference then you could give them a commentary while you demonstrate; or, you could ask them to talk you through as if they were the driving instructor. A kinaesthetic learner might benefit most from no demonstration or explanation at all – just let them have a go.

Practice

Having demonstrated a particular skill or manoeuvre you should then allow your pupil to practise it. You could find that there is a need for prompting if the pupil is encountering difficulties or deviating from what they should be doing. For example, if the pupil is practising the turn in the road and not turning the wheel effectively, you may need to say, 'Use longer movements of the steering wheel and turn more briskly.'

Establishing good habits in these early stages while practising the manoeuvre will pay dividends for the learner later.

When the pupil is practising new skills, check on the body language for signs of stress, frustration or despair. Be prepared to intervene if necessary. Encouragement and reassurance may be needed. Be prepared to change your lesson plan and go back to consolidating previously learnt skills to boost flagging confidence.

Controlled practice will allow the beginner to remain safe, and not be too unsympathetic to the vehicle. It involves the learner in following simple verbal instructions to carry out the component parts of the skill which, when brought together, form complete mastery.

The speed with which the learner interprets and responds to the instruction needs to be considered. This may vary from pupil to pupil. With some pupils it may be necessary to carry out tasks more slowly than normal.

The instructions given should eventually be reduced to prompting. As soon as the learner appears to be able to cope independently, the instruction should gradually be phased out.

The amount of prompting given will depend on the ability and willingness of learners to make decisions on their own. Some learners will require a lot of encouragement to act and think for themselves.

The ultimate objective is to get the learner to carry out each skill under all normal traffic conditions with no prompting from you at all.

Many learners complete their programme of training being able to carry out all the driving tasks required of them, but unable to do any of them particularly well. This is not helpful to the pupils, who may themselves feel that 'all is not well'.

The sequence of development should be:

- controlled practice;
- prompted practice;
- transferred responsibility;
- reflection;
- revision.

Prompting should not be necessary where the learner is about to be presented for the 'L' test!

Pupil involvement

To help maintain the interest and attention of your pupil you need to bring the lesson to life, personalising it and making it enjoyable. At the end of any lesson your pupils should leave the car feeling not only that they have learnt something and achieved the objectives of the lesson, but also that they have enjoyed themselves.

A proportion of your pupils will probably come to you having had lessons with another instructor. Why is this? It is often because they feel they were not making progress with the previous instructor or were not enjoying the lessons.

Don't forget that each pupil is an individual. Use first names during the lesson and make eye contact when discussing things while stationary. Use the different speech elements we discussed in the previous chapter – metaphors, hyperbole and similes – to add interest and perhaps a touch of humour to the presentation.

Use visual aids when explaining things, and make sure that pupils can actually see what it is that you are showing them. So many instructors cover up what they are showing with their hands, pupils cannot see or understand the points being made!

Visual aids

A learning aid is any medium you might use to enable you to present your ideas, concepts, knowledge and skills in a manner that is more easily understood by your learner.

Learning aids can assist the learning process by helping to hold pupils' attention and generate an interest that stimulates the desire to learn.

It has been said that 'The purpose of a learning aid is to liberate the teacher from the limitations of their own speech.' But, while learning aids may help to make a good instructor even better, they will not compensate for bad teaching.

Learning aids range from a simple notepad and pencil to sophisticated driving simulators. Between these two extremes, there is a vast range of aids available to the instructor, many of which are visual. In this section we will concentrate on those aids of a visual nature that can be used in the car.

'A picture paints a thousand words' – provided it is a good picture! It is amazing how many instructors say to their pupils, 'I am not very good at drawing, but I am going to draw you a diagram to explain what I mean.'

The visual aids you use are limited only by your imagination. You can use your hands to explain how the clutch plates come together; you can use your fingers to show 'the thickness of a coin' when explaining the biting point; you can produce pre-prepared diagrams to assist you in explaining various aspects of road procedure, manoeuvres, etc.

Be careful, however, not to overuse visual aids to the extent that they detract from the basic message you wish to put across.

Visual aids offer the following benefits:

- they add structure to your lesson;
- they provide a change of activity for the learner;
- they will assist you by reminding you what needs to be explained;
- they will allow the pupil to recall and visualise previously encountered situations;

- they can help to clarify difficult concepts or show specific positions required when manoeuvring or dealing with hazards;
- they stimulate the interest of the learner and help to maintain attention.

By being skilful in designing, creating and integrating visual aids in your presentation, you will be able to bring the lesson to life.

When using visual aids in the car you should:

- avoid just reading from a script;
- talk to the pupil and not to the visual aid;
- turn the aid around so that the pupil can see it – it is for their benefit, not just for yours;
- avoid covering the visual aid with your hand – you may need to hold it with your right and use your left hand, or a pen, to point to the key parts;
- avoid 'pen-waving' because it can be threatening to the pupil;
- put the visual aid away once you have used it, before it becomes a distraction.

The 'A to E' of visual aids:

Accuracy   –   Try to ensure that the visual aid accurately recreates the situation you are trying to depict.

Brevity   –   Keep drawings/diagrams simple and avoid having too many words or unnecessary detail.

Clarity   –   Ensure that letters or words are big enough to be seen by the pupil.

Deletion   –   Use them then lose them, otherwise they become a distraction.

Emphasis   –   Make sure that the visual aid stresses the key points.

At the end of each lesson ask yourself:

- Did I take every opportunity to use visual aids in order to assist the learning process?
- Were the visual aids stimulating and effective?
- Did I identify any situations where a visual aid could have been useful? If so, should I think about designing one for future use?

The use of questions

Question and Answer technique (Q&A) is an important aspect of driving instruction because it involves the learner in the process and allows the instructor to check that learning is taking place. Coaching questions are very different from traditional Q&A and are dealt with in Chapter 3.

It is the combination of key skills of questioning, building rapport and active listening that enables the driving instructor to establish a balance between instruction and coaching – a balance that is critical in keeping the car safe. There are various questioning techniques that can be employed to help strike this balance.

For details of different types of coaching questions, see the section on effective questioning in Chapter 3.

Intervention

Some learner drivers may fail to recognise potentially dangerous traffic situations in time to employ the necessary procedure or defensive strategy.

Instructors must read the road well ahead. They must also learn to anticipate a learner's incorrect response to situations and be prepared to compensate for it, either by verbal or physical action.

When giving driving lessons you must maintain a safe learning environment for your pupils by:

- planning routes that are suitable to their ability;
- forward planning and concentrating on the overall traffic situation – front, rear and to the sides;
- being alert and anticipating learners' incorrect actions or lack of activity in difficult situations;
- giving clear instructions in good time for them to respond;
- overriding learners' decisions when necessary;
- being prepared to intervene verbally or physically.

Many learners show a reluctance to slow down, give way, stop, or hold back when necessary. This is usually because they have an innate fear of stopping. If they stop, they know they then have to get the car moving again – one of the most difficult things for learners to do in the early stages!

This reluctance to deal with hazards defensively may cause the situation to develop into an emergency. Where the situation is allowed to reach this critical level, there are two possible unwanted reactions: the pupil may do nothing and remain frozen at the controls; the pupil may over-react at the last moment, resulting in harsh, uncontrolled braking, the effect of which is difficult to predict.

It is in situations like this that expert instructors prove their worth. By intervening, either verbally or physically, a possible accident situation can be avoided.

There are four main reasons why you should intervene:

1 To prevent risk of injury or damage to persons or property (including the driving school car).

2 To prevent the pupil from breaking the law, which could lead to you being prosecuted for 'aiding and abetting'.

3 To prevent excessive stress to the learner in certain unplanned circumstances (for example, an emergency situation).

4 To prevent mechanical damage to the vehicle (for example, in the event of an injudicious gear change).

Because intervention can undermine confidence and inhibit the progress of the learner, it should be kept to a minimum. Verbal intervention should, if time allows, be used before considering the use of physical intervention or the dual controls.

Verbal intervention

A verbal instruction or command will usually be successful in dealing with most traffic situations or driver errors, provided it is given early enough.

Verbal instructions and memory prompts will be used more frequently in the early stages of learning to drive and may take the form of more specific instructions such as: 'Use the mirrors well before...', 'More brake!', 'Ease off the brake' and 'Clutch down'.

These more positive commands will often be needed to make sure that your pupil slows down early enough on the approach to a potential hazard.

'Hold back!', 'Give way!' and 'Wait!' are other examples of positive instructions that require a positive response or reaction from the pupil, but which also leave some freedom of judgement.

When using this type of command, the pitch and tone of your voice should be used to convey the degree of urgency to the pupil.

The use of the word 'Stop' should generally be restricted to those occasions when other instructions have not been followed by the pupil or when the pupil has not responded positively. Incorrect use of this command could mean that your pupil over-reacts and stops too suddenly or in an unsuitable position. Unnecessary and too frequent use of the word 'Stop' – for example, when parking – could have the effect that pupils will not respond quickly enough in urgent situations.

Physical intervention

Use of any form of physical intervention, or the dual controls, should be restricted to situations when the verbal instruction has not been followed or there is insufficient time for it to be given or acted on.

In these situations, you may need to consider the main alternatives: use of the dual brake and/or clutch; assistance with the steering.

Using the dual brake/clutch

The following points need to be considered:

- Avoid sitting with your legs crossed when teaching. When approaching hazards, keep your right foot discreetly near the dual brake but not riding on it.

- Avoid unnecessary or 'fidgety' movements of your feet as this may unnerve your pupil.

- Make effective use of the dual mirror before using the dual brake.

- If your pupil has 'frozen' on the gas pedal, avoid using the dual clutch as this could cause a blown head gasket.

- Give the pupil time to use the brake before intervening. If you both use the brake at the same time, this could cause problems.

- Consider using the dual brake to help you to 'buy time' if you have to help with the steering. This applies particularly where the pupil may be trying to turn a corner too fast.

Assistance with steering

This should only be used to make slight alterations to road position. It would be better for you to tell the pupil to 'Steer to the right' or 'Steer to the left'.

Bear in mind the following points:

- Minor corrections with steering are usually more practical and safer alternatives to using the dual brake.

- Use only your right hand when assisting with steering.

- Avoid physical contact. If you get hold of the pupil's hand or arm and he or she lets go of the wheel, you have lost control.

- If you wish to steer to the left, hold the wheel near the top so that you can 'pull down'.

- If you wish to steer to the right, hold the wheel near the bottom so that you can 'push up'.

- If the situation is such that more drastic turning of the wheel is required, it would be safer and much less worrying for the pupil if you used the dual brake.

- Never get into a fight with the pupil over the wheel – you might lose!

There may be occasions when assistance with both steering and braking are required. For example, it may be essential to hold the steering wheel while using the dual brake to prevent the pupil from over-steering. In order to gain more time, you may need to reduce and control the speed of the vehicle with the dual brake, particularly when the pupil has 'frozen' on the gas pedal.

In any potentially dangerous situation, you will need to use your experience to decide which method of intervention is required. You may need to use the dual clutch at the same time as manipulating the gear lever to prevent an inappropriate gear change. This will allow your pupil to concentrate on maintaining the correct speed and position.

Examples of other types of physical intervention that crop up from time to time include:

- selecting a missed gear at a critical time or place;

- preventing an incorrect gear selection by 'covering the gear lever' until the correct speed is reached;

- covering the dual clutch to be ready to prevent the car moving off at an inappropriate time;

- rectifying an error with the handbrake when there is no time to tell the pupil to do so;

- switching off the engine to prevent mechanical damage;
- cancelling an injudicious signal with safety in mind when there is no time to tell the pupil to do so.

The need for any kind of intervention can be kept to an absolute minimum by careful route planning and matching the road and traffic conditions to the ability of the pupil.

You may encounter some resentment towards any form of physical interference or the use of the dual controls. This could result in pupils losing confidence in themselves and in you as a teacher. You should therefore make sure that:

1 You do not get into the habit of using physical intervention or the dual controls excessively or unnecessarily.

2 Having used any physical intervention, you fully explain to the pupil what you did to control the car, and why it was necessary to do it!

05
Driver training

Teaching driving as a life skill in today's traffic conditions is a challenging occupation. So that your pupils become safe and competent drivers, as well as being able to enjoy their future driving you need to:

- understand and be able to apply all the coaching and client-centred skills covered in this book;
- be able to develop confidence and safe attitudes in your pupils;
- structure your training to follow the 'known to the unknown' and 'simple to complex' rules of learning.

In this chapter some of the subjects are dealt with in a relatively formal way, including an introduction, objectives and so on. With others, we give examples of how to set up more of a coaching approach by way of a dialogue with the pupil to encourage more self-learning, self-awareness and motivation. With other topics we simply offer a few guidance notes on the important key points.

With experience, you should be able to decide for yourself the method and approach that will best suit your own style and one that will be most appropriate for any individual pupil or specific circumstances.

This chapter contains a training programme that follows a logical sequence incorporating the above principles. It focuses on the various topics involved in driver training and not necessarily on the requirements of the ADI exam. If you learn how to apply these effectively, you should be well prepared to teach drivers at all levels of experience and ability.

Beginning with the introduction of the car's controls and how to move off and stop, we progress through the different stages of learning to drive in a logical sequence.

Depending on your local road and traffic conditions, as well as the individual needs of your pupils, you may need to teach some of the subjects in a different sequence. Also, if you are dealing with a pupil from another driving school or are preparing for your ADI Part 3 test, you will need to adapt your lesson to suit the level and ability of the pupil, or the limited amount of time available.

You can do this by:

- using your client-centred learning skills to work to an agreed programme;
- adapting your teaching method to suit progress made by a pupil during the lesson; and
- ensuring some positive learning takes place through practice within the time scale.

Throughout this chapter you will find examples of the types of question you could use to suit the pupil's experience, the topic under instruction and the circumstances. You will, of course, need to formulate your own questions, as every pupil has individual needs and each situation is different.

Whatever the subject or level of ability of your pupil, your aim should always be to ensure that some learning takes place and to encourage pupils' development and long-term learning.

Lesson structure

Every lesson, no matter what the subject matter is, should follow a similar pattern. There should always be a beginning, a middle, and an end.

The main ingredients should be:

Beginning

- greeting;
- recapping on the previous lesson;
- agreeing the objectives and aims;
- establishing prior knowledge and understanding;
- agreeing the base line according to the above.

Middle

- working from the known to the unknown;
- applying the appropriate teaching, instructing and coaching skills;
- creating opportunities for learning to take place through practice.

End

- giving appropriate feedback in a summary, including praise where appropriate;
- looking forward to the next lesson.

Example lesson plan

Greeting

'Hello Wayne, how are you today?'
   'I'm fine thanks.'

Recap

'You did really well on your last lesson and were getting quite good at moving off, stopping and changing up and down the gears.'
   'Yes, but I remember crunching the gears a couple of times.'
   'Don't worry about that: if you take your time a little more, your gear changing will soon become smooth.'

Agreeing the objectives

'By the end of today's lesson we should have sorted out that little problem and also learnt how to turn left and right at T-junctions. How do you feel about that?'
   'That would be great.'

Establishing prior knowledge

'So, Wayne, can you tell me what routine you need to apply for moving off and stopping? You know, that little three-letter sequence.'
   'Oh, you mean Mirror Signal Manoeuvre.'
   'Yes, good. And why should we check the mirrors before we stop?'
   'So that we know what's behind.'
   'Good, any other reason for checking them?'
   'I'm not sure.'
   'What about checking to see how close they are and what speed they're travelling at?'
   'If we know they're there, why does all the rest matter?'
   'Because it's going to determine whether we need to signal a little earlier to give them plenty of notice that we intend to stop. By doing this, it will give that following driver more time to respond.'

'Oh right, I never thought of that.'

'So you see how important the M S M routine and how we apply it is!'

'What we've agreed, then, is how to break down that routine into more sections and apply it to turning left and right at junctions.'

Working from the known to the unknown

This pupil knows a little about the basic M S M routine in straightforward moving off and stopping situations, but now needs to learn how to apply it to turn left and right at junctions.

You need to analyse the routine by discussing in detail the M S M (mirrors–signal–manoeuvre), P S L (position–speed–look) and L A D (look–assess–decide) routines. A visual aid will be useful as you can use it as a memory jogger while your pupil will be able to see exactly what you mean.

A demonstration is sometimes useful with a complex topic but when dealing with straightforward tasks such as simple junction work, prompted practice will be more effective.

Apply the appropriate teaching, instructing and coaching skills

The subject in hand, the level of skill of your pupil and the road and traffic circumstances, will all need to be considered when you decide on the most appropriate teaching method to be applied.

A certain amount of talk-through instruction might be needed when dealing with a new subject and, as confidence and skills increase and to develop safe attitudes, coaching will become more appropriate.

Create opportunities for learning to take place through practice

Select a route that will allow plenty of opportunities to apply the appropriate routines and skills. The more time that is allocated to the practice element, the more the pupil is likely to achieve success and confidence.

Give feedback and praise

If you are to encourage your pupils to work with you, and to leave at the end of each lesson wanting more, it's important to give some positive feedback.

This should include:

- praise for procedures and routines learnt and carried out correctly;
- use of appropriate questions to confirm the pupil's understanding; and
- giving advice on where improvements can be made.

See Chapter 2 for guidance on giving feedback.

Look forward to the next lesson

It's always useful to give your pupils something to think about before their next lesson. Tell them what you will be covering and give them an indication of where to find appropriate information. Give them some incentive to do a little research by confirming that you will be asking a few questions at the beginning of their next lesson.

Main car controls

Objectives

Main objectives for this lesson:

1 To get to know your pupil by finding out what has motivated them to want to learn and why they have chosen you as their instructor.

2 To let the pupil get used to you and your style of teaching, and for you to gain their confidence.

3 To introduce the main controls of the car and, if possible, let the pupil have some experience in moving off and stopping.

Getting to know your pupil

One of your main aims, when meeting a pupil for the first time, is to sell yourself by promoting a caring and understanding image and ensuring that you inspire confidence. To do this, try to imagine how your pupil may be feeling about learning to drive, and being in the confined space of a car with a stranger.

For this lesson, you will need to drive to an area that is reasonably quiet, with as long a stretch of straight road as is available to practise moving off and stopping (see route planning in Chapter 4). The area you use will depend on the locality of the pupil's pick-up point and the likely content of the lesson. You will sometimes have to adapt your instruction to suit less than ideal conditions – this is often the case on the instructional ability test.

During the drive to the training area find out if your pupil:

- has a valid and signed driving licence;
- can read a number plate at the prescribed distance;
- is studying for, or has already passed, the theory test.

Get to know a little more about your pupil by asking questions such as:

'Why do you want to learn to drive?'

'How did you hear of me? Was I recommended by someone?'

'Do you have any experience in driving a car?'

'Do you ride a motorbike?'

'When you've been a passenger, have you been watching what the driver was doing?'

If your pupil is a little shy, you may have to 'back off' a little. However, try to avoid silence – this will only make a nervous pupil even more tense.

Remember, part of your job as an instructor is to gain the confidence of your pupils and put them at ease.

Driving deliberately and a little more slowly than usual, give a simple commentary on what you're doing. Focus mainly on the application of the M S M routine and its application to the various situations you meet.

Remember, you are your best salesperson – make sure your driving is impeccable.

Select a training area that is safe, legal and will cause as little disruption to other drivers as is possible – in other words, convenient. Park where:

- you can safely carry out your explanation of the main controls;
- the pupil can get some stationary practice in their use; and
- there is plenty of opportunity to learn how to move off and stop.

Vehicle familiarisation

It is usually more practical to get the pupil into the driving seat so that you can explain where the controls are, and they can practise using them. This makes the most effective use of your time and avoids unnecessary repetition. It means you have plenty of time for the pupil to get practical experience at moving off and stopping before the end of the lesson, which in turn should help to meet some of their expectations.

With an absolute novice, for instance someone with no experience of cars as a passenger, you may decide to give the explanation from the driving seat. This will ensure that the pupil is not tempted to fiddle with any of the controls.

The first thing you need to get your pupil to think about is getting out of the passenger seat, around the car and into the driving seat safely. This should include:

Checking around before opening the passenger door. You could ask something like: 'Is anyone near the car on the pavement?'

Making sure it's safe to walk into the road, around the car and to open the door, ask: 'Is there any traffic coming up that might make it unsafe to step out or that you will affect by opening the door?'

Entering the car and getting into a correct seating position is commonly called 'The cockpit drill' and includes:

- Doors – ensuring they are properly closed.
- Seat – correct adjustment of seat, back rake, head restraint and other ancillaries as are available and necessary such as steering column and seat height.
- Steering – hands can be comfortably moved from top to bottom of the wheel.
- Seatbelts – correctly put on and removed (no twists); driver's responsibilities.
- Mirrors – all mirrors are correctly adjusted.
- Ancillary controls – to avoid overloading your pupil with too much unnecessary information, only cover those that are needed for the conditions, for example wipers and lights.

Main controls

These fall into three categories:

1 foot controls;

2 hand controls;

3 ancillary controls.

It is not essential to cover these in the sequence listed. However, it does help pupils if you deal mainly with those controls that will be used to make the car go and stop – that means the foot controls. Apart from the indicators, the ancillary controls you will need to cover should depend on the weather and light conditions.

Foot controls

Unless you are teaching in a car with automatic gears, confirm that there are three foot controls:

- accelerator;
- footbrake; and
- clutch.

Ask your pupils if they know which foot operates which pedal and what each does, for example:

'Do you know what the pedal on the right does?'
'What's the pedal in the centre for and which foot will you use to operate it?'
'Do you know what following drivers should see when the footbrake is used?'
'What's the pedal on the left for?'

If you are teaching in a car with automatic transmission, then you will need to explain that the right foot is used for the two pedals. You will also need to explain about the gear selector.

Accelerator

Because you will sometimes need your pupil to respond quickly to a request, for example to start slowing down, it's easier to say, 'Off the gas' than it is to say, 'Off the accelerator'.

If you ask, 'What does the gas pedal do?' most pupils will say that it makes the car go faster. Very few will realise that it is also the first means of starting to slow down the car. However, this point should become clear if you use a simple comparison such as how a tap works, explaining that when the pedal is pressed down more fuel will flow into the engine to make it go faster; and when the pressure is eased the flow will slow down. The pedal is sensitive and should be used gently.

Footbrake

Operates on all four wheels to slow the car down and eventually bring it to a stop.

Discuss a few important points such as:

- a mirror check should be made before braking;
- this is also a sensitive pedal and should be used gently and progressively;
- the stop lights will be activated as soon as pressure is applied to it.

Clutch

Consider asking questions such as: 'Do you know what the clutch does?'; 'Do you know when you'd use it?'

Depending on the pupil's responses, using a visual aid, either confirm or explain in simple terms the clutch's main purpose. This is to disconnect the engine from the gearbox to make smooth changes from one gear to another and to ensure that the engine keeps running when the car has been stopped.

Hand controls

Explain that, although there are lots of dials, switches and gadgets in the car, there are three main hand controls:

- steering wheel;
- handbrake; and
- gear lever.

Steering wheel

You can use coaching skills to find out which hand position is most comfortable for your pupils. First, get them to place their hands on the wheel at around 'ten to two' or 'quarter to three' and encourage them to hold it gently with the thumbs along the rim rather than around the wheel. Ask how it feels when they slide their hands to the top and bottom. If it's not comfortable, get them to drop the hands a little and try again. Try this procedure until the pupil can move the hands comfortably around the wheel – provided they aren't at rest too near the top or bottom.

Turning the steering wheel using the conventional method of 'pull–push' does not come naturally to most new drivers and everyone's body and range of movements are different. Use common sense and be flexible about the way the steering wheel is used.

Although 'pull–push' still seems to be the officially recommended method, the main point is that the car should be under complete control and in the correct position on the road. You should also be aware that 'rotational' steering generally results in a much quicker response in most emergency situations and in correcting skids.

Describe how it's natural for the hands to follow the eyes. Ask your pupils if they've ever experienced a situation when they've been walking along and something to the side has caught their attention and when they've looked forward again, they've gone off course. Confirm that this can happen while driving and that's why it's so important to look well ahead up the road at where they want to go.

Handbrake

Confirm that it secures the car once stopped by locking up the rear wheels. As well as for parking, it should be used for stops of longer than a few seconds, on hills to prevent rolling forwards or backwards, and for safety when stopped for pedestrians on crossings. (When driving automatics, the handbrake should be used more often to compensate for the tendency to 'creep'.)

You will need to ensure the car is secure. You can either apply the dual footbrake or, because you also need to encourage an understanding of the relationship between the two braking systems, you could say something like: 'Press the middle pedal down with your right foot.'

The handbrake has three positions: on, off and, when the button is pressed, ready to release. Discuss how to properly release and apply the handbrake and then allow the pupil to practise this a couple of times.

Gear lever

Find out what pupils know about the use of gears. Usually if they have ridden a bike they will have a little understanding. However, in order to develop your practical teaching skills, we will deal with the subject as it should be taught to someone with no knowledge.

First, explain about the power to speed ratio and, while serving as a memory jogger for you, a visual aid may assist your pupil in understanding this principle (see 'Visual Aids', Chapter 4).

Confirm that, because of the weight of the car and its occupants, you will need more engine power to get moving. The lower gears, first and second, are the most powerful and normally first is used for moving off. Second is useful for moving off down hills where gravity will help in getting the car rolling more quickly. We will need to accelerate to build up speed and then change up into the higher gears. These allow us to drive at a wider range of speeds while using less power.

To assist in the pupil's understanding, you might ask:

'When you're walking uphill what happens to you?'
'Do you start to slow down and then have to put in more effort?'
'If you were cycling up a hill, what would you have to do?'

You will then be able to confirm that this is exactly what happens to the car by saying something like: 'Because of the hill slowing the car down, we will need to give it more power by changing into a lower gear.'

You should also discuss the point that, because all cars differ in size and power, the speed at which the gears will need to be changed varies. However, after a few lessons they should become familiar with the sound the engine makes as it 'tells' them when a change is required. Confirm that you will help them to recognise these sounds and to build up their vehicle sympathy so that they will eventually feel the car is part of them.

As one of the main objectives of this lesson is vehicle familiarisation, you should allow plenty of stationary practice so that the pupil will be able to 'find' all the gear positions while looking ahead. This can be done without switching on the engine, but it might be useful to get the pupil to push down the clutch to establish the relationship.

Allow your pupil to take an initial look at the lever and identify the different gear positions. It might help, in the early stages, to relate the position of the first four gears in the form of the letter H to the position of the road wheels so when a change is necessary, and without looking down, they should be able to move the lever in the appropriate direction.

The gear lever in most modern cars is usually 'spring-loaded'. As well as demonstrating (with your right hand) how to select the gears using the 'palming' method, you will also need to emphasise this bias as you talk the pupil through the various changes.

Allow the pupil to practise gear change combinations. That is, as well as showing how to change in sequence up and down, explain about selective changing and talk through these changes with a couple of examples of where they might be used.

This practice is very important because, the more confident pupils become with gear changing while stationary, the easier they will find it when they are on the move.

Other hand controls

Indicators

Remember – new drivers will have been pedestrians and passengers and will be aware of the use of indicators. To avoid being patronising try to get them to discover for themselves where they are and in which direction they will need to be operated. Use questions such as:

'What are the orange flashing lights for on the front, rear and sometimes the sides, of cars?'

'When do you think they should be used?'

'Which of the controls on the steering column do you think is the indicator switch?' If the pupil has a problem, follow this up with: 'OK, find the switch with the arrows on.'

'If you're intending to turn right, which way will you turn the wheel? Now tell me which way you think the indicator switch will need to be operated.'

Allow the pupil to practise switching the indicators on and off (preferably using the fingertips while keeping the hand on the wheel), confirming that the indicator should normally self-cancel after going around corners. Explain the audible and visible warnings that will tell the driver when the indicators are operating.

Horn

Confirm that this is a warning device and should only be used when there is possible danger or potential damage. Discuss one of the main rules about not using it when stationary unless under threat from another moving vehicle. You could then ask them to check up on the other rules because you'll be asking some questions on their next lesson.

Ancillary controls

As your pupils must take on board lots of information on this lesson, it's very important to consider how much of it is likely to be remembered. Overloading them at this stage with information they are unlikely to remember in any case, is going to inhibit their progress and confidence.

Only cover those ancillary controls that are necessary according, mainly, to the weather and light conditions. If it's not raining and light conditions are good, you won't need to cover the lights, washers, wipers or demisters. Confirm that you will show the pupil where these are and how they work on another lesson.

Stationary practice

Demonstrate how to check that the handbrake is firmly applied and that the gear lever is in neutral. Ask your pupil to make these checks and then allow plenty of stationary practice in:

- setting the gas;
- covering the brake pedal;
- finding the 'biting' point.

Moving off and stopping

You would normally have time to include moving off and stopping on the first lesson.

Confirm that your pupil understands about the main controls by asking a couple of questions such as:

'Do you feel happy with what we've covered so far?'

'Is there anything you're not sure about?'

'Is there anything in particular you feel you need to practise?'

Agreeing the objectives

You are now ready to continue the lesson by agreeing the next objective. This is to learn how to move off and stop the car safely. If your pupil is preparing for their theory test, ask if they know anything about the M S M routine and give praise if they have even only a little knowledge. In any case, you will need to give a breakdown of the routine to ensure that all the important points are covered.

Mirrors

Discuss the difference between the flat glass of the interior mirror and the convex glass of the exterior ones. Confirm why any decisions must be based on the true image seen in the interior mirror.

Confirm that not all areas to the rear and sides are covered by the mirrors and demonstrate what a 'blind area' is by selecting a point, such as a driveway, to the pupil's right. Confirm why it's important to look over the shoulder before moving away to make sure no one is at the side of the car. For example, there may be a cyclist or someone emerging from a driveway or side road.

Signal

Introduce *The Highway Code* requirements and discuss the use of signals to warn or inform other road users of your intentions.

Discuss whether there is a need to give a signal if no one is going to benefit from it. Explain that you will help with these decisions to begin with.

Manoeuvre

This means any change in speed or direction. Moving off involves getting the car moving, building up speed and getting into the normal driving position; and stopping involves slowing down, moving back towards the kerb and stopping.

Practice

Moving off and stopping

Make sure the pupil knows and understands how to:

- make safety checks before starting the engine;
- prepare the car to move;
- take full all-round observations;
- move the car when it's safe;
- stop where it's safe, legal and convenient;
- move off on the level and on uphill and downhill gradients (where suitable opportunities arise);
- move off, building up speed and changing through the gears; and
- slow down and stop.

At this stage it is useful to practise stopping from different speeds and in different gears (without changing down!). Controlled stops – for example 'By that next lamppost' – will reinforce the point about slowing and stopping by using the footbrake rather than gears.

Be patient and give help where necessary, particularly with the less able. As skill increases, start dropping off your instruction. However, always be ready to come back with more help when needed.

Fault identification, analysis and rectification

Be positive when you make corrections and give your reasons. Common errors during these early stages of learning are:

- Moving away before or without checking blind areas. Ask: 'Is there anyone in the blind area?', 'Can you see that pedestrian?'

- Lack of coordination between gas and clutch. By being totally in tune with your car, and giving positive instruction, you can do much to ensure your pupil's confidence is built up. By encouraging your pupil to listen to the sound of the engine and feel for the biting point, you can do much to prevent a stalled engine and, at the same time, start to develop vehicle sympathy.

- Looking at the controls. Confirm that the hands will follow the eyes and that's why we need to look well ahead up the road when we're driving.

Feedback

Throughout the lesson, give praise for routines carried out correctly. End the lesson by confirming where progress has been made. Look forward to the next lesson when more practice will take place prior to learning how to apply the M S M routine to turning left and right.

Use of mirrors

Objectives

The main objectives of this lesson are to ensure your pupil fully understands the importance of correct mirror adjustment and effective use of all mirrors.
   Examples of agreed objectives:

- able to adjust all mirrors so that you have the maximum possible view around the car with the minimum of head movement;
- awareness of the areas not covered by the mirrors;
- understand the importance of responding properly to what you see;
- able to apply the M S M routine.

Confirm what your pupil has remembered from previous lessons by asking questions such as:

- 'When you get in the car, how should you adjust the mirrors?'
- 'Tell me which is the offside and which is the nearside mirror.'
- 'Do the mirrors cover all areas around the car?'
- 'What is important about checking over your shoulders before moving off?'
- 'What do you need to consider before deciding on a signal?'
- 'What routine would you apply for moving off, passing parked cars and stopping?'

Give praise for correct answers and discuss where knowledge or understanding is weak.
   Make sure the pupil understands that, when a change in direction is involved, the mirrors should be used in pairs. For example, before moving out to pass a parked car a check of the interior mirror should be made, followed by a check in the offside door mirror. Before moving back in to the left, the

interior mirror should be re-checked and this should be followed by a check in the nearside door mirror. Similarly, before turning left, as well as checking the interior mirror a check should be made to the nearside for any cyclists.

Discuss why it's important to check the mirrors well before deciding when to signal. For example, before signalling to turn right, it's important to know what's behind, how fast it's travelling and whether anyone is going to overtake you. In this case, applying a signal too early may cause confusion all around so it would be better to delay it until the vehicle's gone by. On the other hand, if you intend to turn left and there's someone following closely, giving an early signal will be of benefit as it will give the other driver plenty of warning of your intention and time to react to you slowing down.

This is another subject where practice rather than demonstration will help develop your pupil's awareness and skill in mirror use.

Practice

Unless the pupil has had several lessons, some prompting may initially be required to establish the need for regular checking of all the mirrors. Encourage general mirror checks every few seconds so that eventually, when there's a hazard that requires a change in speed or direction, checking will become automatic.

As your pupil's mirror work develops, drop off your instruction but when any lapses occur, give a reminder. You can do this by either physically watching them or by using an extra mirror trained on their eyes. The latter can be beneficial in that you can avoid giving hints to your pupil to check the mirrors by not having to look directly at them at the appropriate time.

One of the basic ingredients of safe driving is being aware of what's happening all around and responding safely. To establish safe routines, it's extremely important that you identify any weaknesses in pupils' mirror use during their early stages of learning. You will need to watch for pupils:

- not adjusting mirrors correctly;
- exaggerating head movements when checking the mirrors;
- making late mirror checks;
- checking mirrors at the same time as signalling;
- not checking mirrors before speeding up, slowing down, changing direction or stopping;

- playing about with the anti-dazzle setting;
- not checking blind areas;
- not using door mirrors;
- not responding correctly to what is happening.

Always try to give reasons for using the mirrors effectively by explaining the consequences for other road users of incorrect responses.

You then need to create opportunities where you can emphasise the need for using the mirrors correctly and responding safely. This may sometimes mean using prompted instruction until you can see that the pupil's understanding is improving.

Feedback/recap

Give praise where improvement has taken place and confirm by looking back over a few of the situations that arose, where any weaknesses must be worked on.

Remember that feedback is a two-way process. At the end of the session confirm, by using effective questions, that the pupil understands the importance of correct mirror use and ask if there are any points they are not sure about. Discuss with the pupil where any misunderstandings may be occurring.

Use of signals

The use of signals, and response to those given by others, is not a subject that you can teach in isolation. It should be taught from lesson one and as part of the general routine for driving.

Make sure that your pupils are aware of the many ways in which drivers communicate with each other, including:

- indicators;
- arm signals;
- brake lights;
- horn;
- headlights;
- road positioning;

- eye contact;

- signals given by police officers and school wardens.

The emphasis here should be on the need to give signals to warn or inform other road users. If no one will benefit, make a conscious decision not to give a signal. This will encourage more effective use of mirrors and all-round observations.

Sample questions to assess the pupil's knowledge and understanding:

- 'How can we tell other road users of our intentions?'

- 'How does a following driver know when you're slowing down?'

- 'When could you use the horn?'

- 'What does *The Highway Code* say about using hazard-warning lights?'

- 'When would you signal to move away or stop?'

- 'Do you always need to signal to pass parked cars?'

- 'When might you use an arm signal for slowing down?'

- 'Apart from the indicators, how can you tell following drivers that you're going to pass parked vehicles?'

- 'If you wanted to allow another driver out of a side road when it's busy, how could you do this without waving them out?'

- 'Why do you think it might be dangerous to beckon pedestrians onto crossings?'

- 'If someone flashed their headlights at you to turn in front of them into a side, would you automatically assume that your way was clear?'

During pupils' early lessons, you should ensure that they get plenty of practice in applying the M S M routine in all situations. As the basic car control skills improve and the pupil becomes more confident, encourage them to judge when to use signals. They should learn to:

- look all around and check the mirrors before moving, working out whether anyone will benefit from a signal;

- make regular checks of all mirrors and decide on the best way to tell others of their intentions to pass parked vehicles, for example moving out earlier;

- use the brake lights as an early indication of slowing down for lower speed limits;

- respond correctly to other road users' signals for moving off, stopping and turning;

- check for themselves that it's safe to proceed when others beckon them on;

- use eye contact;

- work out when a short beep on the horn might be used to warn others, for example when they see someone reversing out from a driveway or where there is a blind summit.

As this subject will apply to every lesson, you should give the appropriate praise when the correct routines are applied and good discrimination is demonstrated; and positive advice on where more practice is required.

Turning and emerging at junctions

As with all topics, first agree the objectives for the lesson so that you can pitch the instruction at the correct level. Remember, in this chapter we are dealing with how to teach the subject to one of your regular pupils who has no experience of the subject. You can set the baseline, therefore, by asking a few questions relevant to what was covered on the previous lesson. Examples:

- 'Do you remember our discussion on the last lesson about the routine for moving off, stopping and passing parked cars?'

- 'Why do you think that it's important to use the mirrors before signalling?'

- 'What if there is some traffic behind, for example, a motorcyclist who is about to overtake? How would that influence your signalling?'

- 'What do you think you should you look for when you're turning into a side road?'

- 'What does *The Highway Code* say you should do if there are pedestrians who are about to cross the side road?'

Early in the pupil's training you should ensure that your instruction will result in the correct routines being applied. To do this, you will need to start giving your instructions early enough to allow the pupil plenty of time to carry out each individual element comfortably.

As they are less difficult, begin with left turns into and out of T-junctions. Do a few circuits of these and then, as the pupil's skill improves, and their confidence increases, introduce turning right following a similar pattern of circuits.

Where there are any weaknesses or misunderstandings you must create opportunities for more practice on appropriate junctions so that positive learning and improvement can take place. To achieve this, you may find that you have to drive from one area to another to avoid the pupil having to deal with situations that are too complex for their ability. It might be helpful to use these opportunities to give a demonstration with commentary, keeping this to a level that will suit the pupil's capabilities.

For all types of junction make sure that:

- the Mirror–Signal–Manoeuvre routine is applied correctly;
- signals are properly timed, considering any following traffic and the location of the junction;
- road position is appropriate for the direction being taken, the width of the road, and the presence of other road users;
- full control of the car is maintained by effective use of the brakes;
- any downward gear change is done only after slowing down with the brakes – this should be emphasised from the start, otherwise the pupil mistakenly gets the impression that gears are needed for slowing down;
- the car is secured with the handbrake when waiting to emerge for more than a few seconds;
- full all-round observations are made. Keep checking that your pupil is looking effectively, as well as making sure that it will be safe for them to complete the turn or to emerge.

During the initial stages of training you might include questions such as:

- 'How far down the road can you see?'
- 'Have you checked your mirrors?'
- 'What are you going to do about the motorcyclist behind us?'
- 'At what point do we need to change down?'
- 'Have you released the clutch?'
- 'Have you seen the cyclist coming up on the nearside?'
- 'Have you taken account of those pedestrians waiting to cross?'
- 'What will you do if they step out?'
- 'Do you think you've time to turn right before that oncoming car reaches us?'
- 'Have you looked to the right to see what's happening in the new road?'
- 'How far can you see in both directions?'

- 'Tell me what's happening on the main road to our left.'
- 'What's happening at the bus stop?'

As skill increases, transfer the responsibility for decision making and introduce more difficult and busier junctions.

Always bear in mind that, no matter what their level of ability, you are responsible for the safety of all your pupils, other road users and, of course, yourself. Don't let an unsafe situation arise and put someone else at risk when it could easily be avoided by giving a simple instruction such as 'Wait' or, if necessary, 'Stop'.

At the end of each lesson offer a summary, including a few questions such as:

- 'Why do you think that we should look into a junction before turning in?'
- 'How would you deal with a slightly more complex situation such as...?'
- 'Why was it necessary for us to...?'

As well as your use of effective questions to recap on the lesson, allow time for the pupil to ask questions. Make sure your pupils go away with an understanding of the principles covered during each lesson.

Finally, 'look forward' by briefing the pupil on the next training topic. This would probably cover 'crossroads' as an extension of junction work or, if progress is slow, maybe a lesson consolidating junctions.

Crossroads

The introduction to this subject should include a brief recap on turning left and right into and out of minor roads.

A few questions to recap will be appropriate, particularly if there has been a gap between lessons and if the pupil is normally getting private practice. Here are a few examples:

- 'Have you been able to get some practice in?'
- 'How did you get on?'
- 'Why do you think that it's more appropriate for us to slow down by using the brakes, rather than using the gears as your brother/father/ mother says?'

- 'If we can see that we're going to have to stop – for instance at a red light – do we need to change gear?'
- 'Did you check on that *Highway Code* rule regarding pedestrians – what did it say?'

To introduce the subject of crossroads you might use the following types of question:

- 'Have you dealt with crossroads at all while you were practising?'
- 'Compared with a T-junction, what extra observations do you think you'll have to make?'
- 'Who has priority at a crossroads if we are going ahead and the oncoming traffic is turning right?'
- 'Can you explain the sequence of traffic lights?'
- 'What do you think "amber" means?'
- 'Which is potentially more of a problem – a light that's green as we approach, or one that's been red for some time?'
- 'Why do we need to look to the right when we are about to turn left?'

Before introducing more complex situations such as traffic light-controlled junctions, allow for practice at various types of less busy crossroads and include turning:

- left from main roads into side roads;
- left onto main roads;
- right onto main roads;
- right from main roads into side roads.

When the pupil is applying all the principles, particularly the extra observations required at crossroads, select routes where there are different types of traffic light-controlled junctions.

Remember that your job is to produce skilled and safe drivers. This means that you not only have to work on their practical ability, but you also need to develop in them sensible attitudes towards other road users in situations that aren't always straightforward. An example is at traffic light controlled crossroads where there are no markings and decisions need to be made as to whether to turn right using the offside to offside, or nearside to nearside method.

Make sure that your pupils understand the principles involved and that they can make sound decisions based on the size of the junction, its layout and the position of any oncoming, right-turning drivers.

For all types of crossroads, make sure that:

- the M S M routine is correctly applied, particularly when turning right for the first few attempts;
- signals are timed correctly;
- the pupil responds safely to road signs and markings;
- observations are made all around no matter what direction is being taken;
- pupils are fully aware of pedestrians who are about to cross side roads;
- there is a correct response to other drivers, cyclists and motorcyclists.

At the end of the lesson, make sure that your pupil is fully aware of any weak areas of skill or understanding, but balance this against any good points and confirm where improvement has taken place. As with all lessons, allow time for the pupil to ask questions.

Look forward to the next few lessons, confirming that you will be introducing more complex junctions, busier crossroads, dual carriageways and roundabouts.

Meeting and dealing with other traffic

The objectives are to encourage pupils to respond safely to other drivers when:

- travelling on narrow roads;
- there are obstructions on either or both sides of the road;
- passing parked vehicles;
- turning right across the path of others.

Because of the design of roads in built-up and rural areas, the volume of parked vehicles, and the need to keep traffic flowing, pupils should understand how to deal safely with these subjects from quite early on in their learning.

Meeting other traffic

The most common 'meet' situation is where there are vehicles parked at the side of the road. If these are on the nearside, using a visual aid, you could ask your pupil: 'Where are you going to have to drive to pass the parked car?'; 'Who should have the priority then?'

If the obstruction is on the other side of the road, similarly you could ask:

- 'Who will have priority then, when the obstruction is on the other side of the road?'
- 'What if the other driver doesn't wait, though?'
- 'Do you think it might be appropriate to be ready to give way, just in case they keep coming?'
- 'So, it really doesn't matter whose priority it is, does it? You should consider that you never really know what the other driver is going to do. Be prepared to give way.'

Clearances

To encourage the development of sensible and safe attitudes your pupils will need plenty of practice. In the early stages this should be in quiet areas with the occasional parked vehicle, progressing to busier areas where there are vehicles parked on both sides and oncoming traffic to deal with.

Initially, when dealing with cars parked on the nearside, the pupil needs to understand how to give enough clearance to allow for:

- car doors opening and drivers stepping out;
- pedestrians, particularly children, or animals wandering into the road from between the parked vehicles;
- drivers moving off without signalling.

Any discussion should include:

- forward planning and applying the M S M routine for approaching the hazards;
- deciding on whose priority it is and whether to give way;
- the ideal clearance – give a demonstration of this by getting your pupil to check the road and then open their door to see exactly how far into the road it goes;
- at busier times of the day the need to keep the traffic flowing by creeping slowly through some of these gaps – the reduction in speed compensating for the lack of clearance and creating more time to respond should a door open;
- being prepared to move into passing places on the left to allow oncoming drivers through.

Crossing the path of other vehicles

Our drivers need to be courteous in all situations and not to make any other road user have to take avoiding action. The key points to cover are when: turning right – encourage pupils to work out whether they have enough time to turn, that they have checked on what's happening in the new road and that they won't make any oncoming road user slow down; driving in lanes – ensure the pupil checks what's happening all around them before deciding to change lanes.

Practice

Use routes that have varying amounts of parked and moving traffic and encourage the pupil to use early planning and 'holding back' to allow time for hazards to clear and to try to keep the car moving.

Some of the more common faults include:

- lack of planning and response to oncoming vehicles;
- not giving way to oncoming vehicles;
- arriving at hazards at too high a speed and having to stop at the last moment;
- steering in towards the kerb instead of keeping out towards the centre of the road;
- steering out too far for passing;
- driving too close to vehicles parked on the left;
- driving too far out and getting too close to those parked on the right;
- failing to anticipate doors opening;
- lack of response to pedestrians waiting in between parked vehicles.

Feedback

Feedback should always be used to encourage positive improvement. Confirm where the pupil has learnt and shown improvement and discuss where there is room for improvement.

Recap

Apply your coaching skills to help pupils analyse their own actions and discuss the reasons why they might need to vary their approach. Examples:

1

'When we were driving down that steep hill had you considered giving way to
the bus driver?'

'Because the parked car was on his side!'

'Yes, I know, but don't you think it might be difficult to get a large vehicle like
that moving up a steep hill?'

'I hadn't thought about that, I just thought it was my right of way!'

'Well, actually, no one has right of way anywhere and even if it is your priority
it doesn't mean it's always the best way. Try to remember what problems you
used to have moving off uphill and then think about trying to move a bus.'

'I think I see what you mean. So, you think it would have been better for me to
let the bus driver through then?'

'Well, that's what I would have done. So, will you think about that the next time
we have a similar situation?'

2

'On whose side of the road was the parked car when you squeezed through that
gap and made the driver of the black BMW slow down?'

'I think it was on our side.'

'You're right, it was on our side. Whose priority should it have been then?'

'Well, I thought as I'd got there before him that he'd wait for me.'

'But he was driving quite fast and, anyway, it was his priority as you had to
drive onto his side of the road. How do you think you'd feel if he'd done the
same thing to you?'

'I suppose I'd have been a bit annoyed.'

'So, in future will you plan a bit further ahead and consider giving way, no
matter which side of the road the parked vehicle is on?'

You can create this type of discussion around any weaknesses to encourage
pupils to arrive at their own conclusions and, by underlining the reasons,
you will help create much better attitudes towards other road users.

Look forward

Confirm that during all future lessons you will be encouraging your pupil to
develop their planning and decision-making skills. The next lesson will deal
specifically with how to anticipate and make allowances for the actions of
other road users, including drivers, cyclists, motorcyclists and pedestrians.

Overtaking

During normal lessons, you will find that very few opportunities will present themselves for teaching how to overtake. However, it will be your responsibility to ensure that your pupils know about the dangers involved and how to carry it out safely. When driving along dual carriageways opportunities will occur when there are vehicles driving at speeds much lower than the legal limits. In this situation overtaking is much safer as there won't (hopefully) be any oncoming traffic. First you need to stress the following important questions:

Is it safe? Is it legal? Is it NECESSARY?

Points you then need to cover include:

- keeping back from the vehicle to be overtaken;
- looking ahead and working out the speed and distance of any oncoming vehicles;
- checking to see that it's safe by looking for bends, junctions, dead ground, etc;
- checking the mirrors to see what's happening to the rear and sides;
- moving to get a view along the nearside of the vehicle ahead;
- checking the mirrors again and moving out to get a view ahead and deciding on whether anyone (including the driver to be overtaken) will benefit from a signal;
- adjusting the speed, including selecting a lower gear to give sustained power;
- moving out to pass, giving plenty of clearance;
- checking the mirrors and in some circumstances deciding on whether or not a signal will be beneficial (for example on dual carriageways when a driver is approaching from behind at high speed);
- moving back to the left without cutting in;
- accelerating away and changing gear as normal.

Manoeuvres

The driving test syllabus includes:

- reverse parking at the side of the road (parallel park);
- reversing into bays (left and right);
- driving into a bay and reversing out (left and right);
- pull over to the right, reverse about two car lengths and then rejoin traffic.

These manoeuvres are now included in the driving test because they are seen to be more realistic and appropriate for today's driving conditions. They replace the previous exercises of turning in the road and reversing round corners.

Before starting to teach any manoeuvres, it is worth making sure that the pupil is completely skilled and confident with uphill and downhill starts and stops. Experience is also needed in angled starts on up and down gradients, so that the pupil has complete control of the car in all of these circumstances.

For example, moving away straight ahead downhill is relatively easy because you don't need too much coordination between the foot controls and the steering – as soon as the handbrake is released the car is on its way! With an angled start, though, there is a need to introduce the use of the footbrake and coordination between that and the clutch to avoid the car running away too quickly and to allow enough time for steering round the obstruction (or to turn into the main road). This exercise is often neglected by some instructors. The result of this is that their pupils are not properly prepared for similar situations when careful control is needed for stopping and starting uphill and downhill.

The manoeuvres do not necessarily need to be taught in any particular order, but there is a certain amount of logic in dealing with basic reversing before introducing some of the other complicating features of the reversing exercises. A lot of the time it will depend on the availability of suitable parking facilities and corners in your own locality.

Introducing the subject

As always, at the start of the lesson establish previous knowledge. Find out if the pupil:

- has done any reversing while they have been practising;
- understands about low speed control, for example when creeping forwards at junctions;

- appreciates that it is important to make effective all-round observations;
- knows why the normal rules about steering do not necessarily apply.

If the pupil has done a little reversing previously, find out exactly what. The following is a scenario where a pupil has had lessons with another instructor:

'Your driver's record and lesson notes show that you haven't done this
   particular manoeuvre before – is that right?'
'Well, on my last lesson with Bill we did do a bit of reversing in a straight line,
   but not much.'
'OK, so what do you remember about turning to look through the back
   window? You might need to release the seatbelt and turn round more in the
   seat.'
'How do you feel about the steering?'
'Did it feel uncomfortable to maintain the position of your hands on the wheel
   while looking back?'
'Do you think it might be better to put your hands in a different position?'
'Why don't you try with the right hand at the top of the wheel?'

If the pupil has no previous experience of reversing, you could give an explanation using a visual aid.

Demonstration

A demonstration combined with an explanation could be helpful in allowing the pupil to see what's required. The demonstration may be appropriate if, for instance, the pupil is particularly nervous about the manoeuvre, or they obviously do not understand the requirements from your explanations.

A demonstration can often be useful for the manoeuvres, because pupils sometimes find it difficult to visualise the overall requirement or the individual parts of the exercise.

Talk yourself through each element, carrying out the manoeuvre a little more slowly than normal. This will allow the pupil time to take note. Be able, if necessary, to carry out certain parts in slow motion. You may sometimes need to replicate the way in which a pupil has carried out a manoeuvre so that they can compare the two.

Keep any demonstration simple and carry it out at a slower than normal speed.

Key teaching/learning points

- The speed of the car should be kept as slow as possible by effective clutch control.

- Pull/push is not always the most effective or comfortable steering method when reversing at slow speed.

- Explain that there is a delayed action with the steering, because the rear wheels are now being used to steer with.

- Look across the rear corner of the car – not at the side – to judge the amount of steering.

- Avoid 'over-steering' – think about how you only have to make small adjustments to the steering when going forwards. Remember, though, the delayed action on the steering.

Observations

A constant check should be made throughout the manoeuvre, looking all around for traffic. Pupils should be encouraged to watch carefully for pedestrians. Remember that there's a blind area to the right when they're looking over the left shoulder.

Make sure that you emphasise the need to be able to manoeuvre the car as part of a driver's everyday requirements, rather than just 'because it's part of the test'. If the pupil persists with raising the question of the driving test, make it clear that we are dealing with driving safely and manoeuvring for convenience and that test procedures will be outlined in future lessons.

With all of the manoeuvres, it's important to recap on what the pupil has covered on previous lessons by asking a few appropriate questions. For example:

- 'As this is the first manoeuvre you'll be carrying out and good clutch control is required, tell me how you would creep forwards at a junction to get a better view.'

- 'What would you do if your car started to creep forwards before you wanted to move?'

- 'Why is it important to keep the speed very low when you're moving out from behind a parked car?'

With any manoeuvre, always get the pupil to consider – is it safe? Is it legal? Is it convenient?

Confirm that, because they are part of normal everyday driving requirements, the manoeuvres are included in the training programme. This is so that new drivers will have the ability to control and manoeuvre the car in confined areas, including car parks and driveways, and when parking at the roadside.

Practice

Don't expect perfection first time!

For pupils' first attempts use an appropriate amount of 'talk-through' so that a reasonable degree of success is achieved, and they are not put off or demoralised by getting it completely wrong.

Watch for, and correct right from the start, any basic errors of control or observations. However, you should make allowances for the fact that the pupil has not done a particular manoeuvre previously and several elements are being combined. These are: car control skills, observations and accuracy.

On subsequent attempts, transfer some of the responsibility by reducing the amount of 'talk-through'. When a reasonable amount of consistency is achieved, introduce slightly more complex situations.

At the end of the lesson

Use effective questions to obtain some verbal feedback from pupils and to find out how they feel about the lesson.

Give feedback, balancing any discussion on areas of weakness with comments on the good points.

Summarise the overall content of the current lesson, emphasise the reasons for each particular manoeuvre and confirm how to make sure they are legally carried out.

Look forward to the next lesson by discussing what will be covered, confirming any preparation work that you require the pupil to do.

During the latter stages of the pupil's training you will need to point out that they will be tested on some of the specified manoeuvres. These test exercises are included as a means of assessing the pupil's ability to handle the car in confined spaces. This means that, to a certain extent, they are slightly contrived 'test exercises'. It is helpful to focus on the skills needed for any manoeuvre rather than the specific requirements of the subject.

For example, we would not normally reverse into a parking space at the side of a busy road unless the existing parked vehicles were close together – we would simply drive forwards into the gap. When using a car park, rather than reversing in, we might prefer to drive forwards into the space to allow us to load shopping into the boot on our return.

In all these respects, the manoeuvres are included in the driving test to assess, in a controlled environment, the candidate's ability, observations and responses. They are also intended to be realistic examples of everyday driving situations we are likely to encounter.

Reverse parking

Following the usual lesson format, the following are some suggestions for introducing this subject:

> 'You'll remember that on previous lessons we've stopped at the side of the road where there were other parked cars. Do you remember how much space it took to drive in and get parked properly?'
>
> 'About three car lengths?'
>
> 'Yes, why do think we needed that much space?'
>
> 'I'm not sure.'
>
> 'Well, it's to do with the fact that the front wheels do the steering and the back wheels are always straight.'
>
> 'Oh yes, I remember that from reversing around a corner. So that means it'll take a while for the front of the car to push the back in does it?'
>
> 'That's right, so how can we deal with that when the space available is much shorter? Do you think that by reversing we can put the back of the car in, and then the front will follow?'
>
> 'I'll take your word on that one as I'm still not quite sure.'
>
> 'So, to demonstrate what I mean, we'll practise where there's only one car, with nothing behind it. Then when you feel confident, we'll move to where there's a proper parking space in between two cars.'

As the pupil will, by this stage, have had lots of practice at the other manoeuvres, use effective questions to determine their understanding and to establish where to set the baseline for the lesson. Here are a few example questions:

> 'We've dealt with reversing in previous lessons so tell me a couple of the important things you need to do.'
>
> 'Can I just make sure that you've dealt with reversing with your previous instructor?'
>
> 'How did you get on?'
>
> 'Is there anything that you're not sure about?'
>
> 'Before we get on to the reverse park we'll just recap on slow speed car control in forward and reverse by moving slowly forwards and back along here.'
>
> 'That's fine.'

Explain that, under normal driving conditions, this manoeuvre would be carried out where there were two vehicles close together. However, for the purposes of training we'll initially be doing it where there's only one car parked.

This sets up a slightly artificial situation as we'll be able to park at the side of the road before starting the manoeuvre – a luxury that is not available in a real situation when there will usually be following traffic and only a confined space to park in.

Using a visual aid, discuss the key elements:

- M S M to get into position to begin the exercise;
- initial positioning at the side of the leading vehicle;
- getting into a seating position that will allow good all-round vision and control;
- coordination of all of the controls to maintain a low speed;
- all-round observations throughout the manoeuvre;
- responding safely to other road users;
- accurate steering;
- checking clearance given to the leading vehicle;
- straightening up to finish reasonably close to the kerb.

Use effective questions to confirm the pupil has understood the main elements. For example:

'Where do you think we should be looking for other traffic?'
'How does that vary from when we did the left reverse round a corner?'
'What would you do if there was a large vehicle behind you as you approached the parking space?'
'What if you were to move half into the space to allow the following traffic through?'
'What signals would you give?'

Demonstration

As this is one of the more complex manoeuvres you may find that a demonstration is needed more often. If your pupil appears to be a little worried and unsure, give another explanation as you are demonstrating how to park. Remember, keep the speed a little slower than normal and make sure your parking is accurate.

Practice

During the manoeuvre, check on:

- whether the pupil has the driving seat adjusted so that they can turn to look through the rear window while retaining steering control;

- coordination of the foot controls – compare this to the speed of the car when creeping forward at a junction;
- observations for other road users – including pedestrians crossing the road;
- appropriate responses to approaching traffic – whether it would be safer to wait or to continue with the manoeuvre;
- correct observations to the rear for positioning in the parking space.

After a couple of attempts, make sure that you get feedback from the pupil by asking a few more questions, such as:

'Other than indicators, what signals do we have that would warn other people about what we're doing?'

'Would it be a good idea to let other people know what we're doing by giving a signal?'

Only when you are sure pupils can cope, should you start transferring the responsibility to them. It would be wise to drive to another site and give them a change of activity before reversing around another car.

Feedback

As with all lessons, it's important to give and receive some feedback. Use effective questions to find out whether the pupil feels confident about parking. Give praise for those elements that have been improved on and reminders about where more practice is needed.

Look forward

Confirm that more practice will be given on the next lesson and you will also be introducing reversing into a parking bay to the left – such as in a car park. To establish some of the points you have previously raised, ask a couple of questions such as:

'Would it be better to reverse into or out of the space?'

'Why might it be better to reverse in and drive out?'

Fault identification, analysis and rectification

As well as the items listed above under things to check on during the manoeuvre, watch for:

- incorrect application of the M S M for stopping;
- failure to turn enough in the seat to get a proper view;
- starting from the wrong position;
- lack of proper coordination;
- reversing too quickly and passing the point at which to start steering;
- steering too early;
- steering too quickly – particularly prevalent in cars with power steering;
- lack of all-round observations throughout the manoeuvre;
- incorrect response to others;
- not checking the front end clearing the leading car;
- steering back too early or too late;
- finishing at an angle to the kerb.

Bay parking

Traditionally, it has always been regarded as safer to reverse the car into a bay so that you can drive out to leave. This way, it makes it easier to see what is happening all round. There is less risk of someone walking behind the car when you are reversing into a narrow space and far more risk of other vehicles and pedestrians being in the way when you leave the bay. However, it is recognised that most people need to drive into a bay when they go to a supermarket so that they can more easily load up the boot with their shopping. Because of this, parking in a bay is included in the driving test. The manoeuvre can consist of:

- driving into a bay on the left or right and reversing out; or
- reversing into a bay on the left or right and driving out.

Examiners use a wide variety of car parks for the bay parking exercise, such as hotels, retail parks and supermarkets. The manoeuvre can also be carried out at the test centre.

If your pupil has a driveway it is great practice to get them to reverse into their driveway at the end of the lesson. This uses the same skills as reversing into a bay.

Introduction to the reverse bay park

As before, the lesson should begin with a recap that takes the pupil from the known to the unknown, for example:

'When you needed to slow the car down, what did you do with the clutch?'

'Before steering to the left where did you need to look and why?'

'How did you judge when to start steering?'

'How did you judge when to straighten up?'

Demonstration

Remember, your pupils will all learn differently, and they will not all be engaged with a briefing. An explanation with a diagram will not always do the trick. Have a go at varying the methods you use with your pupils. For example, you could hold the following conversation:

'Do you know how you learn best?'

'I like to watch to see how something is done and then I can copy it.'

'Would it be helpful if you got out of the car and watched me manoeuvre into this bay? You would be able to see the position of the car and the way the wheels are pointing, as well as the speed I am going at.'

'Yes, that would be helpful.'

Pupils often learn a lot by watching and copying. Standing back and seeing which way the car is moving and which way the wheels are facing really makes sense to them. Even walking through the manoeuvre can help.

Practice

Build the practice up bit by bit. It is not necessary to do the whole manoeuvre in one go. The pupil might set a goal that just focuses on being able to get the car between the two lines. You can divide up the responsibility for risk and look after the observations for them. Later on, when the pupil has succeeded at reversing between the two lines, you can hand the observations back to them. Choose a bay with no vehicles either side initially and then develop so that the pupil has to judge parking between two vehicles.

This exercise should be introduced when your pupil has become fairly proficient with reversing to the left. Your lesson plan, incorporating all the usual ingredients, therefore, should be to build on these skills.

Your pattern of teaching/coaching should follow the usual routines of using questions to establish whether the pupil understands the reasons for the manoeuvre and to fix an appropriate baseline for the lesson.

Questions at the start of the session might include:

'Why do we need to do this manoeuvre?'

'Because it's part of the test?'

'That's not the best reason. Can you imagine situations where you need to park either by driving in or reversing out?'

Always refer to 'Is it safe? Is it legal? Is it convenient?'

Feedback

Feedback and reflection are vital to the pupil's development. Use your questioning and listening skills to help them self-evaluate their performance. Are they achieving their goal? What went well? What didn't go so well? What do they need to improve? What extra help do they need from you, if any?

After completing the manoeuvre, ask a few questions such as:

'Did that seem OK to you or could it be improved in any way?'

'Do you think that by looking around a bit more and getting the wider picture you would be able to steer more effectively?'

'What do you need to see and be aware of?'

Depending on the pupil's responses, follow up with:

'What you're saying is that you feel that by going a bit slower, you would have more time to steer? OK then, let's try it.'

Or: 'How do think it would work if we did...?'

'Why not try this approach...?'

Faults to watch for are:

- seating position not adjusted to afford the best view;
- poor coordination skills;
- under- or over-steering;
- lack of observations;
- ineffective observations resulting in lack of response to others.

After two or three attempts you could develop a discussion along these lines:

'How did you feel about doing it that way? Were you happier with your control/positioning/observations?'

'Did you feel that you were able to deal with the other traffic and pedestrians that time?'

'Did you feel there was anything different from the first time?'

Recap

At the end of the lesson use questions to recap on the main points. Summarise and give praise on the good points and identify the weaknesses that might need to be worked on. Look forward to next lesson.

Introduction to driving into a bay

Discuss the benefits of driving into a bay and the added risks of then reversing out of a bay. Confirm that this manoeuvre requires the same skills as any manoeuvre, in terms of control, observations and accuracy. Emphasise that the car is more manoeuvrable in reverse gear because you can put the rear end of the car where you want it to be and then steer the front to follow. Therefore, it can be more difficult to drive into a bay initially, as you must steer out further to allow for the rear wheels taking a shorter route.

Reversing out of the bay is also more challenging because you need to consider the front end of the car and allow for it clearing the vehicles either side before starting to steer. Also, visibility is more reduced than if you were driving forwards and you must be far more watchful of the front end of the car swinging out.

Nevertheless, this is a real-life manoeuvre because of the need to have accessibility to the boot of the car when shopping and therefore it will be included on the test as an option.

Practice

Just asking the pupil to steer into a bay with no cars either side will give you both the opportunity to reflect on what went well and what didn't go so well. Remember, this is the benefit of experiential learning, which we discussed in Chapter 1 with Kolb's theory of learning, where the pupil has a go in a safe environment before any kind of explanation is given.

Similarly, letting the pupil have a go at reversing out of the bay without any explanation first will give you both something to discuss and reflect on.

Parking on the right and reversing two car lengths

The examiner will ask the pupil to pull up on the right, reverse for around two car lengths and then rejoin the traffic.

On our busy roads, there will be times when a driver needs to pull up on the right – and they need to have the knowledge and skills to do it safely. It's vital to use a safe and systematic routine, including observations and appropriate signals. These are the skills we'll be assessing.

It's also important that drivers know and understand what factors to take into consideration when looking for a safe, legal and convenient place to stop or park. For example, a busy main road with a constant flow of traffic would not be safe or convenient.

There will be times, once your pupil has passed the test, when a vehicle parks just in front of their car. They will need the skills to reverse a couple of car lengths before moving away again. This will be assessed by the examiner without a 'real' vehicle being parked in front.

The candidate will need to use their understanding of these factors to choose an appropriate place to pull up on the right, when asked by the examiner.

Introduction

The lesson should begin with an introduction of the subject and by agreeing the objective.

Use effective questions to establish the reasons for being able to carry out this manoeuvre and to establish the 'base line' for the lesson. By this stage pupils should be able to respond to this approach much more readily than by giving them a lecture on the subject. For example:

'Why do we need to be able to do this manoeuvre?'

'Because it's part of the test!'

'Well, there are times when we need to use a parking space on the right.'

'But it is part of the test?'

'It's part of the test because it gives an examiner the opportunity to assess your ability to control the car in a confined space and to see how you deal with other traffic at the same time. Anyway, today we're not concerned with the test – that's a long way off, and we'll have more discussions about that another time.'

By using this type of discussion, you can lead in to the topic rather than simply stating an objective.

Whatever the circumstances, as with all the other manoeuvres that have previously been covered, we always need to consider 'Is it safe? Is it legal? Is it convenient?'

Typical questions might be:

'How do you feel about those manoeuvres? Is there anything you're not sure
    about?'
'OK, in view of what you're saying we'll spend a few minutes on a reverse
before moving on to other manoeuvres.'
'How do you think the basic reversing skills are connected to what we're going
    to be doing today?'

With any of these discussions you'll be starting a dialogue with the pupils to
get them involved in the learning process and encouraging them to take
some responsibility for their own learning.

The variations of questions will depend on whether the pupil has previously
been trained by you and on their responses to your questions. Always be ready
with a follow-up question to keep the dialogue moving in the direction you want
it to go so that you achieve your objectives. Either way, you should be able to get
a clear indication within a few minutes of how to plan the rest of the lesson.

Emphasise the need to:

- keep looking all round for other traffic and pedestrians;
- make eye contact with others and either wait for them or carry on as
    appropriate and depending on the other driver's anticipated actions.

Practice

Don't expect perfection first time!

On the pupil's first attempt, give 'talk-through' instruction to support
them where necessary to avoid any errors. This will promote reasonable success and should motivate and encourage the pupil. On subsequent attempts,
or with more experienced pupils, reduce the amount of prompting.

Feedback

After the first attempt you should be able to obtain some feedback from the
pupil by asking a few questions. These might include:

'How did you feel that went?'
'Well, OK, but you were helping me a lot.'
'That's true, but for a first attempt it was pretty good.'
'Would I pass the test?'
'We're not going to deal with what happens on the test yet – you'll be having
    a lot more practice on different roads and with more traffic and with less
    prompting from me. What do you think we need to do to improve?' etc.

Or:

> 'Well, I don't think it was very good.'
>
> 'In what way?'
>
> 'I didn't seem to be in complete control.'
>
> 'Do you mean with the accuracy?'
>
> 'Yes.'
>
> 'Well, for a first attempt it was very good, but how do you think it could be improved?' etc.

After the second attempt, the discussion might be along similar lines:

> 'Did you feel that was better?'
>
> 'What was different?'
>
> 'You're saying that by going a bit slower you might be able to achieve more?'
>
> 'Did you feel that you got in the way of the other traffic?'
>
> 'How do you think we could avoid that situation?'
>
> 'OK, let's try it the way you've just described.'

This type of discussion encourages the pupil because they have made decisions for themselves about how to carry out the manoeuvre.

Recap and summary

As with all lessons, end by using effective questions and give a brief recap on the main points. Give a summary of the good points and some of the weaker areas, trying to balance the two.

Look forward

Discuss the next lesson with the pupil and give an indication of the subjects to be practised or learnt.

Key learning points to include:

- coordination of all the controls to give maximum time for steering and observations;
- looking in the direction the car is travelling;
- making all-round observations throughout the manoeuvre;
- responding safely to other road users, including pedestrians.

Emergency stop

Objective

To stop the car promptly, safely and under complete control.

Introducing the subject

Using effective questions, confirm that your pupil has stopped in various types of situation on previous lessons, for example at junctions, at the side of the road, and in specific places such as 'by the second lamppost'.

Emphasise that an 'emergency stop' is only an extension of what they have done before. The main difference is that the brakes will need to be applied more firmly.

Ask questions to confirm previous knowledge and understanding, for example:

'Why is it necessary to apply progressive braking?'

'Do we need a gear change when stopping?'

'Why is it important to keep both hands on the wheel when we are braking firmly?'

'Do we need a signal?'

'What about the handbrake?'

Discuss possible situations where an emergency stop might be needed, for example if a child ran out from a gateway into the road. Relate this to the pupil's previous hazard perception understanding when they will have been responding mainly to things they could see.

Your initial discussions should include information on:

- the fact that there may not be enough time to check on what's happening behind, because of the need to stop quickly;
- prompt reaction in moving from gas pedal to footbrake;
- use of the footbrake – progressive, firmly;
- maintaining steering control because the weight of the car is thrown onto the front wheels;
- avoiding locking wheels;
- having the clutch down just before stopping;
- securing the car after stopping;
- all-round observations before moving away.

Emphasise the need for both hands to remain on the wheel to keep the car on a straight course, and for controlled braking. Confirm this by giving an example such as, 'There's no point in avoiding the child who's run out if we then slide across the road and hit other pedestrians.'

Confirm the pupil's understanding of braking distances. For example:

'What is the thinking distance if you're travelling at 30 mph?'
'At 70 mph how far would we travel before starting to brake?'
'How does that relate to a number of car lengths?'
'How far do you think it takes to stop from 20 mph? (Or any other speed.)
'Tell me how far that is in terms of the distance from here?'

In preparation for their theory test pupils should be doing some homework on reaction times, thinking distances and braking distances. Make sure they realise that there is a straightforward means of calculating the distances and that they are not random figures. For example: the thinking distance is based on an average reaction time of two-thirds of a second, which equates to about 60 feet (or 18 metres) when travelling at 60 mph (88 ft per second); the braking distance at 20 mph is 20 feet (6 metres) and it increases with the square of the speed, which means that if you travel at twice the speed, the braking distance is multiplied four times.

Confirm that on future lessons, thinking, braking and stopping distances will be discussed and related to practical situations.

Practice

Find an area where it's going to be safe to practise and make sure your pupil understands that you will check there's no following traffic before giving the signal to stop. Explain how you will give the instruction and signal for stopping.

On the first few attempts at an emergency stop check on the pupil's:

- slow reactions to respond;
- prompt movement from accelerator to brake;
- harsh or too gentle use of the footbrake;
- left hand off the steering wheel before stopping;
- clutch being pushed down too early or too late;
- lack of adequate precautions after a stall;
- failure to secure the car when stopped;
- lack of all-round observations before moving off.

Look forward to future lessons by indicating that this exercise will be repeated at different speeds and in varying situations, unless, of course, real emergencies crop up.

Pedestrian crossings

The point at which you introduce pupils to pedestrian crossings will depend, to a large extent, on the area in which they live and where the nearest crossings are situated. However, they should have reached a stage at which they can consistently apply the M S M routine to hazards and be able to cope with more traffic and pedestrian activity.

Objectives

As pedestrians, your pupils will have used most types of crossing. Avoid patronising them by treating the subject as if they know nothing about it.

Indeed, the lesson objective will be to build on this existing knowledge by introducing the differences between how, as pedestrians, they will have used crossings and how drivers should deal with them.

First, recap on the pupil's previous progress, using effective questions to confirm that the pupil fully understands the M S M routine. Find out what they understand about the different types of crossing and then set your base line according to their responses. The following are a few sample questions:

- 'When should you apply the M S M routine?'
- 'Can you name three different types of pedestrian crossing?'
- 'How would you recognise a zebra crossing?'
- 'How would you claim priority at a zebra crossing?'

As always, listen carefully to your pupils' responses and vary the discussion according to their level of knowledge and understanding. In any case you need to ensure that the basic principles in dealing with the different types of crossing are covered.

A discussion with the pupil should include:

- the different types of crossing, ie: zebra, pelican, toucan, puffin and equestrian;
- why these differences are in place;

- signs and markings and what they mean, including the rules relating to waiting, overtaking, parking;
- the sequence of the different traffic lights;
- how to look and plan well ahead, applying the M S M routine in good time to stop safely when necessary, and securing the car;
- the use of arm signals when appropriate.

As this subject is very wide-ranging, and so that the lesson doesn't become a one-way lecture, keep your pupil involved by asking the occasional question. For example:

- 'What do the zigzag lines on approach to crossings mean?'
- 'What's the sequence of lights at a pelican crossing?'
- 'What does the flashing amber light mean?'
- 'What's the difference between a pelican and a toucan crossing?'
- 'What would you do if you saw someone waiting at a zebra crossing?'

Level of instruction

To avoid over-instruction, give your pupils an opportunity to demonstrate their skill in subjects learnt previously. For example, by this stage their car control skills should be reasonably well developed, so they should be able to deal virtually unaided with simple junctions.

When you approach the new situations, and to ensure the pupil is able to deal safely with the crossings, use prompts where appropriate to help with the correct routines and procedures.

Practice

Depending on your area, try to incorporate as many types of crossing as you can so that your pupil will see what the main differences are. Ensure that all the basic routines are carried out, particularly in relation to planning ahead and approaching them at a safe speed.

Initially, as you will be giving some prompted instruction, there should be few faults. However, as the pupils' skill improves, and you start transferring to them the responsibility for making decisions, errors are bound to occur.

Watch carefully for these mistakes and give positive correction. Analyse what happened and explain what should have been done to deal with the situations safely.

Feedback/recap/summary

At the end of the lesson give positive feedback and praise where the pupil improved on skills previously covered and has learnt how to deal with the new topics.

Recap on the most important points that arose and give an overall summary on applying the M S M routine to dealing with crossings.

Look forward

Advise your pupil on which reference materials to study. Confirm that you will be asking a few questions on crossings and getting in some more practice on approaching them during the next lesson.

Roundabouts and dual carriageways

Whichever topic you are dealing with, your lessons should all follow the pattern described previously:

- recap, using questions, to establish prior knowledge and understanding;
- agree the objectives;
- set the baseline;
- work from the known to the unknown;
- feedback;
- look forward to next session.

It is normal to deal with two-way roads, T-junctions and crossroads in order to build up pupils' confidence in applying the basic driving routines before introducing more complex road systems. However, depending on the area you are working in, or where each pupil lives, you may need to be flexible with the introduction of roundabouts and dual carriageways. In any case, in some quieter areas where most basic training should be carried out, there may be mini roundabouts to be dealt with.

In most areas, you will need to deal with roundabouts in combination with driving on dual carriageways.

Mini roundabouts

These are usually sited in reasonably busy areas where the minor roads used to have 'Give Way' or 'Stop' signs. They provide for better traffic flow by allowing drivers in the minor roads to merge more easily. The following are a few sample questions you could use to establish pupils' understanding:

- 'Which routine do you need to apply when you're approaching junctions?'
- 'What does the "give way" sign mean at a T-junction?'
- 'Who will you have to give way to at a roundabout?'

Following on from these questions you will need to transfer pupils' prior knowledge and develop it to include the different rules to be followed. For example:

- looking and planning ahead for signs and markings;
- applying the M S M routine;
- selecting the appropriate position (lane) in the road;
- making full all-round observations;
- giving way to traffic from the right;
- maintaining the correct position through the roundabout;
- checking the mirrors;
- signalling for leaving if appropriate and where it won't affect the steering.

Create plenty of opportunities for practice at as many different mini roundabouts as the training area will allow. Begin with straightforward left turns and then approach from different directions, explaining about the need to adapt road positioning to suit each individual roundabout.

For pupils' first few attempts, you might need to give talk-through instruction on the unfamiliar aspects. The pupil will probably need some guidance and/or prompting when traffic is arriving at the junction from all directions at the same time.

Depending on how quickly they pick up the new routines, gradually transfer the responsibility of decision making when you feel you can.

Some of the common faults to watch for at mini roundabouts are:

- lack of application of the M S M routine;
- failure to respond to signs and markings;
- incorrect lane selection;

- emerging in front of other drivers;
- missing opportunities to proceed;
- not signalling when required;
- signalling when not required or when it interferes with steering;
- not maintaining lane discipline.

Roundabouts

If the training area you are working in dictates that you have to deal with mini roundabouts first, then you will be able to transfer this knowledge and introduce the differences that apply to the larger ones.

To deal with larger roundabouts first, you will need to give a full explanation of all the items listed under mini roundabouts, but more information will be required on signs, markings, lane selection and discipline.

Using a visual aid, explain how to deal with a straightforward four-exit roundabout, beginning with turning left. Use effective questions to confirm pupils' prior knowledge of applying the M S M routine as you talk your way through your diagram. For example:

- 'Who has priority at a roundabout?'
- 'Will you need a signal for turning left at a roundabout?'
- 'Do you always need to stop at a roundabout?'
- 'What does the broken white line mean?'
- 'Where should you be looking?'

Remember that questions should be used to get some feedback and not as an interrogation tool. Pupils often become anxious when faced with new and complex situations, so respond to body language, be prepared to back off and give more help if necessary.

Explain the procedures the pupil will not yet be familiar with and then continue by describing the procedures for going ahead and turning right. No matter which direction is to be taken, emphasis needs to be placed on:

- looking ahead for signs and markings;
- application of the M S M routine and maintaining full control of the car;
- looking early for gaps in the traffic from the right;
- watching for traffic coming around the roundabout from other roads – these often create gaps by preventing the traffic directly to our right from emerging;

- continual observations in all directions so that we know what's happening to the right and in front, and to help maintain our position;
- maintaining position and lane discipline throughout the roundabout;
- signalling for leaving so as not to hold up those waiting to merge into the roundabout.

Practice

Each pupil will have their own individual rate of learning, ability and aptitude. This means that the amount of training each one needs will also vary.

Roundabouts also come in many varieties. As the pupil's competence and confidence improve, plan your routes to cover as many different types as possible, including roundabouts with more than four exits.

Your questions might include: 'How do think you should signal if you were taking the second exit?'; 'Where should you position on approach for taking the third exit that is just beyond the 12 o'clock position?'

As pupils' ability improves in applying the basic routines, you will need to focus on their skills at looking and planning ahead, making good progress and taking safe opportunities to proceed.

Errors will generally be similar to those listed under the heading 'Mini roundabouts'. However, the larger roundabouts are generally busier and carry traffic that's often travelling much quicker. You will need to watch for pupils:

- failing to read and respond to signs and markings;
- approaching too fast to allow themselves sufficient time to start looking;
- making unnecessary gear changes;
- looking only at the traffic in the roundabout and not at the gaps;
- not preparing the car in time to move into suitable gaps;
- failing to take opportunities to move;
- concentrating on making observations to the right – this often results in them not keeping to the left as they move into the roundabout and not being aware of what the driver ahead is doing;
- straddling lanes;
- not checking mirrors before signalling or changing lanes;
- leaving in the incorrect lane.

Recap

Some of the questions you could use to further develop pupils' understanding include:

- 'Why is it important to be planning ahead and looking for signs and markings?'
- 'Who has priority at roundabouts?'
- 'If you were going to travel straight ahead at a roundabout would you need to signal on the approach?'
- 'Which signal should you use for leaving a roundabout and when should you put it on?'
- 'Where should you check before moving across into the left lane?'
- 'Why do you think it's important to keep looking both ways at a roundabout?'
- 'What might happen if you wander across into another lane on a roundabout?'
- 'What might happen if you fail to move into safe gaps in the traffic?'

Develop your own questions and adapt each one to suit the circumstances.

As with all lessons, give positive feedback on areas of improvement and advice on where more practice is needed. Use effective questions and encourage your pupils to ask questions if there are any aspects they don't quite understand.

Look forward

Confirm two main points:

- To become consistently skilful in dealing with these busier junctions, lots of practice will be needed.
- During the rest of their training you will help them become confident and able to cope in as wide a variety of circumstances as the area allows.

Dual carriageways

Before introducing dual carriageways, a recap on driving on two-way roads could include the following questions:

- 'Where do you normally drive on a two-way road?'
- 'What is the most dangerous manoeuvre on a two-way road?'
- 'What's the speed limit in built-up areas and on other roads?'
- 'What routine should you always apply when dealing with hazards?'

Objectives

The objective is to teach your pupils how to join, drive along and leave dual carriageways safely and efficiently. Because there are numerous types of dual carriageway you will not be able to achieve this in one lesson – it will be a gradual process over a series of lessons up to and beyond the driving test.

You will need to confirm that dual carriageways come in lots of different designs and layouts. Some of the variations are the:

- number of lanes;
- speed limit;
- methods of joining – ie roundabouts, T-junctions, slip roads;
- volume of traffic;
- parked vehicles.

The following are some questions you could use to confirm what the pupil knows about dual carriageways:

- 'What's the speed limit on dual carriageways where the national limit applies?'
- 'What's the speed limit in built-up areas?'
- 'Tell me what a "repeater" sign means?'
- 'Where should you normally drive on a dual carriageway?'
- 'What's the right-hand lane for?'
- 'Why do you think it might be important to plan further ahead and use all of the mirrors more frequently?'

It might be useful to use visual aids to help the pupil 'see' what you mean, particularly when you're describing how to turn right onto dual carriageways from side roads. You will need to explain the differences that apply where the width of the central reserve varies. The most important key elements you should include in your explanation are:

- joining from roundabouts;
- turning left onto dual carriageways from T-junctions;
- turning right onto dual carriageways through narrow and wider central reserves;
- driving in the left lane unless passing parked vehicles, overtaking or turning right;
- planning further ahead – for parked vehicles or slower-moving traffic;
- using the mirrors more frequently;
- positioning in the centre of the lane;
- planning for junctions and applying the M S M routine early;
- changing lanes safely;
- keeping up with the traffic flow.

The following are some of the questions you might use to coach the pupil:

- 'Why do you think you might have to look and plan further ahead on dual carriageways?'
- 'How often should you use the mirrors?'
- 'Why do you think you have to start the M S M routine earlier than on normal roads?'
- 'How would you turn right if the central reserve is narrow?'
- 'What would you do if the central reserve is very wide?'

As with any other complex subject, the list of questions is endless; you will have to devise questions that suit each set of circumstances.

Demonstrations

Unless your pupil has difficulty in understanding, 'hands on' experience is the most effective way of learning to apply the different rules. You may, in some particularly difficult situations, decide that a demonstration would be the safest way to initially explain how to deal with them.

Practice

For the first few outings on dual carriageways, practice will need to be guided. Although your pupil should by now have good car control skills and can apply the M S M rules on normal two-way roads and at junctions, you may need to offer a certain amount of prompting in these new situations.

Make sure, at this stage, that your talk-through is restricted to the unfamiliar procedures. If you're not careful, it's very easy to revert to giving basic instructions in those skills the pupil has already mastered.

Depending on the road systems in your area, practice should be given on all the procedures listed under the explanation section.

Some of the problems that arise during the early development of skills in driving on dual carriageways are very similar to those listed under roundabouts. Other faults include:

- failing to look ahead and respond in time to parked vehicles – this can often result in the pupil either becoming boxed in or signalling and pulling out in front of another driver;
- not keeping up with the traffic flow and causing problems for others;
- keeping up when the other traffic is breaking the speed limit;
- not planning early enough for junctions;
- blocking a carriageway by failing to work out the width of the central reserve before pulling across;
- moving onto a dual carriageway and failing to build up the speed effectively.

Feedback, recap and look forward

Following the normal lesson format, give positive feedback and advice on aspects that need more attention, recapping on the strengths and areas of weakness.

Formulate questions like those listed under other subjects in order to coach your pupil and develop better understanding and attitude.

Confirm that, as with roundabouts, driving on dual carriageways requires lots of practice and experience in order to build confidence.

Making progress and road positioning

When you have covered most of the syllabus, you will need to cover some important points:

- how to maintain the correct position on the road;
- how to respond positively;

- taking safe opportunities to merge into traffic at all types of junction;
- driving at appropriate speeds to keep the traffic moving.

The agreed objectives could be something like:

'During your next few lessons we will be driving in more congested areas to build up your confidence and improve your personal driving skills. We will be focusing on:

- road positioning and lane discipline;
- how to judge safe gaps in the traffic to emerge into;
- driving on higher speed and multi-lane roads so that you learn how to keep up with the flow of the traffic.'

By this stage pupils should be able to apply the basic driving routines to most situations. The following are a few examples of questions to confirm understanding:

- 'What's the speed limit in a built-up area?'
- 'Give me a few examples of when and where it wouldn't be safe to drive up to the speed limit.'
- 'At what speed would you drive past a school around lunchtime?'
- 'What's the normal driving position on a two-way road?'
- 'When do you think it might be safer to drive a little further out in the road?'
- 'What's the national speed limit on a two-way road?'
- 'What might a following driver be tempted to do if you're driving too slowly for the conditions?'
- 'When you're waiting at a roundabout, why is it important to look to the left as well as to the right?'
- 'What do you think might happen if you miss a suitable gap in the traffic at a roundabout?'
- 'Where should you position the car when you're driving on multi-lane roads?'

Using effective questions at this stage should help establish in your pupils an awareness of the need to remain alert to the all-round traffic situation.

Through discussion on these points, you should be able to explain to your pupils what is required in order to become a good and confident driver. Listen carefully to their responses and guide them towards the correct answers, giving added information as necessary.

Level of instruction

At this stage, pupils' driving skills should be fairly well developed. Give them the responsibility for making decisions in the types of situation they have previously experienced.

You may need to give some prompted assistance at the busier junctions in order to encourage them to take suitable opportunities to emerge and make good progress along the road.

Practice

By selecting appropriate routes, create as many opportunities as you can to cover as wide a variety of road and junction type as is possible within each session.

As you see confidence growing, back off and transfer the responsibility to the pupil. Obviously, how long this will take will vary from pupil to pupil and you may sometimes have to adapt your teaching to suit their progress.

Fault identification and analysis

As with all other subjects, use your pupils' mistakes as opportunities to coach them into being better drivers. You need to ensure they can:

- move off promptly when safe;
- build up speed and change through the gears positively;
- apply the M S M routine effectively at all types of junction;
- take opportunities to emerge safely into traffic;
- travel at speeds appropriate for the road type and traffic conditions and drive in the correct position;
- look and plan well ahead to minimise unnecessary stops at hazards.

Feedback/recap/summary

This is another area where the use of questions and guided discussion on what occurred during each session can help improve pupils' understanding of the principles involved in becoming effective drivers.

Remember to give praise where pupils demonstrate good decision-making skills and use any incidents that arise as discussion points.

Look forward

At the end of each lesson, confirm to the pupil that on the next you will be introducing even more complex situations in order to build up their experience.

Refer them to any specific reading material that may help in their development.

Anticipating the actions of other road users

Today's roads are really congested, with everyone trying to get from A to B as quickly as possible, often with little thought given to those around them. All your pupils will have been passengers and will probably have observed some of the unsafe actions that have from time to time put them at risk.

Objectives

Teaching anticipation cannot be done in one lesson; it is an ongoing process. Try to use all opportunities that present themselves to encourage the pupil to drive defensively by anticipating what others may do and to work out the safest way to avoid conflict.

By applying coaching techniques, you can use pupils' previous experiences to develop their awareness and anticipation and hopefully, by encouraging them to come to their own conclusions, you will influence safer attitudes.

Using the client-centred skills described earlier in this book and in the lesson plans contained in this chapter, make sure that your pupils are able to deal safely with the following:

- Other car drivers. They may pull out from side roads or turn across their path, push their way through spaces between parked vehicles, overtake unsafely or follow too closely.

- Cyclists and motorcyclists. Be aware of them overtaking on either side of your car, particularly between lanes of slow-moving traffic. Remember that they are less easy to see at junctions. Recognise that cyclists may ride off the pavement onto the road.

- Drivers of larger vehicles, for example anticipating that they may straddle lanes in roundabouts and will require more room when turning into and out of junctions.

- Emergency vehicles. Listen for sirens and watch for flashing lights; encourage pupils to be prepared to make room for them to pass.

- Pedestrians. Expect children to step into the road, to mess around with their friends around school time, to misuse crossings, etc. Expect older people to misjudge speed and distance, to be hesitant and to take longer to cross the road.

- Animals. In both urban and rural areas they are unpredictable. Allow plenty of time and clearance.

- Differing road, light and weather conditions. These influence the driver's needs; for example, being dazzled by the headlights of oncoming or following drivers.

Independent driving and use of sat nav

The driving test includes about 20 minutes of 'independent' driving where the pupil follows a predetermined route. This is done by a set of instructions from the examiner or by use of a sat nav.

It is important you give your pupils plenty of opportunities to take control of the route. This could happen right in the early stages where you discuss what would be a safe road to practise moving off and stopping; or ask them to find their own way home when you know they can control the car reasonably safely; or ask them to pick a route that lasts around five minutes and includes left and right turns. Later on, you can ask them to drive following signs and road markings; or give them an A to Z, pick a road and ask them to take you there; or pull them up at the side of the road and give them three or four directions to see if they can remember them and still plan their approach to hazards and junctions.

A part of the independent drive on the driving test may include the use of sat nav (satellite navigation).

The examiner provides the sat nav and sets it up using a stored route. The candidate doesn't need to touch it.

It doesn't matter which sat nav you use for practice. It could be a built-in sat nav, a mobile phone or stand-alone sat nav. The pupil is not being tested on their ability to set a route in a sat nav – just the ability to follow directions from one.

The examiner will make sure that the sat nav is positioned appropriately and safely.

In most cases, the sat nav will not be fixed to the windscreen – it will be on a special dash-mat so it doesn't move or fall off. However, because of the design of some vehicles, there will be some cases where it will need to be mounted on the windscreen.

Before applying for a driving test your pupils should be able to drive consistently safely in all types of road and traffic conditions and to anticipate and deal safely with other road users.

If you follow a client-centred approach with all your customers, it will make the learning situation more enjoyable for them. By the end of their course, your pupils should also be able to safely share the road with us.

06
National standard for driver training

The 'national standard for driver training' describes the skills, knowledge and understanding needed to be a safe and responsible driving instructor or instructor trainer.

It forms the basis of the work that an effective driver trainer would be carrying out regularly on a day-to-day basis with the whole range of pupils. They are particularly important in the context of the ADI Standards Check, which all ADIs are obliged to undertake at intervals.

Details of the Standard are set out in detail in this chapter as it is essential that you fully understand every aspect, not only for the Standards Check, but as part of your everyday work. However, there are several significant quotes and sections that are worth highlighting and discussing. At the end of the chapter we look at each of these topics in more detail, but as you read through the Standard take particular note of them as they are key issues in understanding and implementing the competencies.

1 'Instructors deliver agreed syllabuses using a "client-centred" approach.' (unit 6.2)

2 'Using a client-centred learning approach is about maximising learning by taking into account the status, prior experience and particular needs of the learner.' (unit 6.2)

3 'A learner-centred instructor is able to adjust an outline programme to meet the needs of the learner by taking account of prior learning and identifying issues as the training progresses.' (unit 6.2)

4 'Use best-practice tools, techniques, and exercises to support transfer of ownership of the learning process.' (unit 6.2)

5 'Plan routes for on-road training sessions that provide safe, legal and effective learning opportunities.' (unit 6.2)

6 '"Client-centred" is taken to mean, broadly, the same as "student-centred" or "learner-centred".' (unit 6.3)

7 'Client-centred learning is not about the learner taking charge of the learning process and deciding what is going to happen. It is about creating a conversation.' (unit 6.3)

8 'Within the learner-centred approach there is a legitimate role for well-delivered explanation and demonstration.' (unit 6.3.2)

9 'Frequent explanations and demonstrations can be supportive for some learners; for others this may be de-motivating.' (unit 6.3.2)

10 'Transfer the balance of responsibility for their learning process to the learner as soon as they are ready to take it.' (unit 6.3.3)

All of these topics are discussed in more detail at the end of this chapter and in Chapter 8 we look at how they are used in the context of the ADI Standards Check.

Introduction

This National Driver Training Standard (the Standard) sets out the skills, knowledge and understanding needed to deliver a programme of driver training. It covers training for drivers of all types of cars, light vans, motorcycles and mopeds for use on the road. It covers training for licence acquisition and post-test driving programmes.

The Standard assumes that any person wishing to teach somebody to drive has:

- a current driving licence;
- mastered all the competences set out in Roles 1–4 of the National Driving Standard;
- demonstrated competence in Role 5 of the National Driving Standard.

In other words it assumes that they have maintained and improved their competence, at both the theoretical and practical levels, since they acquired their licence. Candidates will be expected to demonstrate at least level 3 competence.

This Standard sets out the knowledge, skills and understanding needed to deliver successful learning. It talks about instructors delivering agreed syllabuses using a 'client-centred' approach. The Standard talks mainly about the skills, knowledge and understanding required to work 'in-car' but also acknowledges that some driver training organisations may opt to deliver part of any given syllabus to a classroom group. The knowledge, skills and understanding that apply in the classroom have therefore been included, but not all instructors will choose to train in this way.

The Standard includes some of the skills, knowledge and understanding needed by trainers of instructors (such as role play). It assumes higher-level assessment skills will be covered by a standard assessor unit.

As with all of DVSA's standards, this standard is expected to change in response to further evidence that may emerge and to peer comment. It is expected that the range of units will be extended to cover specialist areas such as the Disability Discrimination Act (DDA) and the delivery of remedial programmes.

Meeting all legal requirements

This unit is about confirming that you meet all the legal requirements before you start delivering training. These cover: the vehicle you intend to use; your status as an instructor.

The core of this unit is that you must know and understand what the law says about using a vehicle for training purposes and about your entitlement to deliver training.

Some of the tasks may be given to other people in your organisation. However, you should still be able to confirm that the vehicle you intend to use is roadworthy and that you are legally able to carry out the training.

This unit contains two elements:

Element 6.1.1 – Confirm that you comply with legal requirements

Element 6.1.2 – Confirm that the training vehicle is fit for purpose

Unit 6.1 – Prepare to train learner driver – meet all legal requirements

Element 6.1.1 – Confirm that you comply with legal requirements

This element is about making sure that you can legally provide training. This includes licence and instructor registration requirements. You must report any change to your health or eyesight, or any convictions, to all those who legally need to know.

Performance standards

You must be able to:

1 confirm that you hold a current, valid licence to drive the training vehicle;

2 confirm that you are registered as an instructor with the appropriate body or bodies, or that you are exempt from registration;

3 comply with organisational and legal requirements to report any change to your status as an instructor, such as:

   a convictions;

   b medical conditions;

   c changes to your eyesight.

4 display your current instructor registration certificate in line with legal requirements.

Knowledge and understanding requirements

You must know and understand:

a) the licence regulations that apply to the training vehicle you are using;

b) whether there are requirements to belong to a register of instructors for the training vehicle you are using;

c) the legal requirements and conditions that apply to gaining and maintaining registration to any appropriate body or bodies;

d) the types of offence you must report under organisational or legal requirements and how they affect your status as an instructor;

e) how changes to your health or your eyesight may affect your status as an instructor;

f) the eyesight requirements that apply for the training vehicle you are using.

Element 6.1.2 – Confirm that the training vehicle is fit for purpose

This element is about making sure the training vehicle meets the relevant legal and organisational requirements for roadworthiness. You should confirm that all necessary documentation is available and valid. You should also be aware of any requirements for a minimum test vehicle (MTV). Routine maintenance and recognising any faults with the vehicle are also covered.

When using a vehicle provided by the learner there are clearly limits as to how far you can go in carrying out checks and taking corrective actions. You should still confirm that the vehicle meets minimum test vehicle requirements, check the documentation, carry out basic safety checks, such as those on tyres and lights, and make sure that L plates (or D plates in Wales) are displayed correctly.

Performance standards

You must be able to:

1 make sure that any vehicle used for training purposes: meets the minimum test vehicle requirements; is correctly marked;

2 make sure that any equipment fitted to the vehicle, such as dual controls, is: legally compliant; fit for purpose;

3 make sure that insurance is in place to cover driver training, and where appropriate driver testing, in the vehicle as adapted;

4 confirm all other vehicle documentation (such as registration, tax disc and MOT) meets legal requirements;

5 confirm the vehicle's service record is in accordance with the supplier's or your organisation's recommendations;

6 carry out vehicle checks and report faults with the vehicle in line with organisational and legal requirements;

7 carry out corrective actions that are within your authority;

8 make other arrangements when a vehicle is not fit for purpose.

Knowledge and understanding requirements

You must know and understand:

a) minimum test vehicle (MTV) requirements for licence acquisition practical tests;

b) the legal requirement to identify a vehicle being used for on-road training of provisional licence holders, by fitting L/D plates;

c) how to check the operation of equipment such as dual controls;

d) any legal requirements or restrictions that apply to the fitting and use of equipment;

e) what insurance you must have in place to deliver driver training for the vehicle involved;

f) the need to inform your insurance provider of any adaptations to your vehicle;

g) the statutory registration, licensing and testing requirements for the vehicle;

h) how to access the service record for the vehicle and confirm that necessary servicing has been carried out;

i) how to access any organisational checklist of problems for the vehicle and carry out those checks;

j) what action to take if the vehicle:

- does not have all the necessary documentation;
- has not been serviced;
- fails any checks.

Designing learning programmes

This unit uses a 'client-centred' learning approach. It is about maximising learning by taking into account the status, prior experience and particular needs of the learner. It assumes that any instructor should be able to respond to the needs of any individual who wishes to be trained. It is unreasonable to expect an instructor to understand, and be able to respond to, the specific needs of every type of special need. However, they should be able to actively manage the process of finding alternative support in these circumstances.

Instructors may be following outline programmes designed by others. As learner-centred instructors, however, they must be able to adjust an outline programme to meet the needs of the learner by: taking prior learning into account; identifying any issues or opportunities as the training progresses.

They must also understand how adjustments will affect the learning outcomes of the programme. They can then make sure that no learning outcomes are missed and that learning opportunities are maximised.

Performance standards

You must be able to:

1 confirm that the learner holds a provisional or full licence for the category of the training vehicle;

2 confirm that the learner's eyesight meets licence requirements;

3 identify the learning needs of the learner, their initial learning status and any special needs, including any need for in-vehicle adaptations;

4 transfer the learner to an appropriate colleague where their learning needs exceed your competence, such as learners with physical or cognitive disabilities with which you are not familiar, or where you cannot provide a suitable adapted vehicle;

5 plan an outline programme that delivers equal opportunities and access to learning, including one-to-one and group-based sessions where suitable;

6 create lesson plans for each session that outline learning objectives, identify any resources needed and take into account any special needs (such as reduced concentration spans or fatigue due to physical conditions);

7 make sure that any resources in the plan will be available, including e-learning and third-party providers;

8 include competent third parties, where this will benefit the learner;

9 agree roles and responsibilities of any third-party providers, including how they will record and pass on relevant information;

10 where accompanying drivers are involved, specify how they can best support each stage of the programme;

11 where applicable, specify how parents, guardians, partners or carers can support learners with physical or cognitive disabilities;

12 specify how you will review learner progress and programme effectiveness.

Knowledge and understanding requirements

You must know and understand:

a) the content and principles of the relevant National Driving Standard;

b) the requirements of licence acquisition for the vehicle being used;

c) the requirements of any other formal, post-test assessment of driving competence;

d) the range of prior-learning inputs that can add to the learning process and how they can be featured in the way the learner is taught;

e) the range of special needs that learners might have and their broad implications for driving the training vehicle;

f) how cultural and religious factors may affect the options available to support the learning process, such as:

- inability to attend sessions on particular days of the week;

- sensitivities about making eye contact;
- the belief that it is 'bad manners' to contradict the teacher.

g) the options available for including non-vehicle-based or third-party learning inputs in the learning programme;

h) best-practice tools, techniques, exercises and activities available to support transfer of ownership of the learning process and delivery of desired learning outcomes;

i) the issues involved in the use of psychometric tools;

j) the learning resources available to support driver learning in general and those with special needs in particular;

k) how to draw up learning programmes that cater for different learning styles and needs, including:

- literacy issues;
- numeracy issues;
- language issues;
- physical disabilities;
- cognitive disabilities.

l) how to plan routes for on-road training sessions that provide safe, legal and effective learning opportunities;

m) how to manage effective working relationships with other providers;

n) the law on accompanying drivers;

o) how to maximise the contribution of an accompanying driver or rider to a learning programme;

p) where appropriate, how to foster effective relationships with the parents, guardians, partners or carers of learners with physical or cognitive disabilities;

q) how to monitor and review learning programmes in the light of:

- learners' changing needs;
- learners' progress;
- any formative assessment requirements.

r) how to gather the learners' views of the learning process:

- formally and informally;
- while maintaining confidentiality and trust;
- while remaining within the stated learning objectives.

s) how to manage confidentiality and data security requirements for learning programmes.

Enabling safe and responsible driving

This unit is about helping and supporting a learner to acquire the skills, knowledge and understanding that they need to drive safely and responsibly throughout their driving career. This means that the unit is not just about teaching a learner to pass a test. Instead, it is about developing the learner's competence and their willingness to continue the learning process beyond their test.

The competences which go to make up this unit are presented in four elements. However, it is important to understand that the first three of these elements represent different aspects, or layers, of a single, integrated, approach; an approach known as 'client-centred learning'. It is not really possible or meaningful to attempt to demonstrate these competences in isolation.

In this context the phrase 'client-centred' is taken to mean, broadly, the same thing as 'student-centred' or 'learner-centred'. In this context this unit is not about teaching learners to perform driving or riding tasks in particular ways. While it is reasonable to encourage learners to practise particular methods for performing a given task because there are clearly explainable benefits to that method, the outcome of the learning process should be that the learner has developed a safe and responsible method which they can apply consistently and reliably; not that they have learnt any one specified method.

The fourth element, which is about group-based learning (typically but not always in a classroom environment) shares the 'client-centred' approach. However, it is presented here as a separate element to reflect the fact that some instructors may choose to never work in this environment.

Client-centred learning is not about the learner taking charge of the learning process and deciding what is going to happen. Instead it is about creating a conversation between the learner and the instructor that is based on mutual respect. This approach is based on the idea that people resist taking on new understandings and resist modifying their behaviour if:

- the person who is trying to teach them fails to respect and value their idea of who they are;
- the person delivering the learning is not seen as 'genuine';
- the person delivering the learning is not seen as having legitimate authority.

In the context of learning to drive, the instructor brings to the learning process their hard-earned knowledge, understanding and experience. If they rely simply on telling the learner what they should do they will probably be able to teach them enough to pass their test. However, all the evidence suggests that learners in this sort of relationship do not really change the way they think and quickly forget what they have been taught. There is a better chance of a long-lasting change in understanding and behaviour if the instructor:

- presents their knowledge, understanding and experience clearly and effectively;
- listens to the learner's reactions to that input;
- helps the learner to identify any obstacles to understanding and change;
- supports the learner to identify strategies for overcoming those obstacles for themselves.

This unit contains four elements:

Element 6.3.1 – Create a climate that promotes learning

Element 6.3.2 – Explain and demonstrate skills and techniques

Element 6.3.3 – Coach

Element 6.3.4 – Facilitate group-based learning

Element 6.3.1 – Create a climate that promotes learning

This element is about creating a relationship with the learner, and a context for their learning, that helps them to take ownership of their learning process. It is the foundation on which the next two elements are built.

This approach is based on the understanding that learners who are not engaged by the training or just receive information, are less well equipped to deal with the wide range of challenges they will meet, when they drive independently, than those who are supported to be active learners.

The element is also about ensuring that every learner has access to the same learning opportunities and is treated with equal respect.

Performance standards

You must be able to:

1 establish an effective verbal and/or non-verbal communications strategy that:

- is free from discrimination;

- does not exploit the learner;
- does not collude with risky behaviour or attitudes.

2 make sure the learner fully understands the objectives, structure and formal assessment requirements of the programme;

3 explain how you expect to work with the learner and how you expect them to work with you;

4 make sure the learner understands what other opportunities, methods and resources are available and how these can be included in their overall learning process;

5 where appropriate, explain how parents, guardians, partners or carers can support learners with physical or cognitive disabilities;

6 where a driver accompanies the learner on private practice, explain how they can be most effective in supporting the learner;

7 explain how you intend to monitor and review the learner's progress during the programme;

8 agree the details of the learning plan with the learner:

- within the constraints of the overall programme;
- with the understanding that you may work with the learner to agree changes if required.

Knowledge and understanding requirements

You must know and understand:

a) how to ensure and improve good verbal and/or non-verbal communication, such as by:

- using good eye contact (where this is culturally acceptable);
- using consistent language;
- breaking things into manageable pieces;
- using graphics, pictures and other visual aids to reinforce your words.

b) the content and principles of the relevant National Driving Standard;

c) the evidence that indicates that an active and lifelong approach to learning reduces the risk of crashes and the long-term cost of driving;

d) how to set clear guidelines for acceptable behaviour within the learning environment;

e) the effect of your own assumptions about particular groups within society on your ability to deliver effective learning;

f) the role of 'individual learning plans' and similar models for agreeing ways forward within learning programmes;

g) how to identify and deal with possible barriers to learning and achievement, including:

- delivery methods;

- times;

- location;

- lack of support for people with special needs;

- lack of facilities.

h) how to explain the objectives and structure of a learning programme, and your choice of methods, in a way that is appropriate for each learner;

i) how to include accompanying driver in the learning process in a way that reinforces learning outcomes;

j) the scope for flexibility within the programme;

k) the credibility of the licence acquisition process with key stakeholders such as parents or employers;

l) the credibility of post-test assessments of driving competence with key stakeholders such as parents or employers;

m) external influences on the learner's attitude to the learning process, such as economic factors and peer pressure.

Element 6.3.2 – Explain and demonstrate skills and techniques

About this element:

Within the learner-centred approach, there is a legitimate role for well-delivered explanation and demonstration. This element sets out the standards for this. Instructors should be able to provide clear, realistic and reliable demonstrations of how to apply practical skills – both stationary and moving. They should be able to explain what they are doing and why they are doing it. Having provided such demonstrations, they should then be able to support the learner in practising the skills and give them feedback.

The element assumes that the process of learning practical skills is helped if the learner understands the reasons why a particular skill is necessary.

Performance standards

You must be able to:

1 select suitable locations for delivering demonstrations;

2 provide timely and appropriate explanations and demonstrations of the skills and techniques required to drive a vehicle safely and responsibly, including the use of adaptations where fitted;

3 encourage learners to ask questions and, where necessary, repeat or alter your answer so that they understand;

4 make sure that the learner understands any theory that links to on-road application of the skill or technique being taught;

5 make sure that learners have enough opportunities to practise the skill demonstrated;

6 give feedback to learners that helps them identify, understand and overcome obstacles to competent application of skills where possible; encourage and help learners to practise skills in a structured way, outside the formal learning environment.

Knowledge and understanding requirements

You must know and understand:

a) how to deliver an explanation or demonstration so that the learner gains the maximum learning, taking into account different learning styles;

b) how to make sure that the learner understands the purpose and content of any explanation or demonstration;

c) how to assess whether a location is suitable for the demonstration of a skill or technique;

d) that while frequent explanations and demonstrations can be supportive for some learners, for others this may be demotivating;

e) how to overcome the limitations of the in-vehicle environment;

f) how to provide explanations and demonstrations in practical driving skills while stationary;

g) how to carry out a moving vehicle demonstration while keeping full control of the vehicle;

h) how to provide a verbal explanation of what you are doing while carrying out a moving vehicle demonstration;

i) the content of *The Highway Code* and the requirements of the licence acquisition theory test;

j) the importance of moving the use of vehicle controls, and other practical skills, from active effort to implicit or procedural memory as quickly as possible;

k) how to check the learner's understanding and progress;

l) how to give formative feedback.

Note: The ability to provide an explanation of what you are doing as you are doing it is considered to be a level 3 competence. The more complex process of 'commentary driving' is considered to be a level 4 competence.

Element 6.3.3 – Coach

This element is about engaging in a conversation with the learner to help them identify obstacles to learning and strategies for overcoming those obstacles.

Note: It is unlikely that a learner will be willing to engage in this process if a secure grounding has not been established in element 6.3.1.

Performance standards

You must be able to:

1 listen to what the learner tells you about the obstacles they experience that prevent them from applying:

- practical driving skills;
- their understanding of theory.

2 help the learner to come up with strategies for overcoming obstacles;

3 work with the learner to help them reflect on:

- their experience of the learning programme;
- your feedback;
- the feedback of other providers.

4 work with the learner to identify obstacles to their ownership of the learning process and work out strategies for overcoming those obstacles;

5 transfer the balance of responsibility for their learning process to the learner as soon as they are ready to take it;

6 at all times, exercise your responsibility for the safety of yourself, the learner and other road users;

7 work with the learner to agree when they are ready for formal assessment of driving competence;

8 accompany the learner to formal assessments when appropriate;

9 work with the learner to help them:

- reflect on their experience of assessment;
- reflect on examiner feedback;
- identify strategies for overcoming problems when they have failed an assessment.

Knowledge and understanding requirements

You must know and understand:

a) how to use a range of learner-centred techniques to help the learner identify and overcome barriers to achievement of learning goals;

b) how to use a range of learner-centred techniques to encourage the learner to join up their understanding of practice and theory and of different parts of theory;

c) how to use a range of learner-centred techniques to support the transfer of ownership of the learning process to the learner;

d) the impact of your own willingness to transfer ownership of the learning process;

e) the importance of providing regular formative feedback;

f) how to use learner-centred techniques while putting your responsibility for safety in the learning environment first.

Element 6.3.4 – Facilitate group-based learning

This element shares the broad objectives of elements 6.3.1–6.3.3; creating a suitable learning environment, providing inputs based on expertise, and working with the learner to identify obstacles to learning and strategies for overcoming those obstacles. It recognises that delivering these objectives when working with a group of learners presents extra challenges and barriers to learning. This calls for extra competences.

Performance standards

You must be able to:

1 make sure all learners feel comfortable and able to express their views and concerns;

2 encourage all learners to ask questions and, where necessary, modify your delivery to ensure understanding;

3 make sure learners understand the purpose, processes and intended outcomes of each group activity, and how it links to the rest of their learning programme;

4 support all learners to take an active part in learning activities;

5 make sure individual behaviours or group dynamics do not isolate individuals or distract from the desired learning outcomes;

6 make sure you do not collude with inappropriate attitudes to other group members or to road safety;

7 promptly and clearly interrupt behaviour that is:

- discriminatory;
- oppressive;
- preventing any individual from benefiting from the learning experience whether by other learners or by colleagues.

8 monitor the progress of individuals and provide feedback to the learner and other providers.

Knowledge and understanding requirements

You must know and understand:

a) how to make sure learners feel:

- at their ease within the group;
- safe;
- able to take an active part in the learning process.

b) how to use a range of learning activities that involve all members of the group so that they gain the maximum learning benefit;

c) how to use learner-centred techniques to help individuals identify obstacles to engagement with the learning process and devise strategies for overcoming obstacles;

d) the potential effect of peer group assumptions on the behaviour of learners;

e) the risk of group dynamics being dominated by sub-groups;

f) how to interrupt individual behaviours or group dynamics which have the effect of excluding individuals or sub-groups;

g) the risk of unconsciously colluding with inappropriate behaviours or attitudes;

h) the risk of being diverted from intended learning outcomes by group dynamics;

i) how to identify opportunities to increase learning that arise in the group, and how to adapt presentations to support that process;

j) how to check an individual's understanding and progress within a group;

k) how to give feedback in a group and on a one-to-one basis;

l) how to provide feedback on individual learner progress to other training providers.

Managing risk

This unit is about actively managing the risks that can arise while delivering driver training and ensuring, as far as is within your control, the health and safety of all involved.

This unit contains three elements:

Element 6.4.1 – Manage the on-road environment to minimise risk

Element 6.4.2 – Manage the risk of violence in the learning environment

Element 6.4.3 – Manage health and safety in the classroom environment

Element 6.4.1 – Manage the on-road environment to minimise risk

This element addresses those risks that can arise in an on-road training session. It assumes that learners will always be expected to take their share of responsibility for the management of risk, while recognising that their competence to take that responsibility will change over the period of their training. It also recognises that correctly understanding the nature of the risks that arise during a training session is central to a learner's ability to assess and respond to risk when they drive independently.

Performance standards

You must be able to:

1 take reasonable steps to make sure the learner is fit to start the session, and take suitable action if they are not fit;

2 make sure the learner fully understands how you will share with them the responsibility for:

- their safety;
- your safety;
- the safety of other road users.

3 give clear instructions (such as when and where to start, stop or turn), make sure that the learner understands your instructions and, if they do not, modify your instructions accordingly;

4 explain when and how you may use verbal or physical interventions to ensure safety;

5 continue to scan the environment and assess hazards while observing the learner and providing training inputs;

6 take suitable and timely action where you identify a hazard that the learner does not appear to be aware of, or believe the learner is unable to respond safely to a hazard;

7 how far you are responsible for the health and safety of yourself and others in the on-road learning environment;

8 use 'client-centred' techniques to make sure the learner is better equipped to deal with such hazards in the future;

9 take suitable and timely action, including stopping the session, where the learner becomes unfit to continue or behaves in a way that places you, the learner or third parties at unacceptable risk;

10 comply with any requirement to record details of situations in which specific risks arise;

Knowledge and understanding requirements

You must know and understand:

a) the signs that a learner's fitness to be trained may be impaired by:

- alcohol;
- illegal or controlled substances;
- over-the-counter or prescription medicines.

b) the signs that a learner may be suffering from a physical or psychological condition that makes them unfit to be trained, including conditions that they are unaware of or are trying to hide;

c) what to do if you believe a learner: is temporarily unfit to be trained; has a permanent physical or psychological condition that they have not revealed;

d) how far the learner is responsible for health and safety in the on-road learning environment;

e) how you can take action, safely, and how this depends on the type of training vehicle;

f) where applicable, how to operate dual controls;

g) how to give feedback about risk-related issues so that you motivate and help the learner to change their behaviour without increasing fear-based responses;

h) what to do if a learner becomes unfit to continue the session;

i) how to promptly interrupt deliberate behaviour that places the instructor, learner or third parties at risk;

j) the instructor's right to interrupt or stop sessions where an unacceptable risk arises;

k) how to record incidents in which a risk situation arises;

l) the impact of your own level of competence and attitudes to risk on your ability to minimise risk;

m) the importance of demonstrating consistent attitudes to the management of risk to make sure that formal messages being given in the learning programme are not undermined.

Element 6.4.2 – Manage the risk of violence in the learning environment

The Health and Safety Executive notes that:

> People who deal directly with the public may face aggressive or violent behaviour. They may be sworn at, threatened or even attacked.

This unit is about taking steps to protect yourself, and learners, from aggressive or violent behaviour, whether from other learners or third parties. The 'Management of Health and Safety at Work Regulations 1999' say that employers must assess the risks to employees and make arrangements for their health and safety by effective:

- planning;
- organisation;

- control;

- monitoring and review.

Therefore, it is assumed that any training organisation will have policies and guidance on how to deal with aggressive or violent behaviour. It is important that instructors understand what actions they can take to protect themselves and others, both to make sure that they are safe and that they comply with legal requirements and limits.

Performance standards

You must be able to:

1 implement and comply with your organisation's policy and procedures for protecting staff from the risk of violence at work;

2 implement and comply with your organisation's policy and procedures for protecting learners from the risk of violence during sessions;

3 manage verbally or physically aggressive behaviour in ways that are consistent with best practice and legal requirements;

4 take appropriate and timely action, in line with your organisation's policy and procedures, including:

- stopping the session;

- calling for assistance;

- leaving the learning space.

5 if a learner's behaviour puts you or others at risk, report details of any situation in which an actual or potential risk of aggressive or violent behaviour arises, in line with your organisation's policy and procedures.

Knowledge and understanding requirements

You must know and understand:

a) your legal responsibility to your well-being, safety and health in the workplace as set out in the relevant legislation for Health and Safety at Work;

b) the extent and limits of your obligation to protect learners from the risk of physical or verbal violence during sessions;

c) your organisation's policy and procedures for the management of violence in the learning environment including:

- stopping sessions;

- summoning assistance;
- leaving the learning space and how they apply to your role and level of competence.

d) how to interpret body language, and the importance of acknowledging other people's personal space;

e) the impact of your own level of competence and attitudes and how they may trigger aggressive or violent responses;

f) the limits to your ability to protect yourself in potentially violent situations;

g) when and how you can safely interrupt behaviour which appears likely to result in violence;

h) how to record incidents in which a risk situation arises;

i) the importance of demonstrating consistent attitudes and behaviours in the management of violence in the learning environment so that messages being given in the overall learning programme are not undermined.

Element 6.4.3 – Manage health and safety in the classroom environment

This element is about those particular health and safety issues that arise when using enclosed premises for the delivery of any part of the training process, in particular where groups of learners are involved. It assumes that the risk of violence in the classroom is covered in 6.4.2.

Performance standards

You must be able to:

1 implement and follow general health and safety procedures and requirements for the delivery of services to the public;

2 implement and follow any specific health and safety procedures and requirements that apply in the buildings you are using;

3 make sure that learners understand the operation of health and safety and emergency procedures that apply in any enclosed premises you are using;

4 in the event of an emergency, carry out your responsibilities as set out in your organisation's policy and procedures;

5 report details of any actual or potential health and safety risks that arise, in line with your organisation's policy and procedures.

Knowledge and understanding requirements

You must know and understand:

a) the extent and limits of your responsibility for learners as set out in the relevant Health and Safety at Work legislation;

b) the application of health and safety regulations in any enclosed premises;

c) the content of your organisation's health and safety policy and procedures and how they apply to your role and responsibilities;

d) the operation of fire alarm and emergency evacuation procedures;

e) the importance of remaining alert to health and safety issues at all times;

f) the importance of demonstrating consistent attitudes and behaviours in the management of health and safety risks so that messages being given in the overall learning programme are not undermined.

Evaluating and developing knowledge, understanding and skills

This unit is about evaluating your own performance against the established and evolving requirements of your role, identifying where there are opportunities for improvement and taking action to respond to those opportunities.

It is recognised that many organisations will have a formal personal development process in place with which an employed instructor will be expected to comply. However, beyond this requirement, any competent instructor should be able to demonstrate that they are actively involved in maintaining and continuously improving their skills, knowledge and understanding whether they are employed or self-employed.

This unit is really talking about CPD (Continuing Professional Development) and the importance of self-responsibility in seeking out training providers and courses that will keep you up to date with everything that is going on in the industry, as well as reading up on all available material and information. Specifically, you are expected to know what is in the Driver Training Syllabus and Standard – as set out in this chapter and the next on the Standards Check.

Performance standards

You must be able to:

1 identify the skills, knowledge and understanding needed for your role and evaluate your own capabilities and performance against these;

2 evaluate your working practices against relevant organisational and legal requirements;

3 keep up to date with training industry issues and recognise when changes in the industry mean that you need to update your knowledge, skills and understanding;

4 actively make use of all sources of feedback, such as:

- performance records of previous learners;
- feedback from line managers;
- feedback from colleagues or other professionals to identify gaps in your knowledge, skills or understanding.

5 set out objectives for the ongoing development of your knowledge, skills and understanding;

6 identify training or development opportunities that will help you update or close any gaps in your knowledge, skills and understanding;

7 keep a reflective log so that you can evaluate the outcome of your professional development activities;

8 comply with any organisational requirements to plan and record your training and development activities and to evaluate the benefits of any training you undertake.

Knowledge and understanding requirements

You must know and understand:

a) the personal and professional benefits of evaluating and developing your knowledge, understanding and skills;

b) the requirements of the National Standards;

c) the requirements of the Driver Training Standards;

d) the DVSA's standards check requirements, and how they will be assessed;

e) any regulatory requirements for continuing professional development;

f) the performance and knowledge requirements of any other body by which you are employed;

g) how to obtain feedback on your performance in a non-defensive way;

h) current developments in driver training practice;

i) how to evaluate your own performance against requirements;

j) how to recognise where gaps in your skills, knowledge or understanding are affecting your performance;

k) the opportunities for formal and informal professional development available through your employers or other providers;

l) how to record and evaluate your professional practice in a reflective log;

m) how to build an achievable development plan and set yourself realistic objectives and priorities;

n) how to monitor your performance against.

Developing and using role-play programmes

This unit is about developing and implementing a programme of role play for those training to be driving instructors. The role play will help trainee instructors to learn how to deal with situations that they may come across with their learners.

You will know when role play is appropriate to use as a training method, and be aware of the strengths and limitations of its use. You will be able to brief the trainee instructor and undertake a variety of roles yourself as a trainer. You will be able to make sure the role play develops the trainee instructor's confidence by using accurate and supportive feedback. You will know when to close the role play and be able to help the trainee instructor to understand the learning achieved.

You will appreciate the importance of, and need to comply with, relevant health and safety practices and road traffic legislation in all role play activity.

This unit contains two elements:

Element 6.6.1 – Develop a programme of role play

Element 6.6.2 – Implement a programme of role play

Element 6.6.1 – Develop a programme of role play

This element is about developing a realistic programme of role play to be used with trainee instructors.

Performance standards

You must be able to:

1 identify when role-play could be an effective training activity;

2 design role-play activities that are realistic, reliable and credible;

3 make sure that the role play is relevant to the needs of trainee instructors;

4 define learning outcomes for each role-play situation;

5 plan routes that are suitable for each role-play situation;

6 plan simulation that makes sure that you, the trainee instructor and other road users are not put at risk.

Knowledge and understanding requirements

You must know and understand:

a) the strengths and limitations of role-play;

b) how to develop role-play situations that meet the needs of the trainee instructor;

c) when the use of role-play is helpful, and when to use other methods;

d) the types of faults and style of driving or riding common to various types of learners;

e) for which situations role-play is not a safe training method.

Element 6.6.2 – Use a programme of role play

This element is about using the programme of role play with trainee instructors, and managing the role play effectively and safely.

Performance standards

You must be able to:

1 make sure that the instructor is briefed on the learning outcome(s) of the role play;

2 brief the trainee instructor on how you will manage the role play, for example how you will communicate with them during the role play and how you will give feedback;

3 make sure the trainee instructor knows when you are in or out of role;

4 make sure that your behaviour is consistent with the brief you have given to the trainee instructor;

5 stay in role while the role play is meeting the learning outcome(s) and close the role play when it is not meeting the learning outcome(s);

6 maintain the focus of the role play on the learning outcome(s);

7 scan the driving space and plan your driving or riding so that you have all-round awareness at all times;

8 make sure that safe practices are followed while in role:

- verbal simulation of high-risk faults where possible;
- threatening unsafe manoeuvres without actually making the manoeuvre;
- portrayal of high-risk attitudes that act as a barrier to safe and responsible driving, where appropriate.

9 manage the balance of risk and simulation so that neither you nor the trainee instructor is overloaded;

10 adapt the level of fault simulation to match the trainee instructor's ability;

11 use situations that develop on road to your advantage, while maintaining safety;

12 show realistic improvement when the trainee instructor identifies and targets a development need;

13 remember details of the drive while in role, so that you can give feedback when out of role;

14 give accurate and supportive feedback to help the trainee instructor to develop good instructional technique and safe practices.

Knowledge and understanding requirements

You must know and understand:

a) how to give the trainee instructor a brief on the purpose of and arrangements for the role play;

b) the importance of supporting the brief by:

- communicating in a way that does not alter the trainee instructor's perception of you as a learner;
- driving or riding in a way that does not alter the trainee instructor's perception of you as a learner;
- reacting realistically to the trainee instructor's responses.

c) how to make it clear when role play begins and ends, and recognise when to end the role play;

d) techniques for scanning the driving space and planning your driving whilst also observing the trainee instructor;

e) the safe practices and legislation relevant to the role play, and:

- that no faults can be committed that contravene the rules of the road or affect other road users;

- that no faults that involve vulnerable road users should be committed;

- how to simulate risky attitudes;

- what types of faults you can simulate verbally.

f) how to deliver accurate and supportive feedback to the trainee instructor.

Notes and discussion points

1 Instructors deliver agreed syllabuses using a 'client-centred' approach.

The emphasis here is on the word 'agreed'. Once the goal for the lesson has been agreed, the instructor needs to discuss with the pupil how best to deliver the actual lesson. This means taking into account the pupil's preferred learning style and determining with the pupil whether they need information before they have a go for the first time and whether that information needs to be in the form of an explanation or a demonstration, for example. To use a 'client-centred' approach means encouraging the pupil to take responsibility for their learning by asking questions and listening carefully to the answers in order to determine the best way forward for the pupil's needs and ability.

2 Using a client-centred learning approach is about maximising learning by taking into account the status, prior experience and particular needs of the learner.

Making an assessment of the individual pupil's stage of understanding and skills is an important element in the process of any client-centred learning. The pupil must be engaged in the learning if they are to benefit from it. The status of the pupil means taking into consideration whether they are a complete beginner, partly trained or a full licence holder and adapting the delivery of the lesson accordingly. The pupil will have prior experience even if this is as a passenger or riding a bicycle or even as a pedestrian. The particular needs of the learner will be determined by assessing their learning preferences or whether they have any specific learning difficulties, such as being dyslexic.

3 A learner-centred instructor is able to adjust an outline programme to meet the needs of the learner by taking account of prior learning and identifying issues as the training progresses.

This includes starting from what the pupil knows and can do, building towards what they do not know or cannot yet do, and then modifying the programme as and when required to suit the individual pupil's needs and the particular circumstances that arise during the training.

4 Use best-practice tools, techniques, and exercises to support transfer of ownership of the learning process.

Client-centred learning and the use of coaching skills involves using all strategies and methods at our disposal to achieve effective learning outcomes. This can include direct instruction, intervention, demonstration, explanation, as appropriate to the particular situation.

Ideally, pupils should be encouraged to take responsibility right from the start. This does not necessarily mean that the pupil has to make difficult decisions about major traffic or safety issues at an early stage, but it does mean that they will feel a responsibility to take ownership of their development as a driver.

This transfer of responsibility is much more effective if the pupil is involved in the decision making by identifying goals and objectives from an early stage.

5 Plan routes for on-road training sessions that provide safe, legal and effective learning opportunities.

Most ADIs, including many experienced instructors, could improve their awareness and expertise in the area of effective route planning. This is a topic that is not often dealt with in instructor training – probably because it is not currently an exam subject. Too often we see instructors using routes that are totally inappropriate for the pupil's capability.

If the routes you choose, just because they happen to be nearby, are not properly planned it will not be possible to assess the pupil's development accurately. In this situation you will not necessarily be able to distinguish between errors that are down to the pupil's lack of skill or understanding and those that have been made simply because of the unnecessary complexity of the route.

A properly chosen route will be within the pupil's capability, but will stretch their ability in a controlled way, by having an appropriate level of difficulty. It will allow your pupils to drive with a reasonable amount of independence without the need for too much control by the instructor.

Ideally, the chosen route will allow the pupil and instructor to concentrate on the particular training topic without too many distractions.

6 **'Client-centred' is taken to mean, broadly, the same as 'student-centred' or 'learner-centred'.**

Although the DVSA use the term client-centred learning in all their documentation, this expression is usually taken to mean much the same as 'coaching'. The main variation is that, whereas the DVSA feel that coaching is only 'one tool in the toolbox', most trainers agree that coaching is the toolbox and that there are techniques that can be used, including direct instruction, demonstration, explanation, effective questioning, etc. It can be helpful to view a client-centred approach as the overall umbrella and then select the appropriate tool to facilitate the pupil's learning most effectively. A client-centred approach is one where the relationship between the pupil and the instructor is equal and the instructor believes that the pupil has all the resources they need in order to learn to drive safely. It is up to the instructor to draw from the pupil the knowledge, skills and understanding. To do this, the instructor, with agreement from the pupil, would sometimes coach and sometimes give direct instruction, especially where it is essential to keep the car safe.

7 **Client-centred learning is not about the learner taking charge of the learning process and deciding what is going to happen. It is about creating a conversation.**

In a coaching conversation the instructor encourages the learner to set their own goals. The instructor needs to facilitate the conversation to ensure that the goal for the lesson is specific, measured, achievable, realistic and time-defined. It is important that the instructor guides this discussion as they are responsible for the safety of the environment. Encouraging the pupil to take responsibility for their learning means that the pupil becomes aware of their strengths, limitations and development needs, and develops skills that they can take forwards into their everyday driving decisions once they have passed the driving test. There is more chance of creating longer-term learning and understanding by using a client-centred approach and using appropriate coaching skills to suit the individual situation.

8 **Within the learner-centred approach there is a legitimate role for well-delivered explanation and demonstration.**

As with coaching, this means using various methods and strategies to suit the individual pupil and the particular situation.

If a particular strategy is required, including direct instruction, in order to achieve the desired learning outcomes it can be used within the context of client-centred learning. Ideally, while setting the goals, the pupil would be encouraged to work out for themselves how best to practice and what information they will need in order to ensure they are able to achieve their goals. The instructor may well need to give an explanation or a demonstration during this process.

9 **Frequent explanations and demonstrations can be supportive for some learners; for others this may be de-motivating.**
A varied approach is needed to suit the individual pupil as well as the circumstances of a particular lesson.

By getting to know your pupils and understanding their particular needs, you will be able to decide as and when they might benefit from a varied approach. Many people are kinaesthetic learners, which means they benefit most from learning through trial and error and trying things out for themselves with little, if any explanation. Providing the instructor ensures that the environment is safe and is ready to step in if a safety-critical situation develops, it is very effective for the pupil to learn by having a go.

10 **Transfer the balance of responsibility for their learning process to the learner as soon as they are ready to take it.**
If the pupil is simply told what to do, any learning will be of a short-term nature, but if they are encouraged to take an active part in 'owning' a particular task, there will be much more longer-term, effective learning. If the pupil and instructor together review the goal that was set at the beginning of the lesson, progress can be measured. The learner needs to be able to work independently and the sooner they feel able to do this, the more effective will be their learning.

Please note:

This chapter contains public sector information licensed under the Open Government Licence v2.0.

Chapter 3 dealt with using coaching skills and client-centred learning. The next two chapters deal with how to apply the National Standard criteria in the ADI Standards Check.

07
Goal setting and risk management

This chapter describes a model for goal setting and risk management. The model can be used in all driver training and ensures that a great lesson is being delivered where learning is taking place and value for money is given. The model works for both the Part 3 exam and the ADI Standards Check because it is a simplified representation of the Standards Check marking sheet.

Over- and under-instruction

Driving instructors often come back from a Standards Check saying the examiner commented that they had over-instructed or under-instructed. This is a difficult comment to understand if it is taken as a broad, sweeping statement. There is no such thing as over- or under-instruction on its own. The comment means that the driving instructor has used the wrong amount of instruction in a given situation or at a given time. It will boil down to the fact that either the goal was not being achieved or the risk was not being managed because the instructor was saying too much or too little at particular points in the lesson.

If it has been suggested that the instructor was over-instructing, they may think that the solution is to talk less during their lessons. But you can guarantee that the instructor will then end up not giving the pupil enough help where it is needed because the instructor hasn't identified where they were over-instructing. Of course, the instructor may just talk too much throughout the lesson and this is where the model is really helpful because it helps identify how much 'talk' or 'input' is needed at each stage of the lesson in order to achieve the goal and manage the risk.

Context

Over-instruction or under-instruction can happen in two distinct areas:

- whilst helping the pupil to achieve the goal;
- whilst managing the risk.

It is important to know the precise context in which the instructor has been over- or under-instructing. Was it whilst helping the pupil achieve the goal? Was the instructor giving full talk-through when the pupil clearly needed to have a go on their own – and, in fact, had asked to have a go on their own? Or did the instructor sit back and say nothing when the pupil clearly needed help? Or, was it whilst managing the risk so that the pupil could achieve the goal? It might be that the pupil has said they want to have a go on their own in terms of the goal they want to achieve, and the instructor has sat back and said nothing. This is okay, but what about the risk? For example, if the goal is something to do with emerging from junctions and it has been agreed that the pupil will have a go on their own and practise emerging from three or four junctions before pulling over to review progress, the instructor still needs to manage the risk. This means that you should consider how much, if any, support the pupil will need in managing any other situations that occur. There is a possibility of both over- and under-instruction around the risk, even if the instructor sticks to the agreed level of support around the goal.

Instructor's input

To deliver a lesson that will ensure learning takes place and value for money is being given, be clear on the level of input needed. Input means, quite simply, what you need to say (or do). This is where the model for goal setting and risk management comes in:

You have two opportunities for input:

- firstly, to ensure the pupil achieves the goal;
- and secondly, to manage the risk, so that the pupil will achieve the goal.

Let's look at each of these in turn.

Goal setting

Going down the left-hand side of the model first, your main priority is to ensure the pupil achieves the goal. This is how learning takes place and it is all part of how you plan the lesson. Lesson planning includes:

- identifying the learner's goal(s);
- agreeing the structure;
- confirming suitable practice areas; and
- adapting the lesson plan if necessary, to ensure the pupil achieves the goal.

The goal for the session needs to be SMART. SMART stands for:

- specific;
- measurable;
- achievable;
- realistic; and
- timed.

It is not always practical to set the goal completely at the start of the session and you may well find that some elements of SMART fall into place later into the session. For example, the measurable, achievable, realistic and timed aspects of SMART may become apparent as you agree the lesson structure, practice areas and get the car on the move.

Here's an example.

Instructor: 'Today we're going to look at roundabouts. What would you like to focus on first?' (SPECIFIC)

Pupil: 'The approach to roundabouts.' (SPECIFIC)

Instructor:	'Okay and what do you want to achieve by the end of the session?' (ACHIEVABLE)
Pupil:	'I want to feel confident about the approach to roundabouts.' (ACHIEVABLE)
Instructor:	'So, on a scale of 0 to 10, where 0 is "I don't feel at all confident about approaching roundabouts" and 10 is "I am totally confident about approaching roundabouts", where are you now?' (REALISTIC)
Pupil:	'About a 3.' (REALISTIC)
Instructor:	'Where would you like to be by the end of the session?' (MEASURABLE)
Pupil:	'A 6 would be good.' (MEASURABLE)
Instructor:	'So, what is in the 3?' (REALISTIC)
Pupil:	'Well, I've done junctions and understand how to deal with these. I'm okay with the MSM and PSL on the approach to junctions – whether I'm turning into side roads or emerging. I can see that roundabouts are similar but I'm concerned about the speed on approach because I know that I should aim to keep the car moving if I can, whereas at junctions I'm more likely to come almost to a stop because the visibility is closed on the approach.' (REALISTIC)
Instructor:	'That's great. You've told me your main concern is the speed on the approach because roundabouts tend to be open and are designed to keep the flow of traffic moving. So, what help do you need from me to get you up to a 6 and how long do you want to spend on this?' (TIMED)
Pupil:	'If I could go and practise a few and you could just help me where you think I need it, that would be good. Could we just spend half an hour and then look at something else?' (TIMED)
Instructor:	'Okay, I have a circuit in mind. There are four roundabouts on it. We go left at the first one, straight ahead at the second, right at the third and right at the fourth, finishing back here. How about if we practise that now? I will aim to let you get on with the approach to each of these on your own, because that's what we have just agreed – the goal is the approach each time. When we pull up again, we can review how you have got on and decide what to do next to

improve. We will just spend half an hour on this and then move on to something else. How does that sound?'

Pupil: 'Great.'

The above example is somewhat contrived to make the point about SMART goals, but what you may notice is that a SMART goal will often address the first three bullet points in lesson planning:

- identifying the learner's goal(s);
- agreeing the structure; and
- confirming suitable practice areas.

As the instructor, you are now clear on what needs to happen in terms of your 'input' once the car gets moving, to achieve the goal. The pupil wants to move from a 3 to a 6 in their level of confidence about approaching roundabouts. You know that they may well struggle with the speed on approach because they have expressed this as a concern. You have selected a route with four roundabouts, and the pupil wants to have a go approaching these on their own.

Managing the risk

Now, you need to work your way down the right-hand side of the model and ensure that the risk is managed so that the pupil can achieve the goal.

You cannot judge what input to have into risk management until you have confirmed the goal. If the goal is too vague and not specific enough, you will not understand how to manage the risk and, therefore, the pupil will not be able to achieve the goal. This is key. The model shows how the two aspects go together – goal setting and managing the risk.

To do this, you need to visualise the route you will be driving on – the four roundabouts – and consider what else is on this route that could interfere with your pupil's ability to achieve the goal. The pupil's goal is to gain confidence when approaching roundabouts. This will happen most effectively if you encourage the pupil to experiment and work things out for themselves. In terms of the roundabouts, the pupil does not need to focus on anything other than the approach, and it is down to you, the instructor, to break the learning down sufficiently so that the pupil can do just this.

The pupil might not deal with the emerge, going around or exiting of the roundabout but these are not part of the goal and it is your job to manage the risk and keep the car safe. It doesn't matter if the pupil has previously been emerging, going around and exiting the roundabout on their own. It is possible that, because they are focusing on the approach, the rest goes to pieces. However, if it is a complete disaster and you are struggling to manage the risk and keep the car safe, you might have agreed a goal and chosen a route that is too demanding for both of you. You might need to adapt the lesson plan because the pupil is not going to be able to achieve the goal and all you are doing is managing the risk, which will feel a bit like fire-fighting, where you are basically dealing with faults. In this situation, learning will not be taking place, because of your input.

Once the goal is agreed and you both know how the pupil wants to practise and learn, you need to manage the risk.

The pupil wants to have a go at this on their own so that they can evaluate their progress and determine what they need to further do each time to improve. We know that people learn best when they can experiment in a safe environment and work out for themselves what they need to do to improve. This is why you need to manage the risk to create the safe environment. Having agreed the goal, the next thing you need to state is how the responsibility for risk will be shared.

You might say: 'You're going to concentrate on the goal, which is to improve your confidence in approaching roundabouts. I will let you have a go at this on your own and will step in if I need to help keep us safe. I will also help you with everything else – you know I've got the dual controls so I can use these if I need to.'

Imagine your pupil is now on the circuit, dealing with the four roundabouts. The goal is to increase their confidence in their ability to approach the roundabouts from a 3 to a 6. They're turning left at the first one, going straight ahead at the second and turning right at the third and fourth. To manage the risk after you have made your statement about sharing responsibility, you need to be able to:

- give clear and well-timed directions and instructions;
- observe the pupil and the surroundings;
- step in verbally or physically appropriately;
- give sufficient feedback for any safety-critical incidents.

If you are in any doubt about your pupil's ability to deal with something safely, you will need to intervene, but note that the word here is 'safely'. The pupil might get it wrong and make mistakes, but with you managing the risk they will be better able to achieve their goal because they can learn from their own mistakes. In other words, you should let your pupil make mistakes in a safe environment because this is how learning takes place; it is your job to create the safe environment by managing the risk.

It can be helpful to see the risk as two-fold – within the goal and outside of the goal.

Risk within the goal

Let's look at two examples.

Example 1   You have agreed that the pupil will complete four roundabouts before pulling over to review progress around the goal. The pupil wants to be able to get on and have a go on their own. You have stated that you will manage the risk and help them where necessary with other things, but let them get on with the approaches. The pupil approaches the first roundabout too fast.

You consider the risk and judge that the approach speed, whilst too fast, is not going to cause a problem on this occasion. It will be a great discussion point when you pull over, and if they can recognise this for themselves and take steps to prevent it from happening on the next practice, they will be well on their way to achieving the goal. You decide to say nothing but keep an eye on it to make sure that if the speed on the approach is too fast on the second, third or fourth roundabout and safety is in any way compromised, you will step in.

When you pull up after the fourth roundabout, you will discuss with the pupil:

- What went well?
- What didn't go so well?
- What needs improving?

This is all around the goal. In the 'what didn't go so well' or the 'what needs improving' parts of the evaluation, the speed on the approach will come up. It doesn't matter whether you bring it up or the pupil does, but the point of the exercise is to make sure the pupil achieves an appropriate speed on the approach to the roundabouts, and therefore goes on to achieve the goal – to increase their confidence about the approach from a 3 to a 6.

Example 2   This example is the same as previously, except that when the pupil approaches the first roundabout too fast, you judge that this is a definite risk and needs managing. It is important to recognise that you still need to leave the learning with the pupil about how to achieve the goal. Your job is to manage the risk, so you are not aiming to get the approach speed perfect; you just want it to be safe. You might therefore say, 'How's your speed?'

Of course, you have other options as well. If the pupil doesn't respond, or you have left it a little late, you might need a direct command like, 'Brake, you're a bit too fast.' Your final resort is the dual brake. If you have intervened either verbally or physically, you will need to consider what the pupil needs to know in order to understand the risk and why you intervened – what would have happened if you hadn't stepped in.

The second, third and fourth roundabouts will need to be prompted as far as the speed on the approach is concerned. You cannot allow the problem to occur again because, by stepping in, you judged it was safety critical. In other words, if you intervene verbally or physically, it is because an incident would have occurred otherwise. Again, you don't have to get the speed on the approach perfect. It just has to be safe.

Pull over after the circuit is completed and ask the reflective questions:

- What went well?
- What didn't go so well?
- What needs improving?

This time you need to ensure that sufficient feedback is used to help the pupil understand any potential safety-critical incidents because you had to intervene to keep the car safe by telling the pupil to slow down more on the approach to the first roundabout. As this is part of the goal, you would need to agree with the pupil what they are going to do next time to ensure they do not need your intervention again, and also, what they need to do to get the approach speed right.

Risk outside of the goal

It is highly likely that there will be potential risk outside of the goal that needs managing. This is because you are teaching the pupil to drive in a safety-critical environment where there are plenty of hazards and risks that will get in the way of them being able to concentrate on achieving the goal. If we could teach someone to drive in a simulator there would be minimal other risks, but we are teaching people to drive in a dangerous environment.

The goal is to do with roundabouts and there are four opportunities for the pupil to practise their approach to roundabouts, but what else is there that has the potential to get in the way? Here are some examples of the kind of things that might get in the way of the pupil remaining focused on the goal:

- everything else to do with roundabouts that is not to do with the approach, such as:
  - identifying the roundabout;
  - emerging onto the roundabout;
  - going around the roundabout;
  - exiting the roundabout;
- ordinary junctions;
- pedestrian crossings;
- meeting situations;
- changing gears smoothly;
- general positioning;
- use of mirrors;
- use of signals;
- use of speed.

Your own learning takes place through reflection and self-evaluation. Reflect on the model after a lesson and consider the amount of input you had in the lesson.

Did I have enough input into the lesson so that the pupil achieved the goal, and did I manage the risk sufficiently for the pupil to achieve the goal?

08
The ADI Standards Check

The ADI Standards Check is a legal requirement for all ADIs. To maintain your ADI qualification you are required to take at least one Standards Check in each four-year period of registration.

The Check is conducted with a DVSA examiner observing a normal lesson lasting one hour. You must provide the pupil and a suitable car. For full details of these requirements, see *The Driving Instructor's Handbook*.

In the previous chapter we gave details of the national standard for driver training. These standards set out the skills, knowledge and understanding that are needed in order to be an effective driver trainer.

During the Standards Check you are assessed against three broad or 'high' areas of competence:

- lesson planning;
- risk management; and
- teaching and learning strategies.

Each of these criteria is dealt with in detail later in the chapter.

These three areas of competence are broken down further into 17 lower-level competences, and a mark is given for each of these competences.

Lesson planning

Did the trainer identify the pupil's learning goals and needs?

Was the agreed lesson structure appropriate for the pupil's experience and ability?

Were the practice areas appropriate?

Was the lesson plan adapted, when appropriate, to help the pupil work towards their learning goals?

Risk management

Did the trainer ensure that the pupil fully understood how the responsibility for risk would be shared?

Were the directions and instructions given to the pupil clear and given in good time?

Was the trainer aware of the surroundings and the pupil's actions?

Was any verbal or physical intervention by the trainer timely and appropriate?

Was sufficient feedback given to help the pupil understand any potential safety-critical incidents?

Teaching and learning strategies

Was the teaching and learning style suited for the pupil's level of ability?

Was the pupil encouraged to analyse problems and take responsibility for their learning?

Were opportunities and examples used to clarify learning outcomes?

Was the technical information given comprehensive, appropriate and accurate?

Was the pupil given appropriate and timely feedback during the session?

Were the pupil's queries followed up and answered?

Did the trainer maintain an appropriate non-discriminatory manner throughout the session?

At the end of the session – was the pupil encouraged to reflect on their own performance?

For each of these competences a mark is given on a scale of 0–3:

3 – Competence demonstrated in all elements
2 – Competence demonstrated in most elements
1 – Competence demonstrated in a few elements
0 – No evidence of competence

Score	Description
3	Keep up the good work
2	Acceptable – there are clear areas of improvement
1	Not acceptable – more work needed
0	Completely unacceptable

These marks are added together to give an overall mark and they will also provide a profile of the areas where you have any strengths and where you might need to do some more development work.

If you get a total score of 43 or more you will be given a Grade A.

With a total score of between 31 and 42 you will be given a Grade B.

You will fail the Standards Check if:

- you get a score of 7 or less for the 'Risk Management' category;
- the examiner stops the lesson because you have put yourself or someone else in danger; or
- you have a total score of 30 or less (out of a possible 51).

In a later section we look at each of the competences in turn and how we can check that they are being addressed. It is important to remember that the Standards Check is simply a way of assessing what we are doing in our day-to-day business and therefore these competences should be part of your everyday driver training. The Standards Check will be straightforward if you are practising these competences on a regular basis.

The key thing to understand is that the lower-level competences can themselves be broken down into elements. You will have to use a range of skills to ensure each of these elements is in place.

Total score	Grade	Description
0 to 30	Fail	Your performance is unsatisfactory
31 to 42	Grade B	You will be added to the register of ADIs or remain on it
43 to 51	Grade A	You have shown a high standard of instruction, and will be added to the register or remain on it

Note: If you do not reach an acceptable standard in three consecutive Standards Checks, the ADI Registrar can start the process of removing you from the register.

For example, the first lower-level competence, in the lesson-planning section, is 'Did the ADI identify the pupil's learning goals and needs?'

To fully satisfy this requirement you must:

- actively recognise the need to understand the pupil's experience and background;
- ask suitable questions;
- encourage the pupil to talk about their goals, concerns etc and actively listen to what the pupil has to say;
- understand the significance of what the pupil says; and
- recognise other indications, for example body language, that the pupil is trying to express something but perhaps cannot find the right words.

Competence standards examples

An ADI who grasps the importance of understanding the pupil's needs and makes a real effort to do so, but who finds it difficult to frame suitable questions, would be demonstrating competence in most elements and would be marked 2. Your performance is regarded as acceptable but there are clear areas where you could improve.

An ADI who makes an attempt, asks a few questions, but doesn't really listen and then goes ahead and does what they intended to do regardless, would be demonstrating a few elements of competence and would be marked 1. This is indicating that your performance is not acceptable and that you may need to do a lot more work, even though you have given evidence of knowing what you are supposed to be doing.

An ADI who makes no attempt to understand their pupil's needs would be demonstrating no evidence of competence and be marked 0.

If the examiner gives a score of 3 they are effectively saying that this is an area where you do not need to do any further work, apart from continuously reflecting on your performance.

The maximum mark is 51 and the score achieved will dictate the final grade. Whatever the overall marks, you will automatically fail if:

- you achieve a score of 7 or less on the 'risk management' section; or
- at any point in the lesson, you behave in a way which puts you, the examiner, the pupil or any third party in immediate danger so that the lesson has to be stopped.

Standards Check Form SC1

INFORMATION

鑾
Driver & Vehicle
Standards
Agency

Trainer Name		Location		Outcome
PRN		Date	/ /	
		Dual Controls	Yes ☐ No ☐	
Valid Certificate	Yes ☐ No ☐	Reg No.		
		Accompanied?	QA ☐ Trainer ☐ Other ☐	

ASSESSMENT

Pupil: Beginner ☐ Partly Trained ☐ Trained ☐ FLH New ☐ FLH Experienced ☐

Lesson theme: Junctions ☐ Town & city driving ☐ Interacting with other road users ☐
Dual carriageway/faster moving roads ☐ Defensive driving ☐ Effective use of mirrors ☐
Independent driving ☐ Rural roads ☐ Motorways ☐ Eco-safe driving ☐
Recap a manoeuvre ☐ Commentary ☐ Recap emergency stop ☐ Other ☐

	Competence			
	0	1	2	3
	No evidence	Demonstrated in a few elements	Demonstrated in most elements	Demonstrated in all elements

LESSON PLANNING

	0	1	2	3
Did the trainer identify the pupil's learning goals and needs?				
Was the agreed lesson structure appropriate for the pupil's experience and ability?				
Were the practice areas suitable?				
Was the lesson plan adapted, when appropriate, to help the pupil work towards their learning goals?				
Score for lesson planning				

RISK MANAGEMENT

	0	1	2	3
Did the trainer ensure that the pupil fully understood how the responsibility for risk would be shared?				
Were directions and instructions given to the pupil clear and given in good time?				
Was the trainer aware of the surroundings and the pupil's actions?				
Was any verbal or physical intervention by the trainer timely and appropriate?				
Was sufficient feedback given to help the pupil understand any potential safety critical incidents?				
Score for risk management				

TEACHING & LEARNING STRATEGIES

	0	1	2	3
Was the teaching style suited to the pupil's learning style and current ability?				
Was the pupil encouraged to analyse problems and take responsibility for their learning?				
Were opportunities and examples used to clarify learning outcomes?				
Was the technical information given comprehensive, appropriate and accurate?				
Was the pupil given appropriate and timely feedback during the session?				
Were the pupil's queries followed up and answered?				
Did the trainer maintain an appropriate non-discriminatory manner throughout the session?				
At the end of the session – was the pupil encouraged to reflect on their own performance?				
Score for teaching and learning strategies				
Overall score				

REVIEW

	YES	NO
Did the trainer score 7 or less on Risk Management? (A 'Yes' response to this question will result in an automatic Fail)		
At any point in the lesson, did the trainer behave in a way which put you, the pupil or any third party in immediate danger, so that you had to stop the lesson? (A 'Yes' response to this question will result in an automatic Fail)		
Was advice given to seek further development?		

Feedback offered to trainer

Examiner Name		Signature	

C 1/2014

The Road Traffic Act 1988 (as amended) states that continued registration as an ADI is subject to the condition that they will undergo a test of 'continued ability and fitness to give instruction', known as a standards check, as and when required by the Registrar. The standards check allows one of the Agency's examiners to check that your instruction is up to the required standard, by accompanying you while you conduct a normal lesson.

Assessment Notes
This form is designed to identify the strengths in your instructional ability and to highlight any areas which you may need to develop. The form is provided in conjunction with verbal feedback with the aim of helping you improve your instructional ability.

Criteria for Scoring
Assessment is against three broad areas of competence:

– Lesson planning

– Risk management

– Teaching and learning strategies

A full description regarding the assessment can be found in the 'National standard for driver and rider training', available on WWW.GOV.UK (Teaching people to drive)

ADI Grades
Assessing the lower competencies will represent a 'profile' of Instructional Competence.

Score	Description	Grade
0 – 30	Unsatisfactory performance	FAIL
31 – 42	Sufficient competence demonstrated to permit or retain entry on the Register of Approved Driving Instructors	GRADE B
43 – 51	A high overall standard of instruction demonstrated	GRADE A

Note: If you score 7 or less in the Risk Management section the standards check will be deemed substandard and a Fail. Also, if the examiner believes your behaviour is placing you, the pupil or any third party in immediate danger they may stop the lesson and record an immediate Fail.

Appeals
You cannot appeal against the examiner's decision. You may appeal to a Magistrate's Court or, in Scotland, the Sheriff's office, if you consider that your test was not conducted properly.

Before you consider making any appeal you may wish to seek legal advice.

The examiner will assess your competence to deliver effective driving instruction. The 'National standard for driver training' is expressed in terms of learning outcomes and there may be more than one way for you to achieve those outcomes. Of course, if you do something or say something that is clearly wrong this will be picked up, especially where it could lead to a safety issue. However, the overall approach by the examiner is focused on recognising achievement and promoting improvement and development – rather than purely identifying faults. Your task is to provide an effective learning experience for the pupil. This is judged to be one in which the pupil is supported to take as much responsibility as possible for their learning process.

Where it is correct and safe to do so, feel free to introduce wider issues from the driving standard into the lesson. This could include assessing the pupil's personal fitness to drive, the use of alcohol or drugs, or dealing with aggression. If, for example, a pupil offers an inappropriate comment about the use of alcohol it would be appropriate for you to challenge this.

Similarly, it would be appropriate for you to encourage the pupil to think through what might happen, in particular situations, if the conditions were different. For example, after negotiating a particularly difficult junction it might be helpful to discuss how different it would be at night or in bad weather. The important thing to remember here is that the most effective learning takes place when the pupil finds the answers for themselves.

If opportunities arise for discussion of issues between you and the pupil while on the move, these can be used, but this needs to be tailored to the pupil's ability and should not create distraction. Too many unnecessary instructions can both de-motivate the pupil and create a real hazard. You may be given more detailed feedback by the examiner relating to the competences against which you have been assessed:

- lesson planning;
- risk management; and
- teaching and learning strategies.

The purpose of feedback from the examiner is to help you understand where you might have failed to demonstrate full competence and where you might need to focus your efforts when undertaking further development.

The Standards Check form shows a 'profile' of your performance, against the individual competences. This will help you to see where you have given a strong performance as well as where you may need development.

Typical lessons

Partly trained inexperienced learner

Drivers at this stage of their career are likely to want/need experience of a steadily increasing variety of road and traffic conditions to enable them to develop their basic skills. They may have areas where they are uncomfortable or not yet competent, such as complex junctions or roundabouts, heavy or fast-moving traffic. They may not have a good understanding of theory, for example, of road signs and markings.

In this context the key objectives of the 'National standard for driver and rider training' include being able to:

- create a climate that promotes learning (element 6.3.1);
- explain and demonstrate skills and techniques (element 6.3.2);
- transfer the balance of responsibility for their learning process to the learner as soon as they are ready to take it.

You should be working to understand where the pupil is having difficulties and how you can help them develop sound basic skills. If you are not making the effort to understand, you are not demonstrating competence. By asking questions or staying silent and listening and watching you are clearly making the effort to understand and demonstrate competence. It doesn't matter if you don't achieve full understanding by the end of the lesson.

In the same way, pupils at this level should not feel they are being patronised or talked down to as this will make them unreceptive. They do not all learn in the same way.

Consequently, there is no single, correct way to transfer responsibility to them and, in any case, this is not going to take place instantly. In this context, just as it is unreasonable to expect a pupil to get it right instantly, so it is unreasonable to expect the instructor to transfer responsibility instantly. The key thing that you must demonstrate is that you understand the need to transfer ownership and make the effort to do so.

It is important to understand that, at this level, a pupil will not always 'get it right' as soon as the instructor gives them some direction or coaches them around a problem. You should understand the issue, at least in principle, and what you need to do in theory. Be willing to try to overcome weaknesses, but remember that your efforts may not always be successful. During the standards check the examiner will not penalise you if you do not immediately 'solve the problem'.

Use a variety of tools to encourage the pupil to analyse their own performance and to find solutions to problems. Be supportive and give suitable and technically correct instructions or demonstrations where appropriate. Of course, where a pupil cannot come up with a way forward you may decide to provide suitable input – especially if failure to do so might result in a risk to anyone else.

Experienced pupil – about ready to take their test

At this stage the key objective of the 'National standard for driver and rider training' is 'to work with the learner to agree when they are ready to undertake formal assessment of driving competence' (element 6.3.3).

Evidence suggests that, by this stage, some pupils may:

- be technically skilful;
- be able to complete manoeuvres competently;
- have experience of driving on a wide range of roads and in a range of conditions.

They may be confident and feel that they are at the stage of refining their competence around 'what they need to do to pass the test'. On the other hand, they may have:

- already developed bad habits, especially if they have been taught by a relative or friend;
- an inflated opinion of their competence;
- a poor understanding of risk;
- not developed the skills of scanning and planning that will help them to cope when they drive independently;
- not developed the skills of reflection that will help them to be life-long learners.

They may not be used to being challenged to analyse and come up with solutions. They could be impatient and resistant to correction if they do demonstrate 'bad habits'. They may well have forgotten a lot of what they learnt when they did their theory test. Responses at this level could vary from enthusiastic acceptance of the information they need, to real resistance to being told things they do not think are relevant.

During the Standards Check you must demonstrate that you understand the key issues that need to be addressed to try to reduce the numbers of newly qualified drivers who crash in the first six months. You should:

- develop a realistic understanding of ability and an enhanced understanding of risk;

- be checking, developing and reinforcing systematic scanning and planning tools;

- strongly encourage reflection;

- be supportive;

- not over-instruct; and

- give suitable and technically correct instructions or demonstrations where necessary.

However, the emphasis is likely to be on the use of tools, such as practical examples, to develop a more joined-up and outward-looking approach.

New full licence holder

This type of pupil will have demonstrated 'competence' against those elements of the national standards for driving that are tested in the theory and practical tests. Remember, however, that these tests are limited in scope. They do not require the pupil to drive on all classes of roads and they do not test understanding of that part of the national standards for driving which calls on learners to reflect on their competence as they go through their driving career. At this stage your objective is to develop the pupil's competence across the full range of driving environments and to support and reinforce their commitment to life-long learning around driving.

Reasons why an individual might come to an ADI for lessons at this stage include the following:

- Wanting to refresh their skills if they haven't driven since they took their test.

- Moving on to a bigger or technologically different vehicle.

- Starting to drive for work.

- Starting a family and wanting to improve their skills.

- Moving from an urban to a rural environment, or vice versa.

- Starting to use motorways.

- A simple desire to become a better-developed driver.

This pupil is likely to be enthusiastic and, in theory at least, open to learning if they have chosen to take training. If, on the other hand, they have been told to take it, perhaps by an employer, they might be resentful and resistant. They may well have already lost the disciplines of the mirror-signal-manoeuvre routine and forward-planning skills. They may not be used to driving in an 'eco-safe' way and may not even understand the term. They may be nervous about increased responsibility and accountability.

During the Standards Check the key thing that you must demonstrate is that you are able to find out exactly what it is the pupil wants from the lesson and put together a plan to deliver that. You must of course identify and deal with bad habits that might have been acquired. However, if all you do is go over what the pupil should have learnt prior to their test you are unlikely to reinforce the commitment to life-long learning.

Experienced full licence holder

At this stage this type of pupil should be more confident and competent than they were immediately after passing their test. They should have gained experience across all or most of the possible classes of roads, at night and in bad weather. They may already be driving for work and are likely to regard themselves as capable drivers, even though their application of safety routines and forward-planning skills may show they are not quite as competent as they think.

Reasons why an individual might come to an ADI at this stage include:

- being required by employers to undertake additional training to keep insurance costs down;
- wanting to drive more economically to reduce business costs;
- having had an accident or near miss that has shaken their confidence;
- returning to driving after a period of ill-health, injury or loss of licence;
- recognising that their driving skills are deteriorating through age or ill-health.

The pupil may be an overseas driver who has significant experience but, having been in the UK beyond the statutory period, is now required to take the tests to qualify for a UK licence.

Depending on their reasons for undertaking training, these pupils could be enthusiastic or very nervous, willing or very resistant. Older pupils may find it harder to learn new skills or to get out of bad habits. They may have

Reflecting on today's lesson	
Please consider filling in this reflective log – it's yours to keep and your comments may help you identify where you can make improvements in your performance.	
What went well today?	
What did not go as well today?	
What could I do to improve?	
Notes	

developed unsafe habits such as not leaving large enough separation distances and failing to carry out systematic observation routines.

In assessment the key thing is that you must demonstrate you can find out exactly what it is the pupil wants from the lesson and put together a plan to deliver that. You should, of course, spot and deal with bad habits that might have been acquired. However, the lesson must take the pupil forward in their learning. If it does not deliver what the pupil is looking for they will not engage with the learning process.

This is not an exhaustive list of possible scenarios, but it should give some indication of the sorts of things that should be considered.

Interpreting the assessment criteria

Lesson planning

The purpose of all driver training is to assess and develop the learner's skill, knowledge and understanding in relation to the contents of the National Standard for Driver Training. Research indicates that this is best achieved by placing the client at the centre of the learning process. In this context the assessment criteria will be interpreted as follows.

Did the trainer identify the pupil's learning goals and needs?

Usually this process will take place at the beginning of a lesson. However, where you and the pupil have been working together for some time prior to the Standards Check, you may have already laid down the basic structure of the pupil's learning goals. This is considered by the examiner when assessing this element.

If you have not worked with the pupil before it is perfectly OK for you to ask the pupil to undertake a demonstration/assessment drive. This should give a good idea of the pupil's level of competence and provide a basis for a discussion of the pupil's needs.

As the examiner observes the lesson they will be looking for indications that the elements which go to make up the low-level competence are being demonstrated. In this case the sorts of things that would show an indication of competence include:

- encouraging the pupil to say what they want from the lesson;
- asking questions to ensure understanding;
- checking understanding as the lesson progresses;
- listening to what the pupil is saying;
- taking note of body language.

During the assessment it's important that you:

- encourage the pupil to say what they want;
- ask questions to check understanding at the beginning and as the lesson progresses;
- listen to what the pupil is saying; and
- pick up on body language.

If you deal with all these topics you are likely to get a 3. If, on the other hand, you do all the listening bits but fail to spot the learner getting very tense and nervous in a particular situation you would probably get a 2. You would have demonstrated your understanding of the need to listen, etc, but have not yet developed the ability to spot non-verbal clues. Indications of a lack of competence could include:

- making assumptions about understanding or experience;
- failing to note negative or concerned comments or body language that show discomfort;
- undermining the pupil's confidence by continually asking questions clearly beyond the pupil's knowledge or understanding;
- pushing the pupil to address issues that they are not happy to talk about, unless there is a clear need, such as an identified risk or a safety-critical issue.

This is all about goal setting. The goal needs to be agreed with the pupil. This is done in the belief that the pupil knows best what they need to learn and achieve in each lesson. This might sound a strange thing to say if you are focused on technical skills and control of the vehicle. However, our behaviour is always motivated by our thoughts and feelings and individually we all think and feel very differently from the next person. The pupil might be reluctant initially to state their goals for a lesson because they may not know what they want to get out of a lesson. However, this is part of the learning curve every pupil is on – it is not just about learning how to control the vehicle, it is also about learning how their thoughts and feelings impact on their behaviour and learning how to regulate and manage their thoughts and feelings so that their behaviour is safe. One of the important first steps in this process is making choices.

Instructors often express reservations about allowing the pupil to choose what they want to do in a lesson because it interferes with what they are used to doing and the syllabus they want to work through. If you are focused on the driving test, then you will find this process difficult. However, while you are practising goal setting it is okay to stick with your syllabus and work on getting the pupil to define what they want to achieve by the end of the lesson' or how they want to feel' or what they most want to improve. You could, for example, say, 'OK, so today we are going to look at the reverse park, so what would you like to achieve by the end of the lesson?'

Was the agreed lesson structure appropriate for the pupil's experience and ability?

The lesson structure should allow the pupil to progress at a manageable rate; stretching them without overwhelming them. For example, a pupil who is concerned about entering roundabouts should not be asked to tackle a fast-flowing multi-lane, multi-exit junction as their first attempt. Neither should they be restricted to very quiet junctions, unless you identify a potential risk issue that they want to check out first.

Indications that all the elements of competence are in place could include:

- ensuring the pupil understands what they plan to do and agrees with that plan;
- a lesson that reflects the information given by the pupil and the learning goals they want to tackle;
- building in opportunities to check the statements made by the pupil before moving to more challenging situations;
- checking theoretical understanding.

Indications of lack of competence include: delivering a pre-planned, standard lesson that doesn't consider the pupil's expressed needs or concerns; failing to build in a suitable balance of practice and theory.

This competency is closely tied in with the previous one about setting a goal for the session. Having asked, 'What would you like to achieve by the end of the lesson?' the next question might be, 'How do you want to do this?' It is important that, having started to give the pupil responsibility for their learning, you don't take it back from them by assuming they need a briefing. It is often inappropriate for the pupil's experience and ability anyway to give a briefing. Many people already know everything they need in order to reverse into a parking space – and it depends on the goal they set for themselves. For example, if the pupil says that they simply want to be able to park accurately there may be no need to give a briefing that includes observations and control. They may simply want to have a go and see how they get on. This is then matched to their experience and ability.

Were the practice areas suitable?

You should use an area or route that allows the pupil to practise safely and helps them to achieve their goals. It should provide some stretch and challenge, but without taking them out of their comfort zone.

Indications that all the elements of competence are in place could include choosing a practice area/route that provides: a range of opportunities to address the agreed learning objectives; which challenges, but is realistic, in terms of the pupil's capabilities and confidence.

Indications of lack of competence include taking the pupil into an area that takes the pupil outside of their competence zone – so that they spend all their time 'surviving' and have no space left to look at learning issues – or exposes them to risks they cannot manage.

This is where you rely on your experience and expertise. It is important that you ensure the practice areas are appropriate and you may have to guide the pupil in this so that if they want to choose the area themselves you decide if it will be appropriate for their experience and ability. The conversation might go like this:

ADI: 'What would you like to do today?'

Pupil: 'Could I try reversing into a parking space?'

ADI: 'Do you have a reason for saying that?'

Pupil: 'Yes, I was watching my brother parking the other day and thought I would like to have a go at that.'

ADI: 'What would you like to achieve by the end of the lesson?'

Pupil: 'I would just like to get the car parked reasonably accurately.'

ADI: 'Okay, how do you want to do this?'

Pupil: 'Well, do you think I could just have a go? I could show you what my brother did.'

ADI: 'Yes, that's fine. Do you want me to give you directions to a suitable area because it's too busy here to do it?'

Pupil: 'Yes please.'

ADI: 'There will be a couple of roundabouts to deal with on the way. Would you like some help from me to deal with these?'

Pupil   'Yes please.'

Was the lesson plan adapted, when appropriate, to help the pupil work towards their learning goals?

You should be willing and able to adapt if your pupil:

- appears to be uncomfortable or unable to deal with the learning experience that you have set up; or

- suggests that it is not providing what they were looking for.

If the pupil's inability is creating a possible risk situation you must adapt quickly. This might require a few extra questions to clarify what is out of line. It may be that the problem is because of the teaching and learning style being used rather than because the overall plan is wrong. Whatever the reason for adapting the plan, you must make sure the pupil understands what they are doing and why.

Indications that all the elements of competence are in place could include:

- comparing the actual performance of the pupil with their claims and clarifying any differences;

- responding to any faults or weaknesses that undermine the original plan for the session;

- responding to any concerns or issues raised by the pupil;

- picking up on non-verbal signs of discomfort or confusion.

Indications of lack of competence include:

- persisting with a plan despite the pupil being clearly out of their depth;

- persisting with a plan despite the pupil demonstrating faults or weaknesses that should lead to a rethink of the plan;

- changing the plan without reason;

- failing to explain to the pupil why the plan has been changed.

Risk management

It is vital that all parties in any on-road training situation understand and are clear about where the responsibility lies for the safety of themselves, others in the vehicle and other road users.

There are two aspects to the management of risk in any training situation:

At all times you are responsible for your own safety, the safety of the pupil and the safety of other road users. In some circumstances this can extend to taking physical control of the vehicle to manage a safety-critical incident. If you fail in this basic responsibility, at any time, you will fail the Standards Check.

From a training point of view, you are also responsible for developing the pupil's awareness of and ability to manage risk (as the driver, the pupil also has responsibilities).

These are the aspects being assessed in this section.

Did the ADI make sure that the pupil fully understood how the responsibility for risk would be shared?

The 'balance of responsibility', between the pupil and the ADI, will inevitably vary in different circumstances. For example, compare the following two scenarios:

A pupil in the very early stages of their training, in a car fitted with dual controls.

In this situation it might be reasonable for you to start a lesson by saying something like:

> At all times I expect you to drive as carefully and responsibly as possible. I will expect you to be aware of other road users and to control the car. However, I do have the ability to take control of the car in an emergency. I will only use these controls when I feel that you are not dealing with the situation yourself. If that happens we will take some time to talk about what happened so that you understand for next time.

A pupil who has passed their driving test but has asked you to give them some additional training in their own car, which is much bigger and more technically advanced than the one they learnt in.

In this situation you might say something like:

> You have passed your test and I will therefore assume that you are taking full responsibility for our safety. I will be talking to you from time to time, but I will try to keep that to a minimum so that I don't distract you. If I am quiet don't worry; that just means I am comfortable with what you are doing. I will, of course, let you know if I see any risk that you appear to have missed.

However, such opening statements are not all that is involved in meeting this criterion. You should be managing this process throughout the lesson. So, for example, if the pupil makes some sort of mistake carrying out a manoeuvre you should, ideally, find an opportunity to analyse that mistake with the pupil. Having achieved an understanding of what went wrong you might then ask the pupil to try the manoeuvre again. At that point you should provide the pupil with clear information about what is required of them.

So, for example, you might say:

Let's try that manoeuvre again. I won't say anything. Just try to remember what we have just been talking about.

On the other hand, you may want to take back a bit of control and might say:

Let's try that again. I will talk you through it this time. Just follow my instructions.

You should work with the pupil to decide the best way of tackling the problem and that might mean a temporary change in the 'balance of responsibility'. The important thing is that the pupil knows what is expected of them.

Under test conditions there are no circumstances in which you can assume that the issue of risk management has been dealt with. Even if you and the pupil have had discussions about risk before the observed lesson, you must show that you are actively managing the issue for assessment purposes.

Indications that all the elements of competence are in place could include:

- asking the pupil what is meant by risk;
- asking the pupil what sorts of issues create risk, such as the use of alcohol or drugs;
- explaining clearly what is expected of the pupil and what the pupil can reasonably expect of you;
- checking that the pupil understands what is required of them when there is a change of plan or they are asked to repeat an exercise.

Indications of lack of competence include:

- failing to address the issue of risk management;
- giving incorrect guidance about where responsibility lies for management of risk;
- failing to explain how dual controls will be used;
- undermining the pupil's commitment to being safe and responsible, for example, by agreeing with risky attitudes to alcohol use;
- asking the pupil to repeat a manoeuvre or carry out a particular exercise without making sure that they understand what role you are going to play.

Once the goal has been agreed you must consider how to share the responsibility for risk. If the pupil has said they would like to practise something on their own, you might simply state that you will keep the car safe. In this instance, for example, the pupil may have agreed they would like to practise emerging from junctions on a route that might last a few minutes and involve three or four different junctions in a reasonably quiet area. The pupil has said that they would like to drive this route with no help from you, their instructor, so that they can concentrate on approaching the junctions, assessing their speed and visibility and choosing a safe gap. You must allow the pupil to do this and, at the same time, be prepared to step in with instruction or the use of dual controls where necessary to keep the car safe. Similarly, if the pupil has agreed that the goal for the lesson is the reverse park and that they will have achieved their goal if they can get the car manoeuvred into the space reasonably accurately, then it might be that you do the observations. This is sharing the responsibility for risk. The pupil will be able to focus on the accuracy and control part of the manoeuvre, while you look after the observations.

In both examples, the risk is shared to ensure that the pupil has the best possible chance of achieving the agreed goal.

Were directions and instructions given to the pupil clear and given in good time?

'Directions' should be taken to mean any instruction, such as 'turn left at the next junction' or 'try changing gear a little later'. Any input from you must be sufficient, timely and appropriate. It is important that you take account of the ability of your pupils when giving directions. Directions given late, or in a confusing or misleading way, do not allow the pupil to respond and can make weaknesses worse.

Too many unnecessary instructions can both de-motivate the pupil and create a real hazard. Remember it is an offence to use a mobile phone while driving because this is known to create a level of risk equivalent to or, in some cases, greater than driving while drunk. It cannot, therefore, be good practice to constantly bombard the pupil with unnecessary questions.

Indications that all the elements of competence are in place could include:

- clear, concise directions;
- ensuring the pupil understands what they plan to do and agrees with that plan;
- directions given at a suitable time so that the pupil can respond.

Indications of lack of competence include:

- giving confused directions;
- giving directions too late;
- giving unnecessary directions; and
- failing to recognise when your input is causing overload or confusion.

If directions and instructions are given clearly and in good time, then you are managing the risk effectively and enabling the pupil to focus on achieving the agreed goal. It might be that the pupil has decided they want to choose the route or drive on a previous route without directions. This is perfectly acceptable and, in this case, you would not be expected to give directions. However, you may still need to give instruction if this is what has been agreed, or if a safety-critical incident occurs. In these situations you must ensure that you are giving your instructions clearly and in good time.

'Right, turn left here' is a confusing direction where the trainer should have clearly stated, 'At the end of the road turn left' to avoid the pupil turning right into someone's driveway. Similarly, the timing of instructions and directions can be very distracting especially if the trainer barks them out late. This can actually increase the risk, of being involved in a crash simply because the pupil becomes distracted and confused and may make mistakes.

Was the trainer aware of the surroundings and the pupil's actions?

This question lies at the heart of the ADI's professional skill. You should be able to:

- take in the outside world;
- observe the actions of the pupil, including comments and body language;
- judge whether those actions are suitable in any given situation; and
- respond accordingly.

Any serious lapses in this area are likely to lead to a zero marking.

Being able to observe the road ahead and behind as well as the pupil's eyes, hands and feet is a vital part of risk management. It is your responsibility to ensure that the pupil is going to be able to cope safely with whatever presents itself on the road and to do this you have to be constantly assessing the whole of the environment.

Was any verbal or physical intervention by the trainer timely and appropriate?

The overall approach should be client-centred. Remember that there is a fine balance between giving enough input and giving too much.

When stationary it would be expected that inputs and interventions would take the form of a dialogue with the pupil. In the moving-car environment, you remaining silent and signalling your confidence in the pupil through your body language, is just as much a coaching input as asking a stream of questions. Clearly the most important 'interventions' are those that manage risk in a moving car. You would be expected to point out situations in which a risk or hazard might arise to your pupil. However, direct intervention to prevent a situation escalating may be needed. This criterion is primarily about your response in those situations.

Indications that all the elements of competence are in place could include:

- intervening in a way that actively supports the pupil's learning process and safety during the session;
- allowing the pupil to deal with situations appropriately;
- taking control of situations where the pupil is clearly out of their depth.

Indications of lack of competence include:

- ignoring a developing situation and leaving the pupil to flounder;
- taking control of a situation the pupil is clearly dealing with appropriately;
- constantly intervening when unnecessary;
- intervening inappropriately and creating distractions;
- undermining the pupil's confidence;
- reinforcing the instructor as the person who is in sole control of the lesson.

Say, for example, the pupil has agreed that they would like to focus on adequate clearance to parked vehicles along the high street. At the start of the session you have looked at the responsibility for risk and agreed that you will share the risk by ensuring that the pupil can focus on their goal while you manage any other hazards. On the route there is a pelican crossing, which, at first glance, looks safe. There is no need to mention the pelican crossing because the pupil's goal is, specifically, adequate clearance to parked cars.

It wouldn't be appropriate to talk about the pelican crossing if the pupil appears to be dealing with it OK and there is clearly no risk – unless pedestrian crossings are part of the goal for the session, or the pupil has clearly said that they want to be alerted to other hazards outside of their goal. This is to do with understanding how people learn and very often driving instructors disrupt the learner's learning by giving partly trained instruction. In many situations the learner will achieve far more understanding about how to practically apply their skills and assess the risk involved if they can carry out the task in silence. This raises their awareness of their personal strengths and limitations and therefore builds their responsibility. Constant verbal instruction while the car is moving can lead to a bombardment of the senses and a task overload where something has to give.

Nevertheless, if you need to intervene to keep the car safe then it really doesn't matter if there is a sensory overload. So, in the example shown earlier let's now imagine that a pedestrian approaches the crossing. You must now assess whether you will need to step in and take control in some way. There are four possible options to choose from:

- Option 1: There is no need to do anything. The pupil has already checked their mirror and eased off the gas in case the lights change.

- Option 2: The pupil has made no response and the lights are now starting to change. It is necessary to say something, and a question will keep the responsibility sitting with the pupil for longer. You could ask: 'Do you think you need to slow down for the lights ahead?' This is a leading question with an implicit call for action.

- Option 3: You decided to wait a little longer to see if the pupil was going to respond. You don't want to interfere too early with their achievement of the goal – adequate clearance to parked vehicles. However, it is clear that the pupil is not responding so a direct instruction is necessary, 'Slow down for the lights.'

- Option 4: You decided not to give a verbal instruction and must now take physical action as the pupil is not responding, the lights are on red and the pedestrian is crossing the road. You use the dual brake.

Was sufficient feedback given to help the pupil understand any potential safety-critical incidents?

If a safety-critical, or potentially critical, incident does occur it is vital that the pupil fully understands what happened and how they could have avoided or dealt with it better. Ideally the pupil should be supported to analyse the situation for themselves. However, it may be necessary for you to provide feedback if, for example, the pupil simply did not see a problem. That feedback should be given as soon as is practical after the incident.

Indications that all the elements of competence are in place could include:

- finding a safe place to stop and examine the critical incident;
- allowing the pupil time to express any fears or concerns the incident might have caused;
- supporting the pupil to reflect clearly about what happened;
- providing input to clarify aspects of the incident that the pupil does not understand;
- supporting the pupil to identify strategies for future situations;
- providing input where the pupil does not understand what they should do differently;
- checking that the pupil feels able to put the strategy in place;
- agreeing ways of developing that competence if the pupil feels the need.

Indications of lack of competence include:

- failing to examine the incident;
- taking too long to address issues generated by an incident;
- not allowing the pupil to explore their own understanding;
- telling the pupil what the solution is and not checking their understanding;
- failing to check the pupil's ability to put in place the agreed strategy.

Teaching and learning strategies

The important thing to remember when considering teaching and learning strategies is that it is about client-centred learning. The examiner's assessment is about whether you have been able help the pupil to learn in an active way.

There will be many times when it is useful to use a coaching technique. The principle that underpins coaching is that an engaged pupil is likely to achieve a higher level of understanding and that self-directed solutions will seem far more relevant. This applies in every situation, including instruction. Direct instruction is useful in helping a pupil in the early stages cope with new situations or supporting a pupil who is clearly struggling in a certain situation. Good coaching will use the correct technique at the correct time, matching the pupil's needs. In some cases you may need to give direct instruction through a particularly difficult situation. That instruction forms part of a coaching process if you then encourage the pupil to analyse the problem and take responsibility for learning from it. A good ADI will take every opportunity to reinforce learning.

Was the teaching style suited to the pupil's learning style and current ability?

You should take into account all that you understand about the pupil. Recognise that different pupils will have different preferred approaches to learning, although these may only emerge fully over a number of lessons. Some pupils may be very willing to learn actively, while others may want opportunities to reflect before they make the next step in their learning. You should at least be able to give evidence of their sensitivity to these issues. In a one-off session this will probably be best demonstrated by offering a range of options. Be prepared to adjust your approach if evidence emerges of a different preferred style.

It is impossible to force learning on a pupil. Progress is always determined by what the pupil is comfortable with. The skill is in recognising when the pupil stops learning. The pace of a session should be set by the pupil. On the other hand, a pupil should not be talked out of experimenting, if this is within safe bounds.

When coaching, you should ensure that the tools used are suitable. If a question and answer technique is used this should match the pupil's level of ability and encourage them to use a higher level of thinking to give a response. Asking closed questions of a pupil who is demonstrating a high level of ability, unless this is to check knowledge, is of little use. Asking open questions to a pupil of limited ability who is finding it difficult to achieve the task they have set for themselves may be very confusing. These are not hard and fast rules. The effectiveness of any question is assessed given the circumstances at the time.

Indications that all the elements of competence are in place could include:

- Actively working to understand how you can best support the pupil's learning process. (You might not achieve a full understanding in the session – it is the attempt that demonstrates competence.)

- Modifying your teaching style when or if you realise there is a need to do so.

- Providing accurate and technically correct demonstration, instruction or information. Giving technically incorrect instruction or information is an automatic fail if that input might lead to a safety-critical situation.

- Using practical examples and other similar tools to provide different ways of looking at a particular subject.

- Linking learning in theory to learning in practice.

- Encouraging and helping the pupil to take ownership of the learning process.

- Responding to faults in a timely manner.

- Providing enough uninterrupted time to practise new skills.

- Providing the pupil with clear guidance about how they might practise outside the session.

Indications of lack of competence include:

- adopting a teaching style clearly at odds with the pupil's learning style;
- failing to check with the pupil whether the approach they are taking is acceptable;
- failing to explore other ways of addressing a particular learning point;
- concentrating on delivering teaching tools rather than looking for learning outcomes;
- ignoring safety issues.

If you are in the habit of giving briefings to every one of your customers then you may be slowing down the learning of some of them, particularly if they have a more kinaesthetic learning preference. It is not necessarily true that the most effective way to learn is following the 'Explain – Demonstrate – Practice' (EDP) route. Unfortunately, for many of us, training to become a driving instructor was all about passing the Part 3 test with very little emphasis – if any – on how people learn; and now we have become conditioned to believe that this is therefore the way things should be.

Consider how you got on at school. Did you have teachers you preferred over others, or favourite subjects? Did everyone in your class share your preferences? 'Yes' and 'No' respectively is probably how you answered those two questions because everyone is different and each of us is unique in how we absorb and process information and therefore how we learn new things. Our interpretation of the world and our individual set of experiences, existing knowledge and understanding influence how we learn new knowledge and experiences.

When you are teaching someone to drive you need to adapt the way you teach to suit the way someone learns most effectively. This is not a hard and fast science and most people process information through several different channels. However, consider a situation where your customer is yawning while you are giving them a briefing. It is not necessarily because they were out partying the night before; it is far more likely to be because they are bored by your lengthy briefing and you need to change your method of communication.

Was the pupil encouraged to analyse problems and take responsibility for their learning?

A key part of the client-centred approach is development of active problem solving in the pupil. This means that you should provide time for this to happen and you have to stop talking for long enough for the pupil to do the work. The main point to remember, however, is that different pupils will respond to this invitation in different ways. Some may be able to do it instantly, in a discussion. Others may need to go away and reflect upon a particular problem. They may need to be pointed at readings or other inputs to help them get a handle on the issue. Pushing a pupil to come up with answers on the spot may be unproductive for some.

Indications that all the elements of competence are in place could include:

- providing time, in a suitable location, to explore any problems or issues that arose during the lesson or that were raised by the pupil;
- providing timely opportunities for analysis; promptly in the case of risk-critical incidents;
- taking time and using suitable techniques to understand any problems the pupil had with understanding an issue;
- suggesting suitable strategies to help the pupil develop their understanding, such as using practical examples or pointing them at further reading;
- giving clear and accurate information to fill gaps in the pupil's knowledge or understanding;
- leaving the pupil feeling that they had responsibility for their learning in the situation.

Indications of lack of competence include:

- leaving the pupil feeling that you were in control of the teaching process;
- failing to explore alternative ways of addressing a problem – in response to evidence of different learning preferences;
- providing unsuitable or incorrect inputs.

There is no need to jump in with the answer every time a fault occurs. If your customer stalls the car, for example, ask them if they know what just happened. This develops their ability to analyse problems, which is a crucial skill when they are driving independently. It might be obvious to you that the reason they stalled is because they have just tried to pull away in third gear; or that they brought the clutch up too quickly; or they forgot to release the handbrake; or they didn't have enough gas. But is it obvious to them? No one gets things right all the time and, particularly in driving, it is easy to make mistakes. However, the ability to analyse why something is not working and put it right is very important and could easily mean the difference between a crash occurring or not.

Were opportunities and examples used to clarify learning outcomes?

While training in technique is core to the learning process it is important to reinforce this input and to link it with theory. The best way to do this is to use real-world situations during the lesson. The use of practical examples and scenarios on a lesson gives the pupil a better understanding of when, how and why to use a particular technique.

This can be done, for example, by asking the pupil to think about why mirrors are important when changing direction.

Indications that all the elements of competence are in place could include:

- using examples identified on a lesson in a suitable way and at a suitable time to confirm or reinforce understanding;

- exploring different ways to use examples to respond to differences in preferred learning style;

- using examples that are within the pupil's range of experience and ability to understand; and

- recognising that some pupils will be able to respond instantly while others will want to think about the issue.

Indications of lack of competence include:

- using examples the pupil cannot really understand through lack of experience;

- using complex examples that the pupil doesn't have the ability to respond to;

- failing to give the pupil time to think through the issues and come to their own conclusion or;
- imposing an interpretation.

Learning outcomes are the same as goals and these were established at the beginning of the session. This links back to the Lesson Planning competency and is about taking advantage of the environment and recognising that there are plenty of opportunities that can be drawn on during the session that will help ensure the goals are achieved. For example, the skills involved in planning and anticipation can be developed on a number of different occasions so a goal, that has been set around deciding whether to give way or continue in meeting situations, could be developed when judging a safe gap on the approach to a roundabout or anticipating whether to give way at a pedestrian crossing.

Was the technical information given comprehensive, appropriate and accurate?

As noted above, giving incorrect or insufficient information, with the result that a safety-critical situation might occur, will result in an automatic fail.

Remember that good information is:

- accurate;
- relevant and
- timely.

Failure to meet any one of these criteria makes the others redundant.

Most sessions will require some technical input from you to help the pupil solve problems or to fill a gap in their knowledge. This input must be accurate and appropriate.

Information given must be comprehensive when associated with a recurring weakness in the pupil's driving. Simply telling the pupil that they have done something wrong is unlikely to help them overcome the problem.

Any practical demonstration of technique must be clear and suitable. The pupil should be engaged and given the opportunity to explore their understanding of what they are being shown.

Information given unnecessarily may not be helpful; for example, continually telling the pupil what to do and not allowing them to take responsibility.

Unclear or misleading advice should also be avoided. Comments such as 'you're a bit close to these parked cars' could be used to introduce coaching on a weakness but are of little use on their own as they are unclear. How close is 'a bit' and is it significant?

Indications that all the elements of competence are in place could include:

- giving clear, timely and technically accurate demonstrations or explanations;
- checking understanding and, if necessary, repeating the demonstration or explanation; and
- finding a different way to demonstrate or explain if the pupil still does not understand.

Indications of lack of competence include:

- providing inaccurate or unclear information, too late or too early in the learning process;
- failing to check understanding; or
- failing to explore alternative ways of presenting information where the pupil does not understand the first offering.

Taking a client-centred approach to learning does not mean that you cannot give information where relevant. Your expertise as an ADI is of vital importance when teaching people to drive safely for life. Some people seem to think that coaching is all about asking questions and nothing to do with giving information. This is an inaccurate interpretation of coaching or client-centred learning. Your role as a driving instructor is to teach someone safe driving skills that they will be able to apply and develop throughout their lives. Using a client-centred learning approach ensures that you engage with them in the way that is most conducive to their learning because research shows that this kind of learning sticks. Telling people how to behave/drive does not necessarily stay with them beyond the driving test. You have to determine when it is necessary to give technical information and when it would be more effective for the pupil to go away and research it. Nevertheless, when you give technical information you do need to be certain that it is comprehensive, appropriate and accurate.

Was the pupil given appropriate and timely feedback during the session?

Feedback is an essential part of learning but the process must be balanced. A pupil needs to have a clear picture of how they are doing, against their learning objectives, throughout the lesson. They should be encouraged when performing well and coached when a problem or learning opportunity occurs. However, a constant stream of words, however technically accurate, given at an unsuitable time may be de-motivating or actually dangerous. Sitting quietly and saying nothing can also be a very powerful form of feedback in some situations.

All feedback should be relevant, positive and honest. It is not helpful if the pupil is given unrealistic feedback which creates a false sense of their own ability. Where possible, feedback should not be negative. Rather than saying somebody has a weakness, consider expressing it as a learning opportunity. However, if they need to be told something is wrong or dangerous there is no point in waffling. The pupil should have a realistic sense of their own performance.

Feedback is a two-way street. It should, ideally, be prompted by the pupil with you responding to the pupil's questions or comments. The pupil's feedback should never be overlooked or disregarded.

Indications that all the elements of competence are in place could include:

- providing feedback in response to questions from the pupil;
- seeking appropriate opportunities to provide feedback that reinforces understanding or confirms achievement of learning objectives;
- providing feedback about failure to achieve learning objectives that helps the pupil achieve an understanding of what they need to do to improve;
- providing feedback that the pupil can understand;
- providing consistent feedback that is reinforced by body language.

Indications of lack of competence include:

- providing feedback a long time after an incident so that the pupil cannot link the feedback to what happened;
- providing feedback that overlooks a safety-critical incident;
- continuously providing feedback when this may be distracting the pupil;
- failing to check the pupil's understanding of feedback;
- providing feedback that is irrelevant to the pupil's learning objectives, for example commenting on their personal appearance;
- refusing to hear reasonable feedback about your own performance.

Giving appropriate and timely feedback is about ensuring the goals agreed for the session will be met within the timescales and lesson plan already discussed. This particular competency indicator is not necessarily about dealing with faults because the overall competency is aimed at assessing your teaching and learning strategies. The use of feedback is a strategy that will enhance the pupil's learning and therefore will be solution focused, taking strengths (as well as weaknesses) into consideration. In this respect, this indicator is linked to the others under this competency heading and, perhaps especially, the one about drawing on opportunities and examples to clarify learning outcomes.

Were the pupil's queries followed up and answered?

Direct questions or queries from the pupil should be dealt with as soon as possible. The response may involve providing information or directing the pupil to a suitable source.

Remember that, wherever possible, the pupil should be encouraged to discover answers themselves. However, if you do need to provide information you must ensure that the pupil completely understands the information given.

Pupils may not always have the confidence to ask direct questions. You should be able to pick up comments or body language that indicate uncertainty or confusion and use suitable techniques to explore possible issues.

Indications that all the elements of competence are in place could include:

- responding openly and readily to queries;
- providing helpful answers or directing the pupil to suitable sources of information;
- actively checking with pupils if their comments or body language suggest they may have a question;
- encouraging the pupil to explore possible solutions for themselves.

Indications of lack of competence include:

- refusing to respond to queries;
- providing inaccurate information in response to queries;
- avoiding the question or denying responsibility for answering it.

With good rapport any driving lesson becomes a two-way exchange of information, ideas and opinions. If the pupil is fully engaged in their learning then they may need to ask questions to check their understanding and assess their progress towards achieving their goal. It is important that you attend to their queries and ensure you are listening and remaining focused on their learning more so than your teaching. This does not mean that pupils' queries should be answered immediately because sometimes this would simply not be safe or appropriate. Deflecting a question until a more appropriate time – pulled up at the side of the road – is all about you applying appropriate teaching strategies to maximise their learning. You might, for example, say, 'Good question – let's deal with this situation first and then we can discuss it in more detail when we are parked.'

Did the trainer maintain an appropriate, non-discriminatory manner throughout the session?

You should maintain an atmosphere in which the pupil feels comfortable to express their opinions. You should create an open, friendly environment for learning, regardless of the pupil's age, gender, sexual orientation, ethnic background, religion, physical abilities or any other irrelevant factor. This implies active respect for the pupil, their values and what constitutes appropriate behaviour in their culture.

You must not display inappropriate attitudes or behaviours towards other road users and should challenge your pupil if they display these behaviours.

Indications that all the elements of competence are in place could include:

- keeping a respectful distance and not invading the pupil's personal space;
- asking the pupil how they wish to be addressed;
- asking a disabled driver to explain what you need to know about their condition;
- adopting an appropriate position in the car;
- using language about other road users that is not derogatory and that does not invite the pupil to collude with any discriminatory attitude.

Indications of lack of competence include:

- invading somebody's physical space;
- touching the pupil, including trying to shake hands, unless it is necessary for safety reasons;
- using somebody's first name unless they have said that this is acceptable;
- commenting on the pupil's appearance or any other personal attribute unless it has a direct impact on their ability to drive safely, such as wearing shoes that make it difficult for them to operate the vehicle's pedals.

There are two aspects to being non-discriminatory. One is ensuring that your attitude and approach to your customer is consistently non-judgemental.

The other is not expressing what might be construed as judgemental views about other road users.

You might find yourself feeling frustrated or impatient with your customer because they don't seem able to grasp the skills you are teaching. Remaining non-discriminatory or non-judgemental encourages you to consider different methods of engaging with them. It might be that the teaching strategy you are using does not suit their learning preferences and therefore they are really struggling to meet your expectations. Pupils are neither thick nor stupid – they simply need a different approach.

Commenting on other road users – whether the appearance of pedestrians or the way someone is driving – does little to accelerate the pupil's learning or achievement of the goal set for the lesson. However, using the way someone is driving, or the potential outcomes of distraction caused by focusing on a particular type of pedestrian, as discussion points can be valid and constructive.

End of the session – was the pupil encouraged to reflect on their own performance?

At the end of the session the pupil should be encouraged to reflect on their performance and discuss their feelings. You should encourage honest self-appraisal and use client-centred techniques to highlight areas that need development if the pupil has not recognised them. Once development areas have been identified the pupil should be encouraged to make them part of future development.

Reflection is a necessary part of learning. Reflecting on one's own performance helps embed the learning that has taken place and determine whether or not the goal has been achieved. Reflection also develops self-evaluation skills and the ability to recognise strengths, limitations and development needs. This is crucial in ensuring your customer has the best chance of reducing their risk when driving on their own. At the end of the session you could ask your pupil to name three things they were particularly pleased with in their driving and discuss these with them so that they are able to articulate what it is that pleased them about each of these three things and whether there is anything they would want to improve on and develop further. This is an ideal opportunity for your pupil to consider what goals they would like to set for next lesson.

Review

In most situations you will maintain your awareness of what is going on around you, give reasonably clear and timely directions and intervene in an appropriate and timely way to ensure that no safety-critical incidents occur.

However, from time to time, situations will arise in which your actions or instruction are of such poor quality that the examiner may decide that they are putting themselves, the learner or any third party in immediate danger.

Example: The learner is approaching a closed junction. They ask the instructor whether they should stop at the Give Way line. The instructor is completely unable to see down the joining roads but tells the learner to 'go, go, go'.

In these circumstances the examiner would be entitled to stop the lesson and mark it as an immediate Fail.

09
Professional development

After passing the exams and qualifying as an ADI, the only continuing check on your professional ability is the Standards Check conducted at intervals by the DVSA. This periodic test is an assessment of your ability to deliver a lesson to a specific pupil on the specified date. In other words, it's only a snapshot of your overall ability as a professional trainer. Within this regime many of the other skills required to offer an efficient service to the public and to run a small business effectively and legally are not formally tested or monitored in any way. For example, customer care skills and business administration are generally not part of an instructor's initial training. This leads to a situation where many instructors feel that the only ongoing training they should concern themselves with is in preparation for their periodic Standards Check. This is clearly not how it should be. To be an effective all-round professional driver trainer and to keep up to date with modern methods of coaching and business skills, you need to continually maintain and develop various areas of skill and knowledge.

As part of your Continuing Professional Development (CPD) you should be regularly:

- improving your instructional/coaching skills to deal with pupils and trainees at all levels;
- improving your driving skills by taking regular courses or exams such as the Cardington special test (for details, see page 277);
- using your driving skills to full advantage by keeping an open mind and not being dogmatic about trends in terms of lane discipline (for progress), signalling, steering, fuel economy and environmental issues;
- improving your customer care skills and your business skills, including legal issues, cash flow, insurance responsibilities and public liability;

CPD has been described formally as:

'specific and planned activities that serve to enhance our performance in our work role; that is, how we:

- carry out our job;

- manage our related administrative and business responsibilities;

- deal with others to whom our job relates, including particularly our employees and customers'.

However, the current and most widely used definition of CPD from the DVSA refines these as *the conscious updating of professional knowledge and improvement of professional competence throughout a person's working life and a commitment to being professional, keeping up to date and continually seeking to improve*.

It also involves:

- an ongoing commitment to being professional;

- keeping up to date with information and best practices;

- constantly seeking to improve and is driven by the individual person's own learning and development needs.

CPD can be both formal and informal professional development, based on the individual person's needs.

To maximise your individual potential, it is important that you maintain a high level of professional competence. You can get involved in CPD in various ways, for example by:

- updating your practical coaching or driving skills;

- attending local or national seminars;

- spending time in developing your business skills;

- networking with other instructors and local business people.

Benefits of CPD

An effective programme of CPD will enhance your job satisfaction, improve your overall performance and maintain or improve your credibility within the profession.

Many instructors are perfectly happy to devote their careers to teaching learner drivers, while others feel that they need to broaden their work to give themselves a wider range of customers. Either way, there is a need for all of us to continually look for ways of developing and improving our instructing and coaching skills and level of professionalism. After all, 'Nothing stays the same forever – it either gets better or it gets worse.' It means that you can't afford to stand still – if you think you are standing still, you will in fact be going backwards!

If you are looking for more variety in your work you could think of developing your practical teaching skills in order not only to improve your levels of driving and instruction, but also to expand your potential market. This applies even if your work is entirely related to teaching learners. Because the driving school market has traditionally focused on the training of learners in preparation for the driving test, many ADIs allow themselves to be limited by this – even to the extent of feeling that anything outside the learner driver market is, by definition, not for them. Instructors in this category are often reluctant to work within a group or to cooperate with other instructors, preferring to do their own thing, remaining completely independent in their own working environment. Many do not even join any of the professional associations. It is probable that one of the reasons this type of person chose to be an instructor in the first place was that they preferred to work alone, at their own pace and in their own way.

This approach may have been acceptable in the past, but nowadays it is not realistic. To be an effective instructor, there is a need to develop all of the required skills, but in particular those relating to instructional and coaching ability – and not forgetting the importance of business skills and your own driving skills.

The general trend in most other professions is for CPD to be much more widely undertaken and indeed is an expectation for most people. For example, in the road transport industry there is a requirement for all lorry drivers to take a minimum amount of refresher training every few years and to hold a Certificate of Competence alongside their vocational driving licence.

There is clearly a need for more development for instructors but, as always, it is uncertain how any CPD courses or initiatives will be funded because it is extremely unlikely that the majority of instructors will take training or extra qualifications unless they are obliged to, or are motivated in some way. Nevertheless, it can be shown that CPD is now even more important in a world that is very competitive.

Providers of CPD training are encouraged to focus on the range of topics covered in the 'Driver trainer competence framework' (for details see below). It is for you to decide what type of CPD to take and which training provider to use.

CPD usually has a cost attached to it, although some courses may be available through grants. If you are self-employed you may find that at least some of the cost could be off-set against tax, but always check with your accountant or your local tax office.

Your CPD should always be compatible with the items outlined in the framework.

Driver trainer competence framework

Monitoring and assessment

- evaluation of road and traffic conditions to drive the trainee's actions;
- supervision of trainee's driving;
- directing trainee in specific actions and manoeuvres;
- monitoring of trainee's progress;
- provision of feedback to trainee;
- recording of trainee's achievement;
- supervision of trainee through assessment;
- directing trainee's future development and training.

Strategy and planning

- lesson delivery;
- instructor development.

Instruction delivery

- demonstration of driving skills and methods;
- coaching of driving skills and methods.

Driving knowledge

- road and traffic knowledge;
- vehicle knowledge.

Driving skills

- vehicle handling ability;
- awareness of driving situation.

Driving abilities

- sensory perception;
- cognitive abilities;
- physical movement and coordination.

Communication skills

- appropriateness;
- watching;
- speaking;
- listening;
- writing and drawing;
- non-verbal communication;
- special needs training.

Personal characteristics

- attitude;
- awareness;
- instruction.

Business practice

- monitoring and controlling resources;
- record keeping;
- health and safety, welfare;
- relationships with trainees, customers and the general public.

Business development

- sales and marketing;
- staff recruitment;
- vehicle selection.

In their advice to instructors the DVSA suggests that you can take CPD in different ways, such as:

- updating your teaching or driving skills;
- attending local or national meetings or seminars;
- researching new vehicles for your business;
- spending time developing your business skills;
- going on formal courses;
- spending time on the internet carrying out research;
- networking with other driver trainers.

The documentation includes a 'development plan' covering the following areas:

- What do you want to learn/develop?
- Which competencies does it relate to?
- Who will you need to contact to achieve this?
- Target dates for review and/or completion.

By carrying out at least seven hours of CPD your commitment can be highlighted to learner drivers using the 'Find your nearest driving instructor' service offered by the DVSA. Through this database, which is part of the DVSA's integrated register of driver trainers, prospective pupils can access details of their local ADIs and see at a glance whether someone has signed up for CPD. Being involved with CPD shows the potential pupil that you are being professional and are keeping up to date.

Note: The situation is slightly different in Northern Ireland. You can still take CPD, but you can't register your commitment to it.

Any properly prepared programme of CPD should include an element of business and customer care skills as well as the personal and instructional skills that were discussed in previous chapters.

Business skills and customer care

Both sets of skills can be important elements in your programme of CPD, as they can enhance your business and maintain professionalism and credibility with your customers.

Business skills

Financial management and planning

- keeping proper business records;
- organising budgets and cash flow;
- overheads;
- holidays and sickness;
- pension planning;
- financing assets.

Business administration

- bookkeeping and accounts;
- income tax and National Insurance;
- VAT;
- banking.

Insurance

- vehicle, premises, personal and public liabilities;
- professional indemnity.

Legal responsibilities

- health and safety matters;
- equal opportunities.

Sales and marketing

- lesson pricing;
- advertising.

Customer care skills

- dealing with enquiries;
- new customers;
- follow-up procedures;
- personal contact.

Customer services

- customer records;

- feedback;

- communication;

- handling complaints.

There are several useful books on running a small business, including *Start Up and Run Your Own Business* by Jonathan Reuvid, published by Kogan Page. For details of this and other books, see Appendix 2.

Customer care

Customer care is an important element of CPD for anyone running their own business or franchise and training for it can be used as a legitimate element of qualification for CPD.

Customers (and, more importantly, potential customers) have a great deal of freedom of choice between suppliers – particularly in the service industry. Furthermore, their expectations of efficient service are greater than previously. Your instruction skills may be top-grade, but if you let your customers down in any way your business and your reputation will suffer.

As well as offering good-quality instruction, think of other areas of your business – personal appearance, punctuality and timekeeping during lessons. Avoid short-changing the pupil: give a little extra rather than a little less time.

Customers' expectations – quite rightly – include:

Efficiency. Be on time for all lesson appointments. A wait of two to three minutes can seem a long time to a waiting pupil – five minutes is unacceptable.

Honesty. Carry out your business and instruction honestly and professionally, but tactfully.

Politeness. Maintain the instructor–pupil relationship in a friendly, but not overfamiliar manner.

Respect. The pupil can rightly expect to be treated as an individual person, and does not want to be patronised or treated dismissively.

Dress code. You are not necessarily expected to wear formal clothing or a traditional business suit, but at least you should be neat, clean and tidy – whatever style of dress you choose.

Be professional, but at the same time be friendly and approachable.

Handling complaints

Complaints from customers can be dealt with in a positive manner. The important issue is to try to ensure that any minor problems are tackled before they become major problems.

Your complaints procedure should be clear, stating that in the first instance clients should approach you with their grievance. If you cannot come to an amicable agreement, clients should be advised to refer to the DVSA to consider and give advice on the matter. In some circumstances the Registrar of ADIs is prepared to offer advice to resolve disputes between instructor and pupil.

The industry has a voluntary code of practice that deals with this subject. For details see *The Driving Instructor's Handbook*, or go to www.gov.uk/adi-voluntary-code-of-practice. You – or your franchiser – should have an effective procedure in place for dealing with complaints. Dealing with complaints properly and fairly can help to maintain good customer relations. The important thing, though, is to try to deal with minor queries before they turn into complaints.

To keep up to date with CPD it is worth joining a local and/or national association to keep fully informed on developments in the industry. All national ADI organisations offer CPD courses.

ADI national organisations

Approved Driving Instructors National Joint Council (NJC)

Established in 1973, the ADI NJC is a non-profit organisation with no commercial interests and no salaried staff. Membership consists of local instructor associations, each of which has representation, with each member organisation having a vote at meetings. Individual ADIs can also take part by joining the Driving Instructors' Group, which is a section of the ADI NJC.

Telephone: 0800 8202 444
www.adinjc.org.uk
Email: secretary@adinjc.org.uk

Driving Instructors Association (DIA)

The DIA was formed in 1978 and is now regarded as the largest trade association for professional driver trainers in the UK. Membership is open to all ADIs and anyone training for the ADI qualification. Although the DIA is a proprietary association, it is guided by a General Purposes Committee elected from the membership. Staff members carry out the main work of the organisation.

Each individual member receives regular copies of *Driving* magazine and *Driving Instructor*. Services provided include training courses and conferences as well as special rates on car, breakdown and health insurance.

Telephone: 020 8686 8010
www.driving.org
Email: help@driving.org

Motor Schools Association of GB (MSA)

The Motor Schools Association was formed in 1935, about the time the driving test was introduced. Full membership is available only to fully qualified ADIs, but trainee instructors may join as temporary members. The Association's main aims are:

- to represent members at all levels of government;
- to provide services that will be of benefit to members;
- to set standards of professional and ethical behaviour for professional driver trainers.

The MSA offers a wide range of services, including professional indemnity insurance, a monthly newsletter, vehicle equipment and special discounts on trainer-related products and services.

Telephone: 0161 429 9669
www.msagb.co.uk
Email: mail@msagb.co.uk

Driving Instructors Scottish Council (DISC)

DISC represents and supports Driving Instructor Associations in Scotland. Formed in 1995, it has full consultative status with the DVSA and is a voluntary organisation with no paid positions. Any local driving instructor association in Scotland can apply for affiliation and organisations from across Scotland are represented.

Telephone: 07713 233805
Email: disc.committee@gmail.com

Local associations

As well as joining one (or more) of the national associations, you should consider getting involved with your local association. This is a good way of keeping up to date with what is happening in your local area and of networking with other instructors, both of which can be part of a programme of CPD.

For details of local associations, check in your test centre or contact one of the main national associations who will be able to provide details.

Driving standards

Each year about 2,000 people are killed on our roads. Over the past 15 years or so the figure has been reduced from about 5,000 and the government has indicated its intention to reduce it by a further 40 per cent over the next few years.

As part of the government strategy, there is a commitment to a programme of improvements in driver training and testing. These measures include:

- Instilling in young people the correct attitudes to safe driving by providing presentations in schools and to youth associations.

- Encouraging learner drivers to take a more structured approach to learning and by emphasising the need for it as a lifetime skill, not just a means of passing the test. The main focus of this is on the introduction of the Driver's Record.

- Raising the standard of driver training offered by instructors through improvements to the ADI exams and the periodic Standards Check.

- Focusing on the immediate post-test period for newly qualified drivers. This has been partly addressed by encouraging a greater awareness of the 'Pass Plus' scheme. Over the past four or five years the take-up for these courses has increased from 7 per cent to around 14 per cent.

- An enhancement of the various advanced motoring qualifications. The DVSA has recently agreed national minimum standards with the organisations that offer advanced tests. These tests are now regularly monitored by the DVSA to ensure that the standards are maintained.

Advanced driving tests

To make sure that your own driving skills are up to date, consider taking one (or more!) of the advanced driving tests that are widely available.

Special Cardington Driving Test

The Cardington test is specially designed and operated by the DVSA for ADIs who – as part of their ongoing CPD – want to demonstrate that they have a high standard of driving competency.

The test is conducted in your own car and is carried out by a specially trained staff member at the DVSA Training and Development Centre at Cardington, Bedfordshire. It involves about 90 minutes of practical driving on all types of road, including motorways, and in a variety of traffic conditions. To pass the test, you have to show a positive, courteous attitude and the ability to control the position and speed of the vehicle safely, systematically and smoothly. In particular you are assessed on your:

- expert handling of the controls;
- use of correct road position;
- anticipation of the actions of other road users and taking appropriate action;
- sound judgement of distance, speed and timing;
- consideration for the convenience and safety of other road users.

There is no element of theory testing and a commentary drive is not required.

More detail about the Cardington test is available from the DVSA on 0300 200 1122 or at www.gov.uk/dvsa-special-tests-for-instructors

Institute of Advanced Motorists (IAM)

The IAM's advanced driving test has been operating since 1956 using Metropolitan Police principles of advanced driving.

You can take the test at various locations around the country. It lasts about 90 minutes and usually covers 30 to 40 miles on all types of road, including motorways if available.

The examiners are holders of the Police Advanced Drivers certificate and all have considerable experience in police driving methods. IAM examiners are not looking for driving faults alone; they are trained to check for positive aspects of the driving as well as any negative points.

For more information, contact the IAM on 0300 303 1134 or at www. iamroadsmart.com

Royal Society for the Prevention of Accidents (RoSPA)

The RoSPA Advanced Driving Test normally lasts about 1¼ hours and is based on the principles in *Roadcraft*, the Police Driver's Manual. RoSPA advanced tests are conducted at locations throughout the UK.

One unique feature of this test is that there is a grading system. At the end of the test the examiner discusses any points that have arisen and allocates a grade according to the overall driving performance of the candidate.

Application forms and further details about the test can be obtained from RoSPA on 0121 248 2000 or at www.rospa.com

During advanced driving courses, and in preparation for a test, you should develop a better understanding of some of the issues relating to driving, such as:

- the importance of fatigue – we all tend to use the roads for much longer periods;
- fuel economy driving – to lessen the impact of our use of world resources;
- the different types of fuel available;
- the growing importance of 'dual-fuel' vehicles.

In our approach to our personal skills, and when teaching our pupils to drive, we need to be much more flexible in today's road and traffic conditions, especially in terms of:

- lane selection;
- selective signalling;
- roundabout procedures;
- right-turn positioning;
- use of steering;
- appropriate use of gears;
- other procedures that might have been regarded as correct when we took our own driving test, but which we now must reconsider in relation to the current conditions on the roads.

Taking one of the advanced tests will not necessarily provide all the answers, but your preparation for it will provoke and stimulate you into possibly re-evaluating your style of driving.

Driving instructor training

After you have gained some experience as an ADI, have regularly achieved a good Standards Check grading and have a consistently high success rate in the driving test, you might consider becoming a tutor or trainer of instructors. This could be as part of your ongoing CPD or supplementary to your ADI work. To prepare for this change, you will need to:

- have a thorough knowledge of the syllabus for the ADI theory and hazard perception test and be able to provide your students with the relevant study materials and necessary support;
- always drive to a consistently high standard;
- have a thorough knowledge and understanding of the official syllabus for learning to drive and of the ADI Part 3 syllabus;
- be able to deliver appropriate practical training;
- adapt your practical teaching skills to suit drivers who will have much more experience than learners;
- be competent in the skills required to train people to teach, including coaching skills;
- acquire and develop your role-play skills;
- undertake training with a specialist organisation.

While preparing for your own ADI exams, you should have become fully aware of the in-depth knowledge required for the theory test and the high standard of personal driving skills required for the Part 2 test. However, training to instruct is very different from teaching people to drive. You will need to develop more of your practical teaching skills to progress into the field of instructor training.

Some of the skills discussed in previous chapters will certainly be beneficial, but one of the most important parts of the tutor's job is having the ability to stimulate and motivate trainees with varying aptitudes, attitudes and personalities. Role play takes up a large percentage of the time spent in training new instructors and you will need to develop this skill so that your simulation of the learner driver becomes credible.

Before making the decision to take a course in the tutoring of ADIs, you should already be able to confidently and effectively apply all the essential practical teaching skills in your everyday work with learners. Prior to committing yourself and embarking on this more challenging aspect of the driving instruction world, you should seek advice and assessment from a recognised tutor. You will find a list of specialised training establishments in ORDIT – the Official Register of Driving Instructor Training – on the DVSA's website.

No matter which branch of driver or instructor training you intend to focus on, if you are to keep up to date and be able to compete, you should seek to continually improve all of your personal and professional skills. We hope you find this book helpful in enhancing your practical teaching skills and your continuing professional development to suit your own individual needs.

Driving instructor qualifications

Pearson SRF BTEC Level 4 Professional Award in Coaching for Driver Development

The course, which is run by Tri-Coaching Partnership, consists of four one-day classroom sessions backed up by a self-development project or assignment. There is also a one-day in-car session.

For more details contact Tri-Coaching on 0800 058 8009 or at www.tri-coachingpartnership.com.

City and Guilds

Various courses and qualifications are available including:

- introduction to trainer skills;
- personal and professional development qualification; and
- learning and development.

For more detail contact City and Guilds on 0207 294 2468 or at www.cityandguilds.com, email: general.enquiries@cityandguilds.com.

Royal Society for the Prevention of Accidents (RoSPA)

Advanced Driving Instructor Diploma.

A five-day course for ADIs to 'reach the next level'.

For more detail contact RoSPA on 0844 543 0033 or www.rospa.com.

Business opportunities

Various business opportunities are available to supplement your learner driver training, and which can be regarded as part of your ongoing professional development.

Although most driving instructors concentrate solely on teaching learner drivers, there are many other opportunities for increasing your scope of work. As well as adding variety to your daily work in driver training, these other activities will offer the opportunity for additional revenue and income streams for your business.

Some of the areas you might consider include:

- pre-driver training;
- Pass Plus training;
- learning materials;
- training for people who have a disability;
- defensive and advanced driver training;
- taxi driver assessment;
- company and fleet driver training;
- minibus driver training;
- trailer and caravan towing;
- assessments for older drivers;
- driver training schemes for local authorities;
- speed awareness courses;
- corrective and driver rehabilitation courses.

Which (if any) of these you decide to offer will depend on your individual interests, experience, qualifications or expertise.

Pre-driver training

If you have access to any off-road facility such as a large private car park, school grounds or a disused airfield, you may be able to offer pre-driver training for under-17s. Training would normally be more cost-effective for groups of pupils rather than one-to-one instruction, so target your local youth groups and schools – through the head teacher or direct with the education authority. If you have a local road safety group, it would be worthwhile liaising with them for course content and for marketing or promotion purposes. It is often beneficial to work with one or more other instructors in your area and to organise the course as part theory and part practical. This has the added benefit of working on attitudes in addition to practical vehicle control skills at an early age. Even if you only have a relatively small training area available, it is still possible to organise the course programme with an emphasis on lower-speed manoeuvring.

Training for people who have a disability

Teaching pupils who have a disability can be extremely rewarding. They are usually very motivated and keen to gain independence with their driving. Training courses for instructors are available at QEF Mobility Services, 1 Metcalf Avenue, Carshalton, Surrey SM5 4AW (telephone 0208 770 1151) or at www.qef.org.uk.

Disabilities and impairments are dealt with in detail in *The Driving Instructor's Handbook*.

Intensive 'L' driver course

Offering intensive courses can be a useful way of generating business – particularly if you are based in an area that people would like to visit.

Before considering this business opportunity, you need to be aware of a few important points:

- If you offer a one-week intensive course with the practical driving test on the final day, the pupil must have already passed the theory test.
- The customer should be made aware that they may not be ready to take the test – in which case, the driving test fee would be lost. What is your policy on refunds?

- Full payment should be taken in advance as you will not want to risk having an empty diary for the whole week.

- Intensive courses are, by their nature, hard work for both the pupil and the instructor. Not everyone responds to them effectively – many pupils would be better off with a less concentrated programme of training consisting of two or three hours of instruction each day over a longer period.

- Intensive or concentrated courses involve having the same customer with you for an extended period – possibly all day, every day for a week or more. You will need to deal with this situation – even with a client who you do not particularly like, or who may have personal hygiene problems.

Pass Plus

If you are going to offer Pass Plus as an extra course of post-test training, make sure that you educate your pupils (and their parents) at an early stage. There is little point in introducing the subject once the pupil has passed the driving test. Make it clear from the start of the training that Pass Plus is regarded as an important and integral part of the whole process of learning to drive.

Pass Plus was originally set up by the DVSA to encourage new drivers to take further training rather than regarding the driving test as the end of the learning process. The intention was (and still is) for the pupil to be trained in a wider range of road and traffic conditions than those that are tested in the ordinary driving test. The course builds on the pupil's existing skills and knowledge and so should be tailored to individual requirements. Although there is no exam at the end of the course, the pupil is assessed by the instructor in each of the modules and must reach an acceptable standard.

Pupils can be encouraged to take the extra training by making sure that they realise the benefit of the extra training and the financial benefit of substantial discounts that many insurance companies offer.

Anyone who holds a full UK licence can take part, but it is usual for pupils to take the course shortly after passing the driving test. By doing this, the new driver can qualify for the special insurance rates.

Your fees for Pass Plus should be more than your normal hourly rate. This is because you will be using more fuel, travelling longer distances and will have an element of office work and DVSA fees to cover. As well as this, there is the probability that the night driving element of the course will involve out-of-hours work.

Pass Plus Syllabus

- Town driving
- All-weather driving
- Driving out of town
- Night driving
- Dual carriageways
- Motorways

The course takes a minimum of six hours, but more sessions might be needed for some pupils to attain a satisfactory standard.

For details of the complete syllabus for Pass Plus, see *The Driving Instructor's Handbook*.

The Pass Plus course can be taken at any time up to 12 months after passing the practical 'L' test and any insurance discount can be deferred for a further two years if the new driver is driving on another person's insurance.

Although the number of drivers taking Pass Plus is gradually increasing, it is still a market where a minority of instructors take advantage of the potential for extra business.

Instructors who are actively involved and are successful emphasise the need to:

- mention Pass Plus and the benefits when pupils first enquire about lessons;
- involve parents at an early stage, getting them to understand the added reassurance that Pass Plus offers;
- remind pupils about the scheme before and after they take the 'L' test;
- inform pupils and parents of the statistics of newly qualified drivers being involved in a disproportional number of accidents.

To register as a Pass Plus instructor, you need to apply to the DVSA for a starter pack.

Vocational driver training

If you have held the appropriate driving licence for a minimum period of three years and if you have sufficient expertise or experience, there are several areas of vocational training for widening the scope of your business.

Minibuses

Anyone who held a full driving licence before 1 January 1997 has entitlement to drive minibuses with up to 16 passenger seats if the vehicle is not used for hire or reward. Drivers who have passed their 'L' test since January 1997 can drive vehicles with up to eight passenger seats. Many minibuses belonging to schools, youth groups and community groups have vehicles with more seats and these can all be potential customers. Instruction can usually be carried out in the customer's own vehicle but be particularly careful of any insurance issues.

Remember, you must have held a licence for that type of vehicle for at least three years.

Car and caravan or trailer

Drivers who passed the car-driving test before 1 January 1997 are allowed to drive a vehicle and trailer combination up to 8.25 tonnes maximum authorised mass (MAM).

MAM is usually taken to mean the maximum permissible weight, which is also known as gross vehicle weight.

For licences issued after 1 January 1997, the driver is restricted in the type of trailer or combination used:

- a car may be coupled with a trailer of up to 750kg MAM so long as the combined weight is not more than 4.25 tonnes.

or

- the trailer may be over 750 kg, provided that the MAM of the trailer does not exceed the unladen weight of the towing vehicle and the combined weight does not exceed 3.5 tonnes MAM.

The effect of these regulations is that most caravans and small trailers towed by cars on a category B licence should be within the threshold, but if not, a separate licence for category B+E must be obtained. This entails higher medical standards and a separate driving test with the car and trailer needs to be taken.

Fleet driver training

For anyone wanting to expand his or her business opportunities, fleet training is a particularly interesting and rewarding area of driver training.

The Fleet Driver Training Register is operated in conjunction with the ADI Register, but with emphasis on coaching and assessment.

Full details of fleet training are available from Fleet Driver Training, DVSA, The Axis Building, 112 Upper Parliament Street, Nottingham NG1 6LP.

As well as formal fleet training, there is also the possibility of offering training individually to local companies, education departments and health authorities as in-service, ongoing training or as pre-employment assessments.

Taxi driver assessments

The driving assessment for taxi drivers usually consists of a practical drive lasting about 35–40 minutes. Some of the skills that are assessed are specific to taxi driving such as making a U-turn and not stopping anywhere that would be dangerous for the passenger.

The driver is tested on his or her knowledge of *The Highway Code* and is also asked to identify several road signs and markings.

During the assessment, the driver is checked on:

- awareness and anticipation;
- effective planning of the prevailing road and traffic conditions;
- correct use of speed;
- emergency stop;
- a manoeuvre involving reversing;
- passenger comfort and safety.

If the taxi is suitably fitted there will be an assessment of wheelchair usage.

The driver needs to complete the assessment with no more than nine minor faults and with no serious or dangerous faults.

Many local authorities are now using this special assessment and you may well find that there is scope in your area for carrying out training, assessments or appraisals.

LGV training

An ordinary driving licence nowadays covers the driver for vehicles up to three tonnes gross weight. For any vehicle over that weight, a special category of licence and a separate test are required.

Vehicles over three tonnes fall into different categories of licence:

C1	medium-sized goods vehicle
C1+E	medium-sized vehicle with trailer
C	rigid goods vehicle
C+E	articulated goods vehicle or rigid LGV with trailer

The only statutory requirement for instructing in lorries is to have held a licence for that category of vehicle for at least three years.

A register of LGV instructors is operated by the DVSA, but it is purely voluntary at the present time. Compulsory training and re-training of LGV drivers was introduced as part of the Driver Certificate of Competence regulations and this has had an impact on the demand for driver training for this category of driver – both for initial instruction in preparation for the driving test and for refresher training for full licence holders.

National Register of LGV Instructors

The Register replaces the original voluntary scheme, which was administered by the DVSA. The new Register is operated by the Road Transport Industry Training Board (RTITB) and supported by both the Freight Transport Association and the Road Haulage Association. The DVSA will be part of the governance committee overseeing the delivery and development of the Register and its associated exam.

You can apply for inclusion on the Register if you hold a full category C1 licence (medium goods vehicle), category C1+E (medium-sized goods vehicle with trailer), category C (rigid goods vehicle) or a full category C+E (articulated large goods vehicle or large goods vehicle with trailer).

To qualify for the Register you must hold a full, unrestricted licence for the category of vehicle in which you intend to instruct. You must not have been disqualified from driving at any time in the previous four years, must have held the appropriate licence for at least three years and must be over 21.

As with the ADI exam, there are three parts to the qualifying exams:

- theory test and hazard perception test;

- practical test of your own driving ability;

- practical test of instructional ability.

For more details contact the RTITB at www.rtitb.co.uk or by telephone on 01952 520200.

CPD can include the development of communication skills, eco-friendly driving, special needs training and business development. You do not necessarily have to attend a formal training course; your involvement can be through informal training or by way of home study.

It is up to you as an individual to decide what type of CPD is most appropriate to your needs and the way you want to undertake it. However, bear in mind that CPD is an ongoing activity and that the DVSA recommend that you should have a minimum of seven hours of CPD training each year.

Apart from formal training courses, Continuing Professional Development can be undertaken in a variety of different ways, including:

- attendance at local or national meetings and seminars;
- spending time developing business skills;
- updating teaching, coaching or driving skills;
- attending formal training courses;
- networking with other instructors.

APPENDIX 1
Useful contacts

Driver and Vehicle Standards Agency (DVSA)

The Axis Building
112 Upper Parliament Street
Nottingham NG1 6LP
Customer Services: 0300 200 1122
www.gov.uk

Theory test enquiries

DVSA
PO Box 381
M50 3UW
email: customercare@pearson.com
telephone: 0300 200 1122

Practical test enquiries

DVSA
PO Box 280
Newcastle-upon-Tyne
NE99 1FP
email: customerservices@dvsa.gov.uk
telephone: 0300 200 1122 (English)
0300 200 1133 (Welsh)

DVSA Training and Development Centre

Harrowden Lane
Cardington
Bedford
MK44 3EQ
telephone: 01234 744000

Driving and Vehicle Licensing Agency (DVLA)

Longview Road
Swansea
SA6 7JL

Drivers' enquiries

Drivers' Customer Services
DVLA
Swansea
SA6 7JL
telephone: 0300 790 6801

Vehicle enquiries

Vehicles Customer Services
DVLA
Swansea
SA6 7SL
telephone: 0300 790 6802

ADI consultative organisations

AA Driving School

telephone: 0330 100 7470
email: driving@theaa.com
www.theaa.com

Approved Driving Instructors National Joint Council (ADINJC)

telephone: 0800 8202 444
email: secretary@njc.org.uk
www.adinjc.rg.uk

British School of Motoring Limited (BSM)

telephone: 0800 316 3811
www.bsm.co.uk

Driving Instructors Association (DIA)

telephone: 020 8686 8010
email: help@driving.org
www.driving.org

Driving Instructors Democratic Union

telephone: 05602 609125
email: info@didu.org.uk
www.didu.co.uk

Driving Instructors Scottish Council (DISC)

telephone: 07713 233805 or 07966 39340
email: disccommittee@gmail.com
www.disc.passwith.me

Motor Schools Association GB Ltd (MSA)

telephone: 0161 429 9669
fax: 0161 429 9779
email: mail@msagb.co.uk
www.msagb.com

Training aids and services

Desk Top Driving Ltd

Unit 6, Gaugemaster Way, Ford,
Arundel
West Sussex
BN18 0RX
telephone: 01903 882299
www.desktopdriving.co.uk

Driving School Aids

telephone: 01132 818199
email: info@drivingschoolaids.co.uk
www.drivingschoolaids.co.uk

Driving School Supplies

telephone: 0121 328 6226
email: sales@d-ss.co.uk
www.d-ss.co.uk

RCM Marketing Ltd

telephone: 01202 949474
email: info@rcmmarketing.co.uk
www.rcmmarketing.co.uk

The Stationery Office (TSO)

PO Box 29
Norwich
NR3 1GN
telephone: 0333 200 2425
www.tsoshop.co.uk
email: esupport@tso.co.uk

Tri-Coaching Partnership Limited

telephone: 0800 058 8009
email: info@tri-coachingpartnership.co.uk
www.tri-coachingpartnership.com

APPENDIX 2
Reference books

The Official DVSA Guide to Driving – The essential skills
DVSA/The Stationery Office

The Official DVSA Guide to Learning to Drive
DVSA/The Stationery Office

The Official DVSA Theory Test for Car Drivers
DVSA/The Stationery Office

Know Your Traffic Signs
DVSA/The Stationery Office

The Highway Code
DVSA/The Stationery Office

The Driving Instructor's Handbook, 21st edition
by John Miller

Coaching for Performance (4th edition)
by John Whitmore

Improve Your Communication Skills
by Alan Barker

Coaching and Mentoring
by Eric Parsloe, Melville Leedham

Start Up and Run Your Own Business: The essential guide to planning, funding and growing your new enterprise
by Jonathan Reuvid

INDEX